UNDERSTANDING
MENOPAUSE

UNDERSTANDING
MENOPAUSE

JANINE
O'LEARY
COBB

KEY PORTER BOOKS

Canadian Cataloguing in Publication Data

Cobb, Janine O'Leary, date
    Understanding menopause

ISBN 1-55013-077-3

1. Menopause.   I. Title.

RG186.C62 1989   618.1'75   C89-090544-4

Editor: Sarah Swartz, The Editorial Centre
Cover design: Linda Gustafson
Drawings: Jackie Heda
Typesetting: Vellum Print and Graphics
Printing and binding: Webcom Limited
Printed and bound in Canada

Key Porter Books Limited
70 The Esplanade
Toronto, Ontario
Canada M5E 1R2

89 90 91 92 93 5 4 3 2

Certainly the effort to remain unchanged, young, when the body gives so impressive a signal of change as the menopause is gallant; but it is a stupid, self-sacrificing gallantry better befitting a boy of 20 than a woman of 45 or 50.

— Ursula LeGuin

CONTENTS

.

INTRODUCTION
.

IT WAS MY INTENTION that my forty-ninth summer be memorable. I planned to spend most of that summer in the country, taking possession of the cottage that we had dreamed about for years. I also planned to give up smoking — this time for good — as a fiftieth-birthday present to myself, and to write a text for a course I had been developing, to be taught as part of the humanities program at Vanier College in Montreal. I had been smoking steadily and heavily for almost thirty years; I needed a peaceful and ordered existence to stop smoking and write a book. Fortunately, four of the five children had summer jobs or were at camp; the youngest would be pleasant company during the week and my husband would arrive on Friday afternoons for the weekend.

The cottage got built, the manuscript was finished, and I haven't smoked since, but that summer is memorable for other reasons. Looking back, I remember the sudden fits of warmth during the night (other than during pregnancy, I had never been *too* warm!), the aching right shoulder (it forced me to swim sidestroke when I preferred the Australian crawl), and the weird dreams of giving birth or of waking to a bed flooded with menstrual fluid. I didn't realize it at the time, but the summer constituted a turning-point — an unconscious farewell to the closure of my reproductive life.

Over the following academic year, I continued to teach my sociology and humanities classes. The usual routine of preparation, classes, and marking was overshadowed by threatened changes to the college system — changes that would both drastically increase the numbers of students in the classroom and shrink the amount of time available for classroom preparation and grading. At the same time, I was coping with a full house: the elder sons had been away from home and had returned to go back to school. I thought I would never live through Christmas with all its attendant responsibilities. By the time classes got underway in January, I was in the throes of a full-fledged depression.

Because I was still menstruating, I never seriously thought of menopause. I believed (from what little I knew) that menopause posed a problem only to women who had time on their hands. As a full-time college professor, wife, and mother, I had no time for menopausal distress. When I complained about my lagging capacity for coping, I discovered that most of my same-age friends shared the feeling. Some were having serious problems with children; some were making noises about leaving their husbands; all were talking about "burn-out" and the inability to feel enthusiastic about their jobs. And *none* of us attributed any of this to menopause.

I celebrated my fiftieth birthday in the south of France — my first trip to Europe and a glorious birthday present from a husband who was, by this time, turning cartwheels in an effort to cheer me up. I continued to feel grim — weepy and pessimistic about everything — but I wouldn't see a doctor because I was convinced I had no *reason* to feel depressed. I refused to discuss the matter and I grew accustomed to the strange glances from family members.

By Christmas of that year (the year we bought a computer as a gift for the children), I had done a bit of research on menopause. I had browsed through the "Health" section of the bookstores, looking for a paragraph, a chapter — anything that would give me a clue. I had found some interesting material (for example, Rosetta Reitz's book, *Menopause: A Positive Approach*, and a chapter in Penny Wise Budoff's first book, *No More Menstrual Cramps and Other Good News*), but I was beginning to get angry about the general lack of information. At my annual check-up, the doctor had mentioned a discussion group on menopause, adding that it was primarily informational (information that I had already found for myself), but that it might provide moral support. I didn't have time to register or to attend — I was about to start a course in word processing. As I became familiar with the capabilities of the computer, it all started to come together.

I got the idea for a newsletter for menopausal women that could be both a source of information and a support group *through the mail*. In March 1984, I carefully printed out a trial newsletter, mailing it to any and every woman I had ever met or heard about who might be interested. Because menopause is a time when a woman often *is* in need, I called the newsletter *A Friend Indeed*.

Since that first tentative mailing to forty women, *A Friend Indeed* has grown steadily. During the first summer, a newspaper article describing the newsletter was reprinted across the country: a week later, I had received more than nine hundred enquiries. After the next Christmas, I taught only half-time and introduced a French version, *Une Véritable Amie*. By September 1985, I was working full time on the newsletter, as I continue to do now.

The success of *A Friend Indeed* is due, in large measure, to the caring and sharing of thousands of menopausal women across Canada. Through their letters, I have learned to esteem highly the knowledge and judgment of women "in the prime of life." Although the decision to invest all my energy in the newsletter meant unaccustomed isolation (me and my computer), when I do emerge from my office to travel to other cities or to attend a conference or workshop, I am warmed by the spontaneous kindnesses and friendly hospitality I receive.

Although I had thought that the newsletter would suffice, readers have persuaded me that a compendium complete with index and "ready reference" might be even more useful and might, in fact, be appealing to many women who are not yet ready to accept the adjective "menopausal." This book is for the women in their early forties who are, all unknowingly, dealing with the minor changes that precede menopause: it is my hope that the information you find may alleviate any irrational apprehension. This book is also for those passing through menopause. Understanding what is happening will, I think, allow you to re-establish cordial relations with a body and mind that may be temporarily out of whack, enabling you to manage your menopause with confidence. I have included excerpts from letters written by readers of my newsletter to give first-hand illustrations of the experiences and feelings of other women going through menopause.

I am grateful to my family who have put up with, and come to the aid of, a wife/mother who takes on too much and is often too intense, too earnest, and too easily upset. I love each of you more than I can say. I am grateful above all to the women who have become my subscribers and my friends, and to the women who were always my friends and have now become my subscribers. You have opened my eyes to new ways of seeing this transitional period in our lives. Let me say it: menopause has been a very *special* time.

CHAPTER 1

■

How to Recognize
the Onset of Menopause

ONCE UPON A TIME, women were deliberately kept in ignorance of the measured steps of womanhood and the role of their own reproductive organs in menstruation, sexual intercourse, pregnancy, and **menopause.** * Each event arrived unheralded and unknown. Today, most females in North American society are encouraged to be informed about each, but the least known of them all is menopause.

Over the last two or three decades, women have become conscious of entrenched sexist attitudes toward many solely female experiences — menstruation, pregnancy, childbirth. These important events in a woman's life have never been taken very seriously by the male political or medical establishments. These attitudes are changing, thanks in large part to the activism of younger women. Mid-life women have not always been so assertive. Many have been faced with not only sexist but also agist attitudes, which discount and dismiss the very real concerns of menopausal women. Rather than label ourselves as "menopausal" and thereby invite the negative stereotype of the middle-aged complainer, too many of us have kept silent.

Isn't it strange that we should be educated in the intricacies of sexual intercourse, pregnancy, and childbirth — which are not experienced by *all women* — and yet left virtually uneducated about a process that touches *each one?* To experience menopause, all we have to do is live long enough. These days, most women do.

■

I didn't recognize the first signs of menopause. I assumed, since I was working full-time outside the home and leading a full and satisfying life, that I would be relatively untouched by it. When I finally saw a doctor about my sore wrists, I was told that it often happened "for no reason" and that there was no reliable cure. When I started feeling depressed, I assumed it was because of the constant insecurity and stress experienced by any woman in my kind of job. It got a lot worse before I belatedly recognized that menopause might be responsible.

* Words in bold type can be found in the Glossary.

5

For most of our adult lives, we are governed by cycles that are more or less predictable. Even those of us who menstruate rarely are accustomed to a predictable unpredictability of menses, or periods. The vast majority of us become accustomed to menstrual cycles that fall within a given time frame. (Always early when you don't want the bother; always late when you count on getting it over with by a certain date!) By age twenty, most of us have learned to gauge the numbers of tampons and/or pads required and to schedule our lives around the inevitable arrival of "that time of the month." We may have even learned to laugh (in retrospect) at our excessive emotionality during the days just before menstruation. Many of us have also learned to get back into the swing after prolonged bouts of pregnancy and breast-feeding. The menstrual cycle is a familiar rhythm and, although we complain that it's inconvenient (or worse), we have grown accustomed to it.

This familiarity with one's own menstrual cycle is very difficult for a man to understand. Because women complain about the way menstrual cycles govern their lives, men think that we hate menstruation and want to be rid of it. But women learn to accommodate the vagaries of menstruation and to make allowances for them. Like an unruly pet, menstruation is something you may complain about but can't imagine doing without.

There is considerable time devoted to the accommodation of menstruation — and the time of adaptation begins even *before* menarche (the first menstrual period) when a girl's body is readying itself for the ability to menstruate. The cycle gradually regulates itself and, once established, there follows the adjustment to the physical and emotional ups and downs that occur every month. A girl who starts menstruating at about age thirteen will probably take at least five years to adjust to, and be comfortable with, her own cycle and its intricate effects — emotional, psychological, and physical. Those of us who can think back to our adolescence should not be surprised if, after thirty-five years, we require five years or more to readapt to *not* menstruating.

This is menopause.

If you look up the word "menopause" in a dictionary, you will not find "a five- or seven-year period marking the end of the reproductive years in women." What you *will* find is "the cessation of menstruation," a time that comes and goes before most of us notice.

There are some problems with this definition. First of all, naturally menopausal women can only acknowledge menopause in retrospect. We never know which menstrual period is the last until there are no more. Second, there are many women who experience a last menstrual period as the result of surgical (or other artificial) interventions but who are not necessarily menopausal. An alternative and more correct term is "**climacteric**," which comes from a Greek term suggesting steps on a ladder and covers the whole mid-life period for both males and females. Changes were thought to take place every seven years and the odd multiples, such as thirty-five, forty-nine, and sixty-three, were considered very important.

But ancient Greek society revolved around the needs and perceptions of men, and this is a book written *by* a woman and largely *for* women, so I'm going to use "menopause" in its commonly accepted sense: as a transitional period marking the closure of reproductive life. "Menopause" in this book refers, according to common usage, to a "time of life" rather than a "point in time."

Menopause usually occurs during mid-life, but not always. The average age of "true menopause" (the last menstrual period) in North America is fifty-one, but it may come earlier in some families and later in others. Age of first menstruation seems to have very little to do with the start of menopause. Smoking will bring on an earlier menopause (up to two years earlier for a heavy smoker) and **hysterectomy** (removal of the **uterus**) and/or a **tubal ligation** (tying or cauterizing of the **fallopian tubes** to ensure infertility) seems to lead to earlier menopause *in some cases*. This information may contradict what you have been told by your doctor but the findings about hysterectomy and menopause are fairly recent and those concerning the effects of tubal ligation are strongly suspected but not yet confirmed.

NATURAL MENOPAUSE

A disturbance in the monthly cycle may or may not be the first sign of onset of menopause. Throughout most of our adult lives, the menstrual cycle operates in a more-or-less expected way, with **hormones** ebbing and flowing at levels just high enough to keep the system in a comfortable balance. As you get closer to the time of true menopause, fluctuations occur — fluctuations that may affect the monthly flow so little as not to be noticed, but that may give you something to wonder about. Many women notice changes in bowel habits or stools; others notice that headaches come and go more frequently. There may be a difference in energy levels or the content of dreams. Many women find that their joints — knees or ankles, wrists or shoulders — start to ache for no reason. Some women experience increased premenstrual distress. Others find that they have many, very *minor* complaints when they have their regular check-ups. It is only hindsight that enables many of us to recognize little changes that occur during our early forties, changes that precede the better-known signs of menopause.

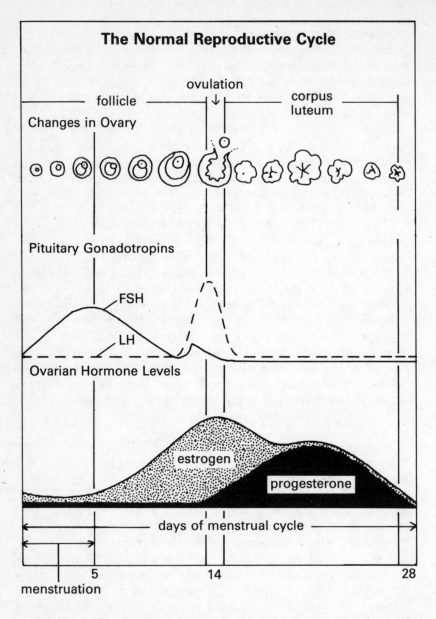

The Normal Reproductive Cycle

ovulation

follicle — corpus luteum

Changes in Ovary

Pituitary Gonadotropins

FSH

LH

Ovarian Hormone Levels

estrogen

progesterone

days of menstrual cycle

5   14   28

menstruation

In early puberty, non-ovulatory cycles (that is, months in which no egg has been produced by the **ovary**) are signalled by heavier and longer bleeding than normal. In fact, many young girls have very heavy or irregular periods *until* regular ovulation is established, at which point their periods settle down to a more tolerable flow and duration. The same happens in reverse as menopause approaches. In the months in which ovulation does *not* take place, periods tend to be heavier and longer. As **pre-menopause** (the time when periods are still regular) moves toward the **peri-menopause** (a term used to designate the transition phase between regular periods and no periods at all), monthly events become more unpredictable. The two or three days of emotional instability that once preceded a period may escalate into a week or more of annoying and unusual premenstrual symptoms.

•

> A few years ago, I went to see my doctor regarding a pounding in my heart and aches in my joints. He never even suggested it might be menopause, stating that, at forty-two, I was too young. Thinking back, I believe it started when I was thirty-nine or forty years old. I experienced minor symptoms as early as this and am only now, at forty-four, able to recognize what these symptoms indicated.

The onset of menopause and its accompanying ailments can be mistaken for any number of slow-acting and terminal illnesses. Unfortunately, most of us think about dying before we think of menopause, particularly when imaginations get out of hand in the wee hours of the morning. This inclination to view menopause as "sickness" is accentuated by our tendency to talk about menopausal *symptoms*. In this book, I have tried to use less loaded terms — "signs," "indications," "ailments." The onset of menopause is remarkable not because of any overwhelming signs that point to the end of our reproductive years but rather because of the cumulative effect of a number of annoying reminders that things are not as they once were.

Menopause, by itself, is rarely devastating. It is estimated that only a small minority (10 to 15 per cent) of naturally menopausal women will experience severe or debilitating ailments related to it. Another small minority (perhaps 10 per cent) will sail through with no problems whatsoever. This leaves the rest of us somewhere "in the middle." Some have a rocky time but cope without drugs or other medical interventions. Others experience only infrequent and mild reminders of their menopausal status. It is the sensation of a loss of control over one's own body that is often the worst problem. If you have a reasonable idea of what to expect, managing the situation is much easier. It is ignorance of our bodily processes that feeds fear.

ARTIFICIAL MENOPAUSE

There can be a significant difference between the menopause experience of a woman who has had her uterus removed (that is, who has had a hysterectomy) and a woman whose organs are intact. A substantial number of women who have had hysterectomies, *whether or not any part of the ovaries has been saved*, experience either premature menopause or a menopause quite different from that of a "naturally menopausal" woman. Women who have both ovaries removed (an **oophorectomy** or ovariectomy) will have a different kind of menopause; women who have other kinds of medical interventions (tubal ligation, complete or partial hysterectomy, radiation treatment, etc.), may not be sure whether they will have a completely natural menopause, premature menopause, or artificial menopause. Rarely are women given a clear understanding of what to expect by their physicians after such surgical intervention.

Many women are unaware of the extent of their own surgery. A "complete hysterectomy," in everyday language, usually means removal of the uterus, **cervix**, ovaries, and fallopian tubes. To a doctor, a "complete hysterectomy" means removal of the uterus and cervix only. It is important for a woman to know exactly what organs are involved in surgery if she is to understand the reasons for, and the possible consequences of, the operation.

For instance, until fairly recently, it was thought that the experience of menopause was similar for any woman who still had her ovaries or part of them — that even a small part of one ovary would continue to secrete enough **estrogen** to allow for menopause at the normal age. We now know that is not true.

The term "artificial menopause" may be applied to: (a) those women who have had their ovaries removed (usually in conjunction with a hysterectomy); (b) those whose ovaries fail following radiation therapy; (c) those who experience a premature menopause as a result of a hysterectomy, even when some or all of the ovaries are untouched.

The women in categories (a) and (b) experience a very sudden menopause. The **hot flashes** start within a few days of surgery (or radiation) and may be brutal in their effects. At the same time, a number of other ailments may strike all at once — headaches, joint pains, fatigue, night sweats, depression, etc. Unless there are strong reasons for artificially menopausal women *not* to have it, **estrogen replacement therapy** (ERT) is started almost immediately and may continue for some years.

The risk of depression is high for women in all three categories, with the incidence highest about two years after the operation. In addition, women who lose their ovaries before age forty will be at increased risk for both **osteoporosis** and heart disease. This is why women under forty should work on developing bone mass, through diet and exercise, and why the experiences of natural menopause and artificial menopause should be considered separately.

Women who retain all or some of their ovaries are less severely affected. However, in one-third to one-half of cases, menopause may occur prematurely. The younger the age at the time of the surgery, the more likely it is that menopause will be advanced; according to recent studies, women who are hysterectomized before the age of forty will experience menopause an average of eight years after surgery.

·

> After undergoing a hysterectomy at age twenty-seven, I believe I am now experiencing menopause. I am forty-one years old. The symptoms started about four years ago and have included tingling sensations, anxiety, hot flashes, severe panic attacks and depression. Lately I've been feeling so poorly that I wish I could go to sleep and never wake up. The three doctors I've seen tell me I'm too young.

Whether we experience natural or artificial menopause, we need information beforehand and, during the period of adjustment, most of us can use some understanding and support. To receive understanding and support, we have to be willing to admit to our own frailties and be prepared to listen to and affirm the experiences of other women. Unfortunately, many women decide to unburden themselves to only one other woman. What if (as it sometimes turns out) this person is one of the small minority who stopped menstruating without any problem? Such women often take personal credit for a problem-free menopause (attributing it to "keeping busy," "not dwelling on things," or "having a sense of humour"). This attitude is not very supportive of the woman suffering from menopausal distress! It is then that we start asking questions: Why am I saddled with all these problems and she gets off painlessly? Is it heredity? Is it diet? Is it the cumulative effect of medication taken over the years? Is it the surgery?

There are no real answers to these kinds of questions. Sisters usually have a similar experience of menopause and go through it at roughly the same age. When there are sharp differences, it forces us to question differences in diet, exercise, sleep habits or the possibility of prior hormone use — for adolescent acne, to induce ovulation, to prevent pregnancy, to induce delivery, to prevent miscarriage, to dry up breast milk, to alleviate hot flashes. The medical world knows very little about the effects of cumulative doses of hormones and what may result from them in terms of timing or quality of menopause.

HOW MUCH IS MENOPAUSE AND
HOW MUCH IS AGEING?

This is the million-dollar question. Because menopause and the sensation of ageing often appear hand-in-hand, the careful separation of one from the other has become a matter of serious academic interest. Apparently, very few of the negatives can be directly attributed to menopause; depression, fatigue, anxiety, wrinkles, and weight gain are more easily linked to factors *other* than menopause. Very recent research suggests that many of the symptoms of **premenstrual syndrome** (PMS) — a few days of severe physical and emotional distress prior to the menstrual period — may be triggered by menopause (natural or surgical) and may continue to be felt for a few years after the last menstrual period. If this is true, it means that chemical messengers in the brain may produce many so-called menopausal ailments, and that menopause takes the blame for ailments that are part of premenstrual syndrome, even when menstrual periods are long past.

On the other hand, many of us know that we *have* visibly aged since our menstrual periods started to falter. Those of us who go grey in our late forties and early fifties, who find ourselves stuck with a substantial weight gain, and who also battle fatigue and aching joints, feel — not too surprisingly — that menopause is responsible. When it comes to real life, it is very hard to separate ageing from menopause.

It is not necessary to gain weight (although some weight gain may have very positive benefits). The onset of menopause is a signal to start watching what you eat. If you feel unexpectedly tired at the end of a normal day, you would be wise to protect yourself from fatigue by cutting down on your commitments — to work, to family, to friends. Aches in joints will probably disappear in time. The good news is that the menopause doldrums will pass. Once your body has adjusted to your new non-menstruating self, you will reach a more stable and pleasant stage of development — the plateau called **post-menopause**.

Post-menopause is established once twelve months have gone by since the last menstrual period. Margaret Mead, the famous anthropologist, introduced the term "post-menopausal zest" to describe the feelings of renewed energy and health that mark women of this age, women from their mid to late fifties onwards. This is where one sees the sharp contrast between the listless newly retired man and his peppy, busy wife! The years after menopause are usually enormously productive.

SOCIAL DEFINITIONS OF MENOPAUSE

The view of menopause differs widely from society to society. In some societies, the onset of menopause is welcomed because it provides a break from stringent rules about what women may or may not do or say. In other societies it is regarded as an inevitable part of growing older and viewed neither positively nor negatively. In North

American society, which makes a fetish of both youth and slimness, menopause is often dreaded. Many of us find, much to our dismay, that we have unconsciously subscribed to our society's very narrow definition of "femininity" and that we are not supposed to look our age. To deal with this, it helps to look at the social standards for men, who are often seen as *more* attractive as they age. Grey-haired and portly, these men appear confident and project an air of prosperity, a well-weathered masculinity. This hard-earned confidence should also be incorporated into women's views of themselves at mid-life, but it often takes a conscious effort to ignore or to see beyond the stereotype of the menopausal woman and to focus on the positive aspects of the menopausal years.

This effort is required because there is, in our society, a sense of loss associated with menopause. It is not that we mourn the loss of the ability to have a baby. Most of us are not interested in being new mothers at age fifty. Nor do we mourn the diminishing of the mother role. Most of us are delighted to see our children step out on their own. What women mourn is the loss of their youthful image, which must now be replaced with a more mature, capable one. The mantle of middle age descends with a thud. As Germaine Greer says: "It isn't a gradual, imperceptible process, but happens in leaps and bounds. You can go on for years being the same age. Your face doesn't change much; your weight remains much the same. You never think of yourself as too old to learn the latest craze, can't wait to [get] off with the old and [get] on with the new. Then, crunch. You're polishing a mirror table and you realize your neck has gone. Just like that."

If there were an expectation of new challenges and new adventures at fifty, menopause would be looked at much more positively. Unfortunately, in this society, the expectations and markers of mid-life are almost uniformly negative. Women approach menopause with attitudes that influence how they deal with it. Because we lack positive images of women coping with menopause, the attitudes tend to be negative.

•

It just seems that menopause takes over one's whole life. I was a year getting over the feelings of I-really-don't-know-what. And all of a sudden I feel "old" and realize that life is now on the down half. Immediately one is no longer young and vital — just old and tired and useless.

And yet, if we keep our eyes open, we can see around us vital and healthy women in their fifties who have overcome this negativity. They have had time to experience the satisfactions of accomplishment, both personally and professionally, and have come to terms with their competence and physical appearance. Look how far we've advanced in relation to the women of fifty or one hundred years ago!

•

Regarding menopause, in all fairness to this process I must tell of spells of great well-being which come rarely, but are so strong and wonderful that I note them in my journal. They last ten to fifteen minutes and, during that time, I am totally content with the world. More than that, really: the sunshine and colours of my surroundings are perfect, my family is totally right and complete, my body and mind are just as they should be, and I am aware that all's right with the world. This is more difficult to put into words than I thought it would be. However, it is a marvellously aware and alive feeling and I think related to our time of life.

Yes, I have anxiety attacks and forgetfulness and mostly sleep loss, especially in the two weeks prior to my body's efforts to menstruate. My periods are getting lighter at last (I'll be fifty-three soon) but these "moments of perfection" are worth it.

FACING MENOPAUSE

Some women choose to deny the existence of menopause. This denial is fairly easy in our society and reflects the common attitude of dread. Unless there are unquestionable medical reasons against it, a doctor can be found to write a prescription for estrogen (and often **progesterone**) so that the monthly menstrual period will continue for some years. However, this means turning a blind eye to the possible side-effects and long-term consequences — in effect, abdicating the responsibility for informed choice. The women who choose to deal with menopause by avoiding it entirely are not hard to spot. Strenuous dieting, consistent application of hair colour, and skillful make-up may minimize the effects of the years, but how long can these women avoid it? What happens when time (and nature) catches up with them? How will they deal with a new "self" and an ageing body — as someday we all must?

Some women, on the other hand, give in to menopause and ageing immediately. The first flinch of joint pain is interpreted as arthritis, and a sure sign of disability. Weight gain is viewed as both inevitable and an excuse for inactivity — particularly sexual activity. Anxiety and irritability are expected, often because a close friend or relative was in bad shape at this age. With this kind of attitude, it is easy to sink into depression. As aches and pains multiply, visits to the doctor become more frequent. Because these women are the ones who turn up at doctors' doors, they have come to represent the menopausal woman. These women are victims of our society's negative view of ageing and illness, and these are the women who give menopause a bad name.

A few women will reach menopause and sail through without a twinge and without a backward glance. We don't know why such women are spared, although — like the research on happy marriages — it would be nice to spread the good news.

The vast majority of naturally menopausal women will be bothered to some extent by minor ailments that come and go over a period of years. With some basic information about diet, exercise, and non-prescription remedies, most women can live and cope very well. If they are also blessed with empathetic and supportive friends, most women can navigate the trickier stumbling blocks of menopause.

Individually, we can confront the negative stereotypes and attitudes associated with menopause. Until our society does an about-face and learns to value the capabilities and appearance of healthy fifty-year-old women, we will have to put up with it. But we can recognize that it is something that *can* be changed, that such attitudes are typical of *one* society at *one* point in history. Unfortunately, all members of our society are affected by it. This will give us some understanding of the attitudes of our husbands, our lovers, our doctors, our friends, and — more importantly — of our own reluctance to age. By thinking through our own attitudes toward menopause and dealing with it as positively and competently as we can, we will be doing something to change the situation — if not for ourselves, then for our daughters and grand-daughters.

CHAPTER 2

.

Physical Ailments
at Menopause

SOMETIMES IT'S HARD to believe that women have been going through **menopause** for centuries. We have very little information about what the experience was like for women before us and, until someone delves into the letters and diaries of our "foremothers," we have only the misleading accounts of the men who treated them. Because there *has* been so little information available about menopause, we tend to view it as an impediment that must be overcome so that we can get on with our lives. This view, in turn, has led to reassuring articles that tell us that we will be past it in a few months or, at most, a couple of years. The purpose is to downplay the interruption and regard adult life as a continuous line. I feel this does grave disservice to the experience of menopause and its effects.

Most other animals die as soon as their reproductive lives are over. The human female is the only one to survive for such a long time after the end of her reproductive life — an average of twenty-five or thirty years, or more than a third of the normal lifespan. This uniquely human capacity is presumed to have evolved from the needs of the newborn human, who has an extraordinarily long dependency period, and ensures that "mother" will be on hand for the needs of the last-born. Even those who accept this as an evolutionary benefit, however, sometimes wonder why menopause operates in the way it does. Why does nature have to add so many hormonal upsets to the end of ovulation?

According to the theories of developmental psychology, all people go through stages of personality growth — periods of disruption followed by the incorporation of new learning and another step on the road to maturity. Each stage leads to new attitudes and behaviour that reflect the new learning. This is how we mature.

Most of us know something about the stages of childhood. We know that the path to maturity is marked with upheaval and that, all being well, the crises are followed by the emergence of a wiser and more self-sufficient child. The crises, of course, vary. It is hard sometimes to see the similarities between a two-year-old's tantrum, the stomach ache of a seven-year-old who doesn't want to go to school, the door-slamming of a teenager, and the heartbroken sobs of a lovestruck adolescent. But the "downs" of each of these episodes is usually followed by an "up" — a painful period of self-recognition and a new stage of self-knowledge on the way to adulthood.

When we look back on our adult lives, we can often pick out similar "growth spurts" — crises faced and dealt with and new insights gained as a result. At work, these steps can be fairly easily charted. Most of us can look back at a particular rocky period that marked the taking on of more responsibility or a new level of confidence about the job. Marriage or the dissolution of marriage, for example, require a non-stop accommodation to another personality, to another situation. Out of the pain comes growth and, eventually, stability, either with someone else or alone. Motherhood demands new skills every few years, skills that are not easy to command. The best mothers of babies are not always the best mothers of adolescents (which is why many of us grow nostalgic about the simpler needs of very young children). To view our own adulthood as one unbroken line that moves onward into old age is to disregard the bumpy road that we have all travelled.

One of the myths of menopause is that one enters it, weathers it, and goes back to being the same woman, only older. This is to deny the essential truth of menopause — that it is a crucial stage of development on the road to maturity, and that the experience will change us. Although only 31 per cent of menopausal women were found to agree with the statement "This is the best age to be," nearly twice as many post-menopausal women (average age, fifty-eight) found this statement to be personally true for them. This tells us that most women reach a new plateau of contentment *after* menopause.

In order to understand what you are (or will be) experiencing during menopause, it is important to recognize a range of ailments — both physical and psychological — that commonly affect women during this time of their lives. Although you almost certainly will not experience more than a few of these ailments, it helps to have heard about them in case you *do* experience them.

Menopausal Ailments

menstrual irregularity
hot flashes and/or flushes; night sweats
dry vagina
insomnia and/or weird dreams
sensory disturbances (vision, smell, alterations to taste)
funny sensations in the head
lower back pain (crushing of vertebrae)
waking in the early hours of the morning
onset of new allergies or sensitivities
fluctuations in sexual desire and sexual response
annoying itching of the vulva (area around vagina)
sudden bouts of bloat (waistline expands by two to three inches for
    an hour or two)
chills or periods of extreme warmth
indigestion, flatulence (wind), gas pains
rogue chin whiskers
overnight appearance of long, fine facial hairs
bouts of rapid heartbeat
crying for no reason
aching ankles, knees, wrists, or shoulders
waking up with sore heels
thinning scalp and underarm hair
greying scalp and pubic hair
mysterious appearance of bruises
sudden inability to breathe ("air hunger")
frequent urination
urinary leakage (when coughing or sneezing, or during orgasm)
prickly or tingly hands with swollen veins
lightheadedness, dizzy spells, or vertigo
weight gain and in unusual places (on the back, breasts, abdomen)
sudden and inappropriate bursts of anger
sensitivity to touching by others ("touch impairment")
inexplicable panic attacks
tendency to cystitis (inflammation of the bladder)
vaginal or urethral infections
anxiety and loss of self-confidence
depression that cannot be shaken off
painful intercourse
migraine headaches
easily wounded feelings
crawly skin ("formication")
disturbing memory lapses

Despite the documented occurrence of all of the ailments listed, most medical texts recognize only three major physical ones — menstrual irregularity, **hot flashes**, and **dry vagina** (or genito-urinary distress). **Osteoporosis** is occasionally listed as a problem related to menopause but it is, in fact, a condition that exists long before menopause but worsens during the menopausal years. Psychological ailments (anxiety, panic attacks, and depression) are viewed very differently, depending on the source or the professional you consult. The three major physical ailments (sometimes expanded to four with the addition of osteoporosis) are usually the only ones that most doctors are prepared to discuss and treat.

MEDICALLY RECOGNIZED PHYSICAL AILMENTS

Menstrual irregularity
The most common sign of menopause is a fluctuation in the menstrual cycle. Although this may not be the *first* indication of menopausal onset, it is the one most women look for. Periods may continue to arrive on time, but there are often minor changes. The woman who once could relax for an hour or two between the first "show" and the need for a pad or tampon may find that she is now very quickly staining her clothes. The period that lasted three or four days may last for two or for six. The colour of the flow may change — rather than moving from red to brown, it may be brown, then red, then brown again. All of this is normal, as is the tendency (as time goes on) to skip a period now and then, or to have two or three periods back to back. If you are familiar with your own rhythm, you will be more exasperated by all this than alarmed.

•

The cessation of my menstrual periods was gradual. It lasted for approximately three years, and the uncertainty was most irritating and often quite embarrassing. I experienced minor symptoms of menopause, such as lightheadedness and hot flashes, during this time. However, now that my periods have ceased altogether, menopause has arrived in full force. I am experiencing hot flashes, mood swings, and dry vagina. I realize now that it is specifically during the first signs of menopause — i.e., erratic menses — that one should take the opportunity to inform oneself fully about the years to follow.

What is *not* normal is bleeding between periods. If you experience this, you should check it out with your doctor.

Hot flashes and night sweats

Another very common physical symptom is the hot flash. Some say "flash" and some say "flush"; they are not the same thing. A hot flash is the sudden sensation of heat (it may be experienced as a result of stress in the absence of menopause). A **hot flush** is the red neck or face that is visible to others. (You may have a red chest or back as well). You can have a flush without feeling a flash, and you can feel a flash without "giving it away" with a flush. Hot flashes experienced during the night are called night sweats. Some women experience flashes but no night sweats. Some experience only night sweats; some experience both.

Many of us do not recognize the onset of hot flashes, which are often heralded by the unexpected return of the old-fashioned "blush." Many women find their faces reddening in the absence of any sensation of warmth. The first experience of a hot flash may be nothing more than a feeling of unusual warmth; you may throw the covers off or remove a jacket or sweater and not think about it further. It is estimated that between 75 and 85 per cent of women experience hot flashes — some for only a few weeks and some for as long as fifteen to twenty years. And the real thing is unmistakable. Many women are aware of it before it even starts, with feelings ranging from slight nausea to a sense of doom: "something terrible is about to happen." In studies done of hot flashes, women are often able to say, "Here comes one!," before the medical instruments start to show any differences in skin temperature or blood circulation. After the "advance signal" there is often a rapid build-up — usually, but not always, concentrated in the chest and upper body — followed by a rise in body temperature and a feeling of unbearable heat. The veins of the hands may tingle and swell. Perspiration may bead at the hairline, between the breasts, down the back. Hot flashes can last from one minute to one hour, but most are over in two to three minutes. There may be a chilly sensation for a few moments afterwards. (A variation is the chill without the flash.)

∎

I would like every man and woman to have just one of my hot flashes! First, a sudden, unexplained what's-the-point-of-it-all feeling which lasts only five or ten seconds. I know that within the next thirty seconds I'm going to have a hot flash — waves of heat travelling up my body, perspiration breaking out all over and running down my forehead, a terrible feeling of weakness and exhaustion. I have to sit down or lean against a wall if no seats are available. I'm left with damp clothes (which quickly start to feel cold) and I feel as if I've just finished a hard game of squash — a game I had to give up some years ago. Sometimes I can feel my head pounding during the flash, and sometimes it leaves me with a headache. This can happen from once an hour to four or five times in an hour.

Hot flashes tend to appear during the time when menstrual periods are acting erratically and to peak during the year of the last menstrual period. They seem to occur most often just before rising and just before bed (6:00 a.m. and 10:00 p.m.) and, for a great many women, seem *not* to be due to unusual stress or worry. Most women report equally heavy flashing during times of rest or relaxation with friends. The night-time version of the hot flash is usually more severe. Perspiration may be so profuse as to require a change of clothing or of bed linen. Night sweats that are severe and/or frequent contribute to fatigue and depression. Fortunately, flashes this severe happen to very few naturally menopausal women.

Dry vagina and urinary distress
With the onset of menopause, there is a tendency for the tissue of the urethra and vagina to thin out and become more fragile. The vagina may also become shorter and both urethra and vagina become more vulnerable to inflammation and infection. Dry vagina (also known by the medical, but unacceptable, terms "senile" or "**atrophic vaginitis**") may mean that a woman's own lubrication is inadequate for pleasurable penile penetration. In extreme cases, the vagina may be so dry as to make routine movements like walking uncomfortable. This condition is likely to occur a few years after menopause (i.e., usually during a woman's late fifties or early sixties) or as a result of artificial menopause (involving removal of the **ovaries**).

Recurring **cystitis** (a burning sensation when urinating) or other urinary problems may occur after **hysterectomy** as a result of the surgery, rather than from natural ageing. Damage to the bladder or ureters (tubes running from the bladder to the kidneys) is not uncommon following this operation, particularly if the procedure was done through the vagina — as, for instance, to repair a prolapse.

Even when vaginal or urinary problems are relatively minor, many woman complain of frequent urination and a tendency to "leak" when coughing or sneezing, or during orgasm. This is known as "stress incontinence" and is different from "urge incontinence" where one feels the need to urinate even when there is only a small amount of urine in the bladder.

Osteoporosis
Osteoporosis means "porous bone" and is a condition that results from excess loss of bone tissue. The onset of osteoporosis is usually painless (which is why it is not listed as a menopausal ailment), and osteoporotic women rarely get advance warning of its onset, except for periodic back ache (often of the lower back) as crush fractures occur.

Because the pain eases after a few days and then goes away, few women suspect that a vertebra has collapsed. For most women, the first awareness of osteoporosis follows from a broken bone, often a wrist fracture. This fracture may lead to a series of them.

Strictly speaking, osteoporosis is *not* a symptom of menopause, since its onset is based on many factors in addition to menopausal status, and most particularly on bone density at about age thirty-five — long before menopause starts. Bone continues to strengthen (that is, become more dense) until the mid-thirties after which we start to lose bone — at first slowly and then more quickly as we reach the late forties and early fifties. Once menopause is past, bone loss slows down again.

It is suspected that osteoporosis may comprise a number of different conditions and there is still a great deal to be known about it. However, we *do* know that there are at least two types of bone involved — cortical (the hard, shiny outer layer) and trabecular (the honeycomb structure of inner bone or vertebrae). Each type of bone may be affected by a number of factors and, unless you have worked hard to build good bone during your young adulthood (that is, consumed a lot of calcium and had regular, vigorous exercise), you may have grounds for concern. If you are slight and fair-skinned; if you smoke, do not exercise regularly, have never borne or breast-fed a child, and have a history of broken bones in your family, you should take steps to prevent excess loss of bone.

Aside from menstrual irregularity, hot flashes, dry vagina, and osteoporosis, there are a number of ailments, minor and major, that are often part of life for the menopausal woman. What such complaints have in common is that they are only rarely blamed on menopause, whether in books or articles, or in the opinions of most medical practitioners. Indeed, it is sometimes difficult to know whether they are caused by menopause or by ageing — a situation that is likely to persist until we get more solid research.

ADDITIONAL AILMENTS

At present, if you mention one of these "additional ailments" to your doctor, you are likely to have it dismissed. It very much depends on the person you consult. A knowledgeable or experienced doctor may take some of these ailments seriously, but it is hard to know which complaints will be attended to and which will be trivialized.

Joint pains
This common ailment often appears before either menstrual irregu-

larity or the first hot flash. When **bursitis** of the shoulder, tennis elbow, trick knees, aching wrists, sore heels, or "funny" ankles trouble a woman, menopause is rarely suspected, but joint aches appear to be linked to the **adrenal glands** where cortisone, the substance that keeps joints moving freely, is manufactured. Studies have shown that from one-fifth to one-half of menopausal women experience joint pain at one time or another. It appears to afflict women of all sizes and shapes, whether they engage in regular, vigorous exercise or are more or less sedentary.

Joint pain is usually restricted to one or two joints and should not be considered in the same class as chronic aches and pains that may recur for years. Chronic and severe aches and pains may be due to fibrositis or, more accurately, **fibromyalgia**. Women with fibromyalgia are often mistakenly diagnosed as either arthritic or osteoporotic although there is no muscle inflammation, damaged tissue, swollen joints, or broken bones. There seems to be a biochemical link between fibromyalgia and depression, but this is still under investigation. It is not likely to happen to you, but it is worth knowing about fibromyalgia for those women who have exhausted every other possibility in the search for an explanation for massive aches and pains.

Migraine

Migraine headaches begin with a spasm in an artery close to the surface on either the left or right side of the head. Since it is confined to one side of the head, a migraine headache is quite different from a stress headache (which usually comes on slowly) or the "hatband" sensation of a tension headache. Some women will experience bouts of dizziness, strange tingling sensations, or episodes of pronounced heartbeat (**"palpitations"**) — these may be forms of migraine activity *without* the headache. Some women will notice strange "pings" in the back of the head, or what feel like strange surges of blood. Although it is wise to check any such symptoms with a doctor, it is also helpful to know that these experiences are not that rare.

•

I experienced severe attacks of vertigo intermittently over a one-year period and they only stopped after a self-imposed regimen of vitamin supplements — Vitamin B_{12}, Vitamin C, and a multiple-vitamin tablet.

The attacks usually came on when I got out of my car in the company parking lot to walk the 150 feet to the entrance. During an attack, if I got up from my chair too quickly, I felt as if I would fall over and, while walking the hallways, I would literally bump into the walls. Now that it is over, I can only attribute the spells of vertigo to stressful situations.

The relationship between migraines and **hormones** has been inferred from the onset of common migraine at puberty, the cyclical nature of the symptoms, and the tendency for migraines to disappear (in about 80 per cent of cases) during pregnancy, and to return again until **post-menopause** when, in the majority of cases, they disappear for good.

Some women, however, develop migraines for the first time just prior to menopause. The migraines, whether in the form of headaches or not, occur most commonly during the menstrual period or in the few days following the period. The timing is assumed to be related to low levels of **progesterone**, but other patterns — headache at ovulation or just prior to menstruation — may be related to **estrogen** levels. Or it may be the ratio of estrogen to progesterone that triggers the migraine.

Some women will experience the typical **aura** (or "prodrome") that precedes a migraine without ever having the headache. The aura is a subjective sensation warning that a migraine is about to start. The aura may take many forms — dizziness, numbness, tingling of the extremities, heightened sensitivity to smells or noise or taste, restlessness, yawning, etc. — but the more common aura is a visual disturbance marked by spots floating before the eyes, then a shimmering outline that gradually obliterates most of the visual field.

Other migraine equivalents are abdominal pain with nausea, vomiting, or diarrhoea; acute pain in the chest, pelvis, or extremities; attacks of rapid heartbeat ("tachycardia"); sudden attacks of dizziness for no apparent reason ("benign paroxysmal vertigo"); or **bloat** occurring on a cyclical basis (repeated after a predictable number of days). Each of these may or may not be accompanied by a headache.

There is no one simple test to establish the presence of a migraine and, even less so, of a migraine equivalent. If you suspect that you are experiencing a migraine equivalent, you might ask your doctor to arrange for medical tests to rule out other possibilities. (Inner-ear infections, for instance, could be responsible for the dizziness.) Or you may wish to see a neurologist with a special interest in migraine. You can obtain a list of specialists in your area from the Migraine Foundation (see page 200).

Burning-mouth syndrome
Some women experience dry mouth during menopause, a condition that is often aggravated by caffeine and antihistamines, as well as some prescription drugs (e.g., **clonidine** and some kinds of antidepressants). This drying out of the tissue appears to be related to the more widely recognized phenomenon of dry vagina. Others suffer from an extreme case of dry mouth, called burning-mouth syndrome (BMS)

estimated to affect only 2 per cent of the general population, of whom as many as one-fifth may be post-menopausal women. Burning-mouth syndrome often prompts a visit to the dentist with complaints about a chronic burning sensation in the mouth and gums, but the cause is not yet understood. Research on burning-mouth syndrome is underway at the University of Toronto Dental School under the supervision of Dr. Miriam Grushka.

Indigestion, flatulence, bloat
Many women complain about indigestion or flatulence. Some of us find ourselves longing, just fleetingly, for those ancient panty girdles that contained unexpected wind so effectively! Some of us also occasionally experience "bloat" — the lower torso (waist and belly) swells and stays swollen for two or three hours. A very uncomfortable feeling — and one that many of us remember from pregnancy!

Sleep problems
Changes in sleep habits are very common. Many women find it hard to get to sleep, to stay asleep, or to sleep past the light of early dawn. The average number of hours spent sleeping diminishes from about eight hours at age twenty to around six hours at age fifty, and there is a concurrent increase in awakenings. Some of this may be due to hot flashes that, although not severe enough to warrant the name "night sweats," are enough to waken. Once wakened, many of us head for the bathroom. It's hard to know what provokes the wakening — the sensation of warmth or a full bladder.

Most physicians assume that hot flashes cause sleep disruption and that the alleviation of the flashes (using estrogen) will result in restful sleep. Sometimes this is true, but some women experience severe sleep problems that cannot be remedied with **estrogen replacement therapy** (ERT).

Menopause may also be marked by episodes of **"air hunger,"** a sudden and unpleasant sensation of suffocation — gasping for air for a few minutes until it passes. A variation is "sleep **apnea**" where breathing stops for a few, interminable seconds. Both sensations last for only a short time but can be very frightening.

■

I have had several unpleasant episodes of sleep apnea over the last two years, two of them severe enough to warrant hospitalization. I really felt quite crazy when I was explaining that I had stopped breathing for a few seconds, but a friend who accompanied the recent Everest expedition had similar symptoms due to the altitude. Unfortunately, my doctor can't offer any help or explanation for this distressing complaint. Neurological tests show nothing wrong.

Weight gain

This is not, strictly speaking, an ailment since it is more common than not. However, many of us find ourselves being chided by our doctors and this, on top of our own frustrating efforts to stay slim, makes it *feel* like a medical problem. Most of us do not eat more than usual. The weight gain is a feature of ageing, but hastened by menopause when the metabolism slows down. Not only are the extra pounds both unexpected and unwelcome but they often accumulate in strange places — on the back, bust, and abdomen — rather than on the hips and thighs.

Skin and hair

Some women complain of a crawling sensation. There is a proper medical term for this — **formication**, which is related to the word for "ants." It feels as if ants are crawling on the skin. Patterns of hair growth may change, with underarm hair, pubic hair, and scalp hair thinning out and changing texture, while unwanted facial hair may make an appearance. If scalp hair is thinning, a dermatologist should be consulted. The cause is assumed to be excessive **androgen** production and, thus far, little has been available in the way of treatment.

■

> I am taking estrogen and, so far, have had no problems with it. However, my unhappiness now — and yes, I can call it that — is that my hair, once curly and pretty, is thinning *drastically*. Of course, I have changed my hair style and tried various "cosmetics" for hair to keep it up and back. I try to ignore the situation, but am privately terrified. I'm fifty-four years old and want to continue my busy, productive life without the threat of a wig!

If scalp hair is thinning too rapidly and in patches, the condition may be **alopecia areata**, which, so far as we know, is not related to menopause. More often, thinning scalp hair results from a change in texture and density that accompanies or follows menopause. There seems to be a family tendency to thinning hair.

Sensory disturbances

Many women experience what are known as sensory disturbances during menopause, either briefly or for a more extended period of time. They may feel their vision is on a downhill slide and need new spectacles, or they may merely see spots in front of their eyes now and then. Some women report that they hear bursts of sounds more loudly than usual. Some women smell phantom aromas for weeks or months at a time — woodsmoke, wet grass, or a dimly remembered scent impossible to place. Some develop a sensitivity to certain tastes, or lose the sense of taste almost entirely. (This latter may also be due to use of **corticosteroids.**) Some women experience **"touch impairment,"** a sensitivity to being touched, which makes them shrink from human contact, or an inability to respond to previously welcome touching by others. These are nearly always temporary conditions.

Miscellaneous complaints

In addition, there are a potpourri of annoying physical changes, some of which may be linked to menopause (such as swollen, tender breasts) but most of which may be caused by ageing. Many women feel overwhelming fatigue. This may be the result of interrupted sleep (although one is not necessarily conscious of the interruptions) but may also be the result of underactivity of the thyroid, a sympathetic reaction to other hormonal upsets. Some women get "rubber legs," the temporary, but frightening sensation that their legs are going to give way underneath them. Some notice weird bruises on their thighs or trunk. It has even been reported that, because of hormonal changes, menopausal women are more likely to suffer from bad breath!

There is no way of predicting who will experience what ailments, who will have a tough time and who will have an easy time. Nor is there any magic formula to decide who can cope and who cannot. The experience of menopause is as individual as the experiences of pregnancy or childbirth.

If your ailments are more nuisance than anything else, you can probably deal with them on your own. Many of the physical ailments of menopause can be managed by alterations in daily routines to eliminate bad habits (smoking and caffeine consumption), to include regular exercise, to add key nutrients to the diet, or to cut back on commitments in order to relieve the stress on your system. Because your immediate interest is in resuming a regular routine, the knowledge that these ailments are likely to be temporary and that they are experienced by many women in menopause will help to restore a sense of control. From this control comes the confidence to deal with the passing inconveniences of the menopausal years.

If you are feeling sick and unable to deal with day-to-day responsibilities, you should look for professional help. Unfortunately, many doctors do not think of menopause in relation to many of these ailments and, if they do, often do not share this information with their patients. The attitude seems to be that menopausal women are eager to complain, and ready to "adopt an ailment" and call it their own. If your ailments are medical, you will need a good physician. In her book, *Patient Beware*, Cynthia Carver provides clear advice about how to find helpful medical expertise. If your menopausal ailments derive from poor nutrition or poor general health, or if they affect your relationships, you may want to see a holistic health practitioner, a naturopath, a counsellor, or a psychotherapist. If you are fortunate, you will find a professional who will work *with* you to find answers to your questions and relief from the most worrisome complaints.

CHAPTER 3
·

Strategies and Remedies:
Medical and Non-medical

THE DECISION TO SEEK medical help is often a difficult one. Because **menopause** has never been a major part of medical studies, many physicians don't know much about it, and don't take it seriously enough. Rather than listening to their patients, they simply tell them to keep busy or to stop thinking about themselves. At the other extreme, gynaecologists — the specialists who are *expected* to know about menopause — are often so occupied with women who are truly ill (usually those who have been hysterectomized), that they view menopause as worse than it really is. Only a few naturally menopausal women have a dreadful time but, because the medical view of menopause defines it as a disease rather than as a normal transition, a specialist may be *too* ready to offer powerful drugs.

If you view menopause as a natural transition (as I do), you may be interested in preventive steps and alternative (non-medical) remedies to help you get through menopause as smoothly as possible. Many menopausal women have been helped by naturopaths, nutritionists, chiropractors, and acupuncturists. By trying readily available alternative remedies, you may be able to manage your own menopause without resorting to prescribed medication.

However, be aware that non-medical remedies often do not provide immediate relief. The benefits of regular exercise, vitamin or diet supplements, not smoking, etc., take time to be felt. If you decide to experiment with an alternative remedy, be prepared to wait for results. Give each product a fair trial — a month or two — before abandoning it. Because more is not necessarily better, it is dangerous to take more than recommended amounts. If you do your shopping in health-food stores, you may find leaflets and publications that make extravagant claims for various products. Be wary of the far-fetched claims made by some manufacturers or packagers. Alternative remedies are not policed with the same vigilance as are prescription drugs.

MENSTRUAL IRREGULARITY

Before you make an appointment with a doctor, it is wise to jot down just what is bothering you. If it is menstrual irregularity, keep track of your periods for a few months. Write down the frequency and duration of each period as well as lightness/heaviness and colour of the flow. Some women have found relief from a heavy flow by taking anti-histamines, although this is not an approved use for these medications, or supplementary **Vitamin A**. [Note that Vitamin A can be toxic in excess. The recommended daily amount is about 5,000 international units (IUs.)]

Many women have avoided minor surgery by keeping records. One woman, for instance, did not menstruate for three months. She then had a prolonged period (fifteen days of heavy flow) that might have warranted further investigation. However, her notes on the colour and consistency of the flow established that it was three periods back to back.

Keep track of when and where you experience any unusual symptoms. Did something happen beforehand that might account for it? Have you had similar experiences in the past?

HOT FLASHES OR NIGHT SWEATS

If you experience **hot flashes**, write down the dates, times, and duration of each. The booklet by Ann Voda, *Menopause Me & You*, provides charts and detailed instructions about how to record hot flashes. If you suspect that certain situations trigger a hot flash, keep track of them. You may find that you can eliminate or manage heavy flashing by giving up caffeine, reducing or eliminating your intake of alcohol, and keeping track of foods, activities, or times of day that seem to bring flashes on. Some women find that they can quickly get rid of or ward off a hot flash by drinking iced water or by splashing the face with cold water. And, of course, you will find it easier to cope if you dress in layers and in natural fibres that breathe, rather than in synthetics.

One of the least known but most effective ways of minimizing hot flashes is to gain weight. The upsets of menopause are, to a large degree, caused by the erratic and diminishing production of **estradiol** (a form of **estrogen**) by the **ovaries**, and the shift to **estrone**, an alternative and less powerful form of estrogen. It is useful to know that menopause is *not* the end of estrogen production but rather a time when the body "shifts gears" and begins to utilize estrogen of a different kind at a different level. Estrone is produced from androstene-dione from the **adrenal glands**, which is then converted into estrone in the adipose, or fatty, tissue of the body. This conversion process becomes more efficient and more effective with age and with a healthy ratio of body fat.

To encourage this shift to estrone production, many nutritionists and geriatricians are encouraging menopausal women to tolerate a gain of ten to fifteen pounds over "ideal weight." The added weight is also helpful in combatting **osteoporosis**. So don't be *too* downhearted if a few extra pounds are accidentally slipping onto your frame. The slender women you have always envied may have a much tougher time with hot flashes and may also be more prone to broken bones in old age.

Non-prescription remedies

The most popular products to combat hot flashes are **Vitamin E**, evening primrose oil (often recommended for **premenstrual syndrome**), bee pollen, and ginseng and/or Dong Quai.

Vitamin E is measured in international units (100, 200, 400 IUs, etc.) and bottles of the capsules are available in drugstores and health-food stores. Vitamin E is said to be effective for one-half to two-thirds of women with hot flashes, but it may take from two to six weeks to feel the difference. Women with diabetes, high blood pressure, or a rheumatic heart condition should take only very small quantities, a maximum of 100 IUs daily. *Vitamin E should not be taken by someone on digitalis.* Most women will be comfortable with 600 to 800 IUs, preferably taken after a meal containing some fat. Some advocates of Vitamin E recommend that it be taken with Vitamin C. Vitamin E is also available in the form of cream or oil to aid healing of minor cuts, or to relieve itchiness. If you are unsure of the types and amounts of diet supplements that might help your particular situation, you may want to consult a nutritionist, a naturopath, or a doctor versed in holistic medicine. A Directory of Health Care Practitioners is listed under Resources for this chapter.

Evening primrose oil is also sold in bottles of capsules and contains gamma-linolenic acid, which is related to prostaglandin activity. Prostaglandins are fatty acids involved in the contraction of blood vessels. Evening primrose oil is promoted for relief of menstrual cramps, swollen and tender breasts, and hot flashes. This product is expensive and generally available only in health-food stores. Women who use it regularly swear by it, although there are, as yet, no reputable studies establishing its effectiveness. The recommended dose is two to eight capsules daily.

Bee pollen is similar to evening primrose oil, in that its popularity and effectiveness are sustained by the menopause grapevine. The product usually mentioned is "Melbrosia pld," available in health-food stores. These are pleasant, chewable tablets and the recommended dose is one a day. This product is also expensive.

Ginseng and Dong Quai (the spelling varies) are herbs originally imported from the Orient, although most ginseng is now grown here. The ginseng root (*panax schinseng* or *panax quinquefolius*) is recommended for both men and women as a way of increasing the metabolic rate and regaining energy. Ginseng is processed as tablets, capsules, liquid, powder, or tea. However, people with asthma or **emphysema** are advised to avoid it because of its **histamine**-liberating action. Dong Quai or Tan Kwai (*Cimicifuga racemosa*) is often sold as "female ginseng" and is said to have **hormone**-like properties capable of relieving severe hot flashes. I have found it in tablets and powders. (It is interesting to know that, in China, the use of such herbs and preparations is supervised by pharmacists who spend six years learning their profession. Medical doctors in China go to school for only five years.)

■

A few years ago, I first became aware of occasionally feeling hot all by myself; no one else seemed to find it too warm. I remember a drive from Vancouver to Banff with all the car windows open, myself dressed in two layers of batiste cotton and my torso sheeted with pouring sweat. I had neglected to renew my supply of ginseng about a week before the trip.

My experience was that, so long as I kept ginseng and Vitamin E as part of my morning regime, I experienced no hot flashes or any other discomfort. The whole business was over in three years with not a ripple of reminder since.

Prescription remedies

Clonidine is the generic name of a hypertensive drug (commonly prescribed as Dixarit) that is sometimes successful in controlling hot flashes. Clonidine is not recommended if you have a tendency to depression as it may contribute to it. It appears to be more effective if it is started before flashes become really severe. Even so, it works for only 30 to 40 per cent of women who try it. The usual dosage is one 0.5 mg tablet twice daily and you should feel a difference within two to three weeks if it's going to work. Potential side-effects are dry mouth, constipation, headaches, and (occasionally) wild dreams. It is recommended that use of the medication be discontinued after three to six months and that the situation be re-evaluated.

The most common prescription drug used to treat hot flashes is a synthetic or "conjugated" form of the female hormone, estrogen. Synthetic estrogen is produced in a laboratory; conjugated estrogen is produced from the urine of pregnant horses. The bulk of prescriptions specify **Premarin** (a word and a product made from *pregnant mares'* urine). Because this estrogen is produced by an animal, as opposed to a laboratory, it is often referred to as "natural estrogen," although it is natural only to horses. Premarin tablets are available in different strengths — 0.3 mg, 0.625 mg, 0.9 mg, 1.25 mg, and 2.5 mg. The 0.625 mg tablet (once daily) is the most widely prescribed.

Estrogen is also available in vaginal creams, in injections, in patches, in pellets (which are surgically implanted under the top layer of skin on the abdomen or inner thigh), in lozenges that are placed under the tongue to dissolve in the mouth, and in combination pills similar to the hormone combination used in contraceptive pills. The pellets, lozenges, and combination pills are not yet approved by Health and Welfare Canada for the relief of menopausal symptoms.

COMMON ESTROGEN PRODUCTS

BRAND NAME	GENERIC NAME	DOSAGE
Tablets:		
C.E.S.	conjugated estrogens	.625 mg or 1.25 mg
Estinyl	ethinyl estradiol	.02, .05 or .5 mg
Estrace	17-beta estradiol	1 or 2 mg
Menrium	esterified estrogens (E) & chlordiazopoxide (Librium)	.2 (E) & 5 mg (L) .4 (E) & 5 mg (L) or .4 (E) & 10 mg (L)
Ogen	estropipate (estrone)	1.5 or 3 mg
Premarin	conjugated estrogens	.3, .625, .9, 1.25 or 2.5 mg
Premarin with methyl testosterone	conjugated estrogens (E) & methyl testosterone (T)	.625 (E) & 5 mg (T) or 1.25 (E) & 10 mg (T)
TACE	chlorotrianisene	12, 14 or 72 mg
Patch:		
Estraderm	estradiol	25, 50 or 100 mcg
Injection:		
Climacteron	testosterone & estradiol	1 ml ampuls or 5 ml vials
Delestrogen	estradiol valerate	5 ml vials
Premarin	conjugated estrogens	25 mg powder (added to 5 mL sterile water)
Vaginal Creams:		
Dienestrol	dienestrol	1 mg/g of cream
Premarin	conjugated estrogens	.625 mg/g of cream

Estrogen offers speedy relief of debilitating hot flashes. Although it will not eliminate *all* flashes for *all* women, it is the most effective prescription remedy available. Because the decision about whether to seek or to accept **estrogen replacement therapy** (ERT) remains the central issue for many menopausal women, additional information on use of ERT is outlined in Chapter 5. Here are some points that should be kept in mind:

1. The precise way in which estrogen works is not completely understood. Some women who suffer from severe hot flashes may take ERT, have the hot flashes relieved, and then stop taking the estrogen after six months or a year and have no further problems. Some women find that, as soon as they go off the ERT, the hot flashes return with renewed intensity. They are forced to continue to take the medication or to wean themselves very gradually while coping with severe flashes. We don't know why this "rebound" effect occurs in some women but not in others.

2. Estrogen is known to sometimes cause endometrial cancer (cancer of the lining of the **uterus**) because estrogen acts to increase the number and density of cells inside the uterus. When too many cells are present, it may lead to a pre-cancerous condition. This is not a a problem if your uterus has been removed. Many doctors now mimic the natural menstrual cycle by prescribing estrogen (which stimulates new cells) and then adding synthetic **progesterone** (which causes the cells to slough off as in a normal menstrual period). This combination of drugs is known as **hormone replacement therapy** (HRT). The "**withdrawal bleed**" is presumed to eliminate the build-up of pre-cancerous cells in the uterus. If you have *not* had a **hysterectomy** or if you are *unwilling* to deal with "monthly bleeds," you should not accept a prescription for estrogen.

3. There are specific contra-indications to the use of estrogen. This means that women with certain medical conditions, or with a tendency to these medical conditions, should not take estrogen. Women with some kinds of heart disease, with high blood pressure, with a tendency to **thromboembolisms** or **phlebitis**, or to gall-bladder disease or gallstones are rarely given ERT. Similarly, women with migraines, diabetes, liver disease, uterine **fibroids**, or a history of (or strong family tendency toward) breast cancer should not take estrogen. Obese women — those who are 20 per cent or more above "ideal weight" — should not be on ERT because they are more prone to cancer.

4. There are also potential side-effects from ERT — nausea, vomiting, cramps, dizziness, light-headedness, fluid retention, weight gain, **bloat**, headaches, breast swelling and tenderness, rashes or itchy skin, visual disturbances (spots floating before the eyes), or

changes in sexual desire. These are not common reactions but you should be aware of them when you have your prescription filled. Estrogen therapy comes in many forms: it may be possible to change the dosage or to switch to another formula. (One product that is *not* recommended is a tablet called **Menrium**, a combination of estrogen and a strong tranquillizer — one with the potential to become habit-forming.)

Although injections are used less and less often now, you may have a doctor who prefers these to tablets. (Tablets must be metabolized in the liver whereas other products bypass the liver and enter directly into the bloodstream.) If you have any negative side-effects from the injections, you will not be able to halt the reaction that will continue to run its course for four to six weeks or more. One injectable estrogen (**Climacteron**) also contains **testosterone**, the so-called male hormone produced in the male testicles but also produced, in small quantities, in the female ovary. Aside from the possibility of delayed side-effects, any product containing testosterone may cause virilization (more masculine voice, increased body hair, etc.). If you are using estrogen for the first time, it would be wise to evaluate the effects of estrogen alone before exposing yourself to a combination drug. It is also a good idea to use a form of the drug that can be quickly discontinued should there be unpleasant side-effects.

Many physicians are now switching to the new estrogen patches that are put on the skin twice a week and that release a controlled amount of estrogen into the system. This form of estrogen, which has only been on the market in Canada for a few months (and in the United States for a year or two), is absorbed directly into the bloodstream, bypassing the liver.

Although hot flashes *can* be debilitating, only a small number of naturally menopausal women suffer significantly from them. Most of us suffer more from fatigue, caused by the physiological stress of constantly adjusting to internal temperature changes, and from embarrassment when we have a hot flash in public. If the social stigma of this kind of "flashing" were removed and the embarrassment eliminated, we would all feel better. Perhaps it is time to revive the use of the fan! Wouldn't it be nice if a menopausal woman felt free to slip a delicately folded fan from her purse and to use it in public?

It is hysterectomized and, most of all, oophorectomized women who suffer from the most severe hot flashes. For these women, and for the small minority of naturally menopausal women who are incapacitated, estrogen provides the only certain relief. Unfortunately, there is still a great deal we *don't* know about estrogen. Until more definitive research can tell us the long-term consequences of estrogen use over a period of years, we will have to make individual and informed choices based on what we *do* know.

DRY VAGINA AND/OR URINARY DISTRESS

The naturally menopausal woman may notice changes in the frequency and pattern of urination while she is still menstruating. On the other hand, the problem of **dry vagina** is more likely to occur months or years into her **post-menopause**. Dry vagina may be detected during regular medical examinations when insertion of the fingers or a speculum is found to be painful. More often, however, a woman notices that penetration by a penis is now uncomfortable.

Problems may occur at an earlier age to the hysterectomized woman, since the bladder or ureters can be damaged during hysterectomy (particularly vaginal hysterectomy), and **oophorectomy** often causes dry vagina.

Healthy tissue in and around the vagina may be encouraged by switching to natural fibres, which allow better air circulation. This means cotton panties and pantyhose with cotton crotches or with the crotch cut out. Some women have reverted to stockings with garters or to the new stockings that cling without garters. Skirts are preferable to slacks, particularly if the slacks are tight-fitting. This may not be so important when you're younger because the **labia** (lips) around the vagina tend to seal it; with age, the labia are not so efficient.

Vaginal discharges should be monitored very carefully. Cutting down on dairy products, sugar, and artificial sweeteners may help chronic vaginal infections. If there is irritation, a change in colour of discharge, or an unpleasant odour, make an appointment with the doctor. A douche may relieve it temporarily but will not cure an infection; it is better to have it checked.

•

> My greatest problem is urinary leakage. Intercourse has become uncomfortable for me because of this. It is most distressing. The doctors and the specialist I have seen say there is nothing that can be done.

Many women notice the need to urinate more frequently, even though they are voiding smaller amounts (urge incontinence), or an involuntary dribbling when coughing, sneezing, or during orgasm (stress incontinence). Both conditions result from the thinning and shortening of tissue in the genito-urinary tract and relaxation of the pelvic floor as a result of ageing.

One can adapt to frequent urination, but the best way to prevent leakage is to make a habit of Kegel exercises. These exercises (promoted by a Dr. Arnold Kegel) involve isolating the sphincter muscle, which controls urination, and strengthening it. If you faithfully practise tightening and loosening this muscle — an exercise that can be done anytime and anywhere — you may find that it not only alleviates incontinence problems, but also enhances the ability to respond sexually.

If you find that you are prone to recurrent bouts of **cystitis** (bladder infections that produce a burning sensation when urinating), make a habit of drinking large quantities of water. Some women find that drinking cranberry juice on a regular basis controls the incidence of such infections. It may also be useful to know that diaphragm use for contraception has been associated with increased risk of cystitis, and that progesterone (either alone or in conjunction with estrogen) may aggravate bladder troubles.

The safest remedies for dry vagina and urinary leakage are a combination of regular orgasm (which encourages natural lubrication) and Kegel exercises. If you do not have a regular partner, you may decide to masturbate in order to keep your vagina healthy. If intercourse is painful, this may be the time to explore other forms of sexual expression — oral/genital sex, mutual masturbation, etc.

Non-prescription remedies
Many women find intercourse more comfortable with the help of a water-based lubricant, such as K-Y Jelly or Lubafax. These products are available at the drugstore and can be inserted into the vagina or smeared on the penis prior to penetration. Note that, despite all jokes to the contrary, petroleum-based lubricants — such as Vaseline — are not recommended since they may damage fragile vaginal tissue. Despite the shame that some women feel about having to use supplementary lubrication during sex, there are many young couples who have always depended on water-based lubricants. Buying a tube of lubricant is not necessarily proclaiming middle-aged inadequacy!

Because the dryness of the vagina is partially due to a change in the chemical environment, some women have had success using natural yoghurt to restore a healthy vaginal climate. Rosetta Reitz, author of *Menopause: A Positive Approach*, recommends equal amounts of yoghurt and polyunsaturated oil (corn, peanut, safflower, sunflower, or soybean) both as a weekly regimen to keep the vaginal walls elastic, and also as a way of lubricating oneself prior to intercourse. Yoghurt can be inserted using the kind of applicator available with douches or foam spermicide, or even with a plastic tampon inserter. Because of

KEGEL EXERCISES

To locate your pubococcyygeal (PC) muscle, simply stop your flow while urinating; it's the PC muscle that contracts to do this. Practise a few times to get the feeling of this muscle. Stop and start urinating at will. Try some stronger and weaker contractions until you can contract this muscle when not urinating. This will help you become familiar with this muscle. You can do your PC exercises anytime you wish; while waiting for a bus or walking down the street, or just after waking. Try them in fitness class when you are working on your abdominals — especially during the pelvic tilt. These two exercises go well together.

Three and Three
Contract your PC muscle for 3 full seconds and then release it for one second. Repeat 6 times, 3 times a day for a few days. Then repeat 12 times a day for a week.

One and One
Contract your PC muscle strongly for one second and release it for one second. Repeat 20 times, 3 times a day. Speed up the contractions so that you get a "fluttering" feeling here.

Ten and Five
Contract the PC muscle for 10 full seconds, working at holding the intensity of the contraction for the full period of time. Relax for 5 seconds. Repeat 5 times, 3 times a day.

Elevator
As you become more aware of your PC muscle, you will notice that you can feel the difference between your anal and vaginal muscle area. When you start to feel this difference, try the "elevator." Start with an anal contraction (bottom floor) and then move it along the PC muscle into the vaginal area and up to the "top floor." Repeat 6 times, 3 times a day.

Once you have improved your PC muscle tone and can do all of these exercises competently, try maintaining the strength and endurance of your PC muscle by doing your exercises once a day instead of three times. As with most exercise routines, it helps to set aside a specific time and place to ensure that you don't forget.

Source: Fitness Leader, September 1983

the consistency of this solution, it is better to be horizontal and to stay horizontal for some time after insertion. And you may want to place a towel under you to protect the bed clothes — or a bearskin rug, depending on your mood!

The tissues outside the vagina, sometimes the whole area around the crotch, may become dry and itchy. If you are already wearing cotton next to the skin, itchiness can often be relieved using "hygienic wipes" — small pads of cotton impregnated with witch hazel and glycerin. You can find hygienic wipes at the drugstore, often close to products for hemorrhoid relief. If the itchiness is serious and is felt inside the vagina, you may have contracted an infection. As the tissues thin out, many women become more vulnerable to infections that are not necessarily sexually transmitted.

Prescription remedies
Estrogen cream is commonly prescribed for dry vagina. It is not a good idea to take two forms of estrogen, so if you are already taking tablets, using the patches, or have had an injection, report this to your doctor. Estrogen cream comes with its own applicator calibrated in grams for insertion into the vagina. The recommended dosage on the package is two to four grams daily, on a cycle of three weeks on and one week off. This is often more than most women need.

The most popular estrogen cream is Premarin, which contains 0.625 mg of conjugated estrogen *per gram*. Since estrogen cream is absorbed into the system — with effects on the whole body, not just on the problem area — use of two to four grams of cream daily would be equal to a daily dose, in oral tablets, of from 1.25 mg to 2.5 mg — two to four times the normal amount. Most women find that a fraction of this dosage will serve to restore the vagina, although it may take three weeks to reverse the situation. Once the vagina is comfortable again, you can experiment with less frequent use — perhaps two weeks on and two weeks off or, after time, one week of regular use of the cream every month.

The applicator supplied tends to deposit the cream deep into the vagina, but it should also be smeared just inside the opening of the vagina; this is the area that is usually most painful. Estrogen cream, unlike water-based lubricants, is a medication and should *not* be used just prior to intercourse since it will also be absorbed by your partner. If you have an intact uterus and if use of the estrogen cream is continued over a period of months, a course of synthetic progesterone may be advisable to make sure that the cells of the **endometrium** are not adversely affected.

OSTEOPOROSIS

The best prevention against osteoporosis is to have strong bones. This means lots of calcium (milk, cheese, dark green vegetables) during the childbearing years, and regular exercise that puts stress on the bones. Since bone is built as the result of the mechanical pull of the muscles, exercises that involve use of the whole body are best — walking, running, rope-jumping, and racquet sports. At one time, it was thought that swimming would not be particularly beneficial for osteoporosis because of the buoyancy factor. A recent study suggests that swimming does help, although it cannot offer the same degree of necessary stress to the bone as is supplied during weight-bearing exercise. Bicycle-riding will help the bones of the lower body but may not strengthen the bones of the arms and shoulders. (A cyclist who plays the piano regularly may have no problem.)

Bone loss is intensified if you consume a lot of caffeine (in coffee, tea, or soft drinks) and phosphorus (primarily in red meat and cola drinks), if you smoke, if you *don't* get regular weight-bearing exercise, if you don't receive sufficient **Vitamin D** ("the sunshine vitamin"), and if your diet does not include adequate levels of two essential minerals, manganese and magnesium. *If you have experienced surgical menopause (removal of both ovaries), the risk doubles.* Fortunately, there is usually a nine- to ten-year delay between the first steep loss of bone (as menopause begins) and the first broken bone. Time is on your side.

Non-prescription remedies
There is a great deal of controversy over the role of calcium, and particularly calcium supplements, in the prevention of osteoporosis among women who are pre-menopausal (still menstruating regularly), peri-menopausal (having erratic or skipped periods), or post-menopausal (last period at least twelve months before). It now seems certain that the official nutritional guidelines for adult women are inadequate and that most women consume only about 500 to 600 mg of calcium in their daily diet. Women *not* on estrogen should aim for 1400 to 1500 mg daily; those on estrogen need about 1000 mg.

Dietary sources of calcium are shown on page 41. To consume enough daily calcium, a woman must diligently drink a quart of skim milk daily, or maintain a high intake of tinned salmon or sardines (including bones), plus green, leafy vegetables. If this is impossible on a regular basis, it may be wise to depend, at least to some extent, on a calcium supplement.

Calcium supplements, tablets designed to add calcium to your diet aside from that provided by food, appear to offer inadequate protec-

CALCIUM EQUIVALENTS

Listed below are amounts of different types of foods needed to supply the amount of calcium found in one cup of whole milk (i.e., 250 mL). Some of these may be easy to substitute for milk; others are simply ridiculous. While you may find a few practical substitutions on the list, you can see how hard it is to get all the calcium you need from your diet if your intake of dairy products is low.

Dairy Products	Approx Measure
Buttermilk	1 cup
Cheese, American	
pasteurized process	1½ oz.
Cheese, Cheddar	1½ oz.
Cheese, Cottage,	
creamed and lowfat	2 cups
Cheese, Cottage, dry curd	6 cups
Cheese, Swiss	1 oz.
Cheese Food, American	2 oz.
Cheese Spread, American	2 oz.
Half-and-Half	1 cup
Ice Cream, Vanilla	1¾ cups
Milk, Chocolate	1 cup
Milk, Dry Whole; 1 oz.	
to 8oz. of water	1 cup
Milk, Evaporated, as is	½ cup
Milk, Evaporated, 1	
part to 1 of water	1 cup
Milk, Instant Nonfat Dry;	
3.2 oz. to 1 qt. of water	1 cup
Milk, Lowfat	1 cup
Milk, Skim	1 cup
Milk, Sweetened	
Condensed, as is	⅓ cup
Milk, Sweetened Condensed,	
1 part to 1.5 water	1 cup
Pudding, Chocolate	1 cup
Yogurt	1 cup

Meat, Poultry, Fish, Eggs, and Peanut Butter

	Approx Measure
Beef, Roast	5 lb.
Chicken, Fried	4½ lb.
Eggs	10
Frankfurters	97
Ham, baked	5 lb.
Meat Patties	5½ lb.
Peanut Butter	29 tbsp.
Perch, Fried, Breaded	2 lb.
Pork Chops	6 lb.
Salmon, Red, with	
Bones and Oil	4 oz.
Sardines	2¼ oz.
Tuna	7¾ lb.

Combination Foods

	Approx Measure
Beans, Baked, Pork and	
Tomato Sauce	2 cups
Custard, Baked	1 cup
Macaroni and Cheese	¾ cup
Pizza, Cheese	¼ of 14" pie
Soup, Cream of Tomato	1¾ cups
Tacos, Beef	1½

Fruits & Vegetables	Approx Measure
Apples, medium	29
Bananas, medium	29
Beans, Green	4¾ cups
Beans, Lima	3¾ cups
Broccoli	2 cups
Cabbage	1½ heads
Carrots, 5" long	15
Corn	36 cups
Greens (collards, kale,	
mustard, turnip)	1 cup
Oranges, medium	5
Orange Juice	13 cups
Peas, Green	10 cups
Potatoes, Baked, large	22
Potatoes, French-fried	448 pieces
Potatoes, Sweet medium	7
Strawberries	9 cups
Tomatoes, medium	11
Watermelon	21 cups

Grains

	Approx Measure
Bread, White, slices, enriched	15
Bread, Whole Wheat, slices	13
Cornbread, 2½" x 3¼",	
enriched	3 pieces
Cornflakes (without milk)	73 cups
Crackers, Saltines	485 crackers
Noodles, Egg, enriched	18 cups
Oatmeal	13 cups
Rice	14 cups
Rolls, Frankfurters or	
Hamburger	10
Rolls, Hard	12
Tortillas, Corn, 6"	
diameter, enriched	5
Waffles, 3½" x 5½",	
enriched	5

Others

	Approx Measure
Bar, Milk Chocolate	4½ oz.
Beer	6 qts.
Butter	3 lb.
Cake, Devil's Food	½ of 9" cake
Cake, Sponge	1 10" cake
Coffee, Black	73 cups
Cookies, Sugar	18
Doughnuts, Cake-Type	22
Mayonnaise	6 cups
Pie, Apple	4 9" pies
Popcorn, Plain	291 cups
Potato Chips	364
Sherbet, Orange	10 cups
Wine, Rosé	2 qts.

Reprinted from *Stand Tall! The Informed Woman's Guide to Preventing Osteoporosis,* by Morris Notelovitz M.D. and Marsha Ware. Copyright 1982 by Morris Notelovitz. Reprinted by permission of Triad Publishing Co., Gainesville, Fl.

tion for women at high risk. But calcium supplements, *in combination with regular exercise*, appear to make a difference to some forms of osteoporosis. These supplements come in many forms: the most common are calcium carbonate, calcium gluconate, and calcium lactate. If you carefully read the label of the jar, you will find that calcium carbonate is 40 per cent elemental calcium; calcium lactate contains only 13 per cent elemental calcium, and calcium gluconate, only 10 per cent. *It is the amount of elemental calcium that is crucial.*

In other words, a 600 mg tablet of calcium carbonate gives you 240 mg of calcium, while the same size tablet of calcium lactate provides only 79 mg of calcium. Calcium gluconate provides even less. The labels of any calcium product available in a drugstore will tell you just how much elemental calcium you are getting. If you take the price of the bottle and divide it by the units of elemental calcium, you will have a guide to the cost of this particular supplement. What you are looking for is the most economical product to do the job.

Some forms of calcium are tolerated better than others. It is recommended that you consume the supplement in conjunction with something else (milk or yoghurt) and, for maximum benefit, just before you go to bed. More new bone tissue is laid down while you sleep. If you have a bad reaction — indigestion, bloat, wind, constipation — to a particular calcium supplement, don't give up on supplements entirely. Try another product until you find one that you can live with. Again, try to avoid products that include other nutrients, such as vitamins A or D. If you are evaluating a product, better to deal with one nutrient at a time.

Prescription remedies

If your physical make-up and family history strongly predispose you to osteoporosis, you may want to consider taking estrogen. Recent research suggests that 0.625 mg of Premarin (the most commonly prescribed form of estrogen) daily will *halt* the loss of bone. Note, however, that it does not build new bone and that it may have to be continued for life. As soon as estrogen is stopped, bone loss takes place as if estrogen had never been taken.

Once a woman is post-menopausal, estrogen therapy can be of limited use as a preventative. The period of rapid bone loss is almost over. This is valuable information because estrogen is often prescribed as if it works equally well for all women, and as if all women were equally in need of it. It may be helpful to the woman who has been diagnosed as osteoporotic but is of doubtful value to women seeking to avoid this condition. You should be aware of possible risks of estrogen (see Chapter 5) before you agree to it. The "Osteoporosis Risk Profile" below will give you an idea of your own needs. Use this profile to help decide if estrogen is for you.

THE OSTEOPOROSIS RISK PROFILE*
By Diane Palmason

This chart is intended to help you assess the extent to which you are at risk for spontaneous fractures of the spine, hip, and wrist that occur in persons with post-menopausal osteoporosis. Listed below are a number of factors that affect your risk profile, including those that you can affect through your lifestyle ("takens"), as well as those that are genetically determined ("givens"). Beside each factor find the statement that best applies to you, note the number beside that statement, and write the number down in the right-hand column.**

GIVENS

Score

AGE:
Female—under 35 ..... 1 35–50............ 3 51–65............ 7 Over 65........ 12 _____
Male—under 50........ 1 51–65............ 2 66–80............ 3 Over 80......... 4 _____

HERITAGE:
Black .... 1 Oriental......... 2 Mediterranean   Nordic
                                                  Middle Eastern . 3 Anglo-Saxon... 5 _____

COMPLEXION:
Dark .... 1 Ruddy/Olive.... 2 Fair/Pale 5   _____

HEREDITY:
No known   Relative over   Parent with   Relative under
bone problems   60 with   bone disease.... 4 60 with
in family .... 1 bone disease.... 3   bone disease.... 5 _____

WRIST SIZE:
Over 6¾"............... 1 6" to 6¼"....... 2 5¾" to 6"....... 3 under 5¾".......: 4 _____

HEIGHT:
over 5'8".............. 1 5'5" to 5'8"..... 2 5'2" to 5'5"..... 3 under 5'2"....... 4 _____

BODY TYPE:
Mesomorphic (high   Endomorphic   Ectomorphic (low
(high muscle, low fat) . 1 high fat, low   fat, low   _____
                        muscle).......... 6 muscle).......... 6

GYNAECOLOGICAL STATUS:
Still menstruating   Menopausal or   Earlymeno-   Surgically
or post-menopausal   post-menopausal pausal   menopaused
after 50.................. 1 46–50............ 3 45 or under..... 5 before 45........ 7 _____

TOTAL OF GIVENS . . . .   _____

* Originally appeared in *Fitness Leader*, October 1984 issue. Reprinted with permission.

** Deduct 5 points if estrogen replacement therapy was started within one year after surgery or early menopause, 3 points if started more than three years after surgery or early menopause.

TAKENS

EXERCISE:

Total body exercise 4 or more times weekly 0	Total body exercise 1 to 3 times weekly ... 3	Total body exercise at least 3 times monthly . 6	Avoid physical activity .... 12 _____

EATING HABITS:

a) Calcium Intake•••

4 or more servings of low-fat dairy products, daily 0	More than 2 servings of dairy products daily .. 3	2 or fewer servings of dairy products daily .. 6	Avoid dairy products .... 12 _____

••• Subtract 3 points if you take a calcium supplement that provides from 500 to 1500 mg of calcium daily.

b) Protein Intake —

Avoid red meat altogether 0	Seafood and white meat of poultry only 1	Meat 3 times weekly or less .. 3	Meat 4 times weekly or more . 6 _____

DRINKING HABITS:

a) Caffeine Intake

Avoid Caffeine and tanneine beverages 0	Decaffeinated drinks and/or tea only 2	3 or fewer cups of coffee/tea daily 3	4 or more cups of coffee daily .... 6 _____

b) Alcohol Intake

Weekly average fewer than 2 beers or 8 oz. wine or 3 oz. spirits 0	Weekly average 2–4 beers or 8-16 oz. wine or 3–6 oz. spirits 2	Daily average up to 2 beers or 8 oz. wine or 3 oz. spirits 4	Daily average more than 4 beers 16 oz. wine or 6 oz. spirits ..... 8 _____

TOBACCO USE:

Non-user 0	Occasional cigarette only, fewer than 14 weekly 2	Daily smoker, fewer than 10 daily 5	10 cigarettes daily or more... 8 _____

TOTAL OF TAKENS _____

FINAL TOTAL _____

Assess your risk according to the following: 8 to 25 — risk well below average; 26 to 48 — risk below average; 49 to 59 — risk generally average; 60 to 82 — moderate risk; 83 to 100 — considerable risk. Note that this chart is not intended to diagnose whether you are, or will be, osteoporotic. It is simply an indication of the extent to which you are similar to women who have been found to have osteoporosis. For an accurate diagnosis, it is necessary to have a bone scan.

Currently, a number of research projects are underway to evaluate the bone-building potential of such medications as sodium fluoride, medroxyprogesterone acetate (**Provera**), and **calcitonin** (a hormone produced by the thyroid, which influences the level of calcium in the blood). Sodium fluoride definitely builds new bone, but the bone is structurally different from normal bone, and it remains to be seen if it can withstand the same kinds of stresses. In addition, sodium fluoride cannot be tolerated by all; many women have to stop taking it because of negative side-effects. Current research studies using any of these medications generally also schedule regular weight-bearing exercise for the women under study. Such studies are highly individualized, with each woman receiving medication and exercise related to her particular diagnosis. Before being released for general consumption, each medication will have to prove itself effective for large numbers of women in less supervised situations.

Although we tend to think of osteoporosis as one generalized condition, experts suspect that it may comprise at least three, and as many as eight syndromes, each of which may affect different types of bone in different ways. There are promising studies of the treatment of osteoporosis using electrotherapy — the weak electric current used by physiotherapists to aid the knitting of broken bones — and full-spectrum lighting, which enhances the absorption of calcium. Other studies have suggested that low levels of manganese in the diet are related to poor calcium absorption and that the diets of most menopausal women are chronically short of manganese. In other words, current dire predictions may be overly pessimistic. Within a few years, new and safer methods may be available to prevent the onset of osteoporosis.

Irregularity of periods, hot flashes and night sweats, dry vagina, and the fear of osteoporosis are legitimate concerns that you may wish to discuss with your doctor. You deserve a sympathetic and supportive hearing and, since these complaints are commonly associated with menopause, you will probably receive some counsel about the advantages and disadvantages of medication. Other complaints may not be taken so seriously.

JOINT PAIN

If you experience long-standing joint pain, you may want to have it checked out. Many women have found that extra **Vitamin B$_6$** (1.5 to 2.0 mg daily), or combinations of **Vitamin C** and cod liver oil (**Vitamin D**), relieve the ache. Your doctor may suggest a cortisone shot (which masks the pain without relieving the cause) or you may consult a physiotherapist about appropriate exercises to ease the stiffness and/or pain. However, on the basis of all those women (including myself) who have been diagnosed with "frozen shoulder," or "tennis elbow," or any other affliction that is not so much incapacitating as annoying, it may be something to "wait out." It may just go away.

MIGRAINE

.

Migraine headaches have been a bane of mine for years, but they have had no regularity. Mine fall into the "common" category. Sometimes I feel they are caused by food allergies, cosmetics, smoke and stress. I usually wake up in the morning with a migraine, don't have any warning symptoms, and the bad ones last three days with nausea, vomiting (which usually provides relief), a peculiar metallic taste in my mouth, and a feeling of general malaise.

Countless experiments have been conducted to alleviate migraine with hormonal preparations — estrogens, progesterones, combinations of these and other hormones. However, because so many young women suffer their first migraine after starting on "the pill" and because the hormonal status responsible is not yet understood, migraine sufferers are generally discouraged from taking any form of supplementary hormones. Since the blood vessels in the head are dilated during migraine, there is concern that hormone use might promote blood-clot formation — clots that might come loose, be carried into the brain, and cause a stroke.

Migraines can be triggered by loss of sleep, fasting (low blood sugar), oversleeping, falling barometric pressure, glaring sunshine, flickering fluorescent or strobe lights, etc. Many migraine sufferers (migraineurs) cannot adequately process foods containing certain types of **amines**, although the headache may not start for hours after eating the foods responsible. Some of the most common culprits are aged cheese (cheddar), chocolate, vinegar, sour cream, yoghurt, yeast products, nuts, onions, citrus fruits, bananas, pork, caffeine-rich beverages, cured cold meats, and alcohol. This reaction to food is not an allergy in the common sense of the term; the amine-containing substance can only rarely be isolated using standard allergy tests.

Other migraine sufferers may have yeast infections (systemic **Candida albicans**, an overgrowth of a normal flora found in the body) or **temporomandibular joint syndrome** (faulty articulation of the hinged joint of the jaw bone; a condition that may cause, in addition to headache, dizziness or ringing in the ears). It is suspected that a tendency to migraine may also result from a major trauma earlier in life.

As soon as a migraine starts, the most effective therapy is to go to bed in a quiet, darkened room. Other preventive measures are splashing the face with cold water, or stepping into a steamy, hot shower (to dilate the blood vessels in the head) and then gradually switching to cold water (to contract the blood vessels). Not an inviting prospect!

Many migraine sufferers have learned to control their headaches with variations of **biofeedback**, relaxation therapy, and visualization. Biofeedback is usually taught at a headache or pain clinic and usually includes, as part of the training, exercises in progressive relaxation. One form of biofeedback teaches the person to raise the temperature of the hands using visual imagery (that is, imagining one's hands in the sun or dipped in a basin of warm water). As the hands warm up, the headache starts to go away. Another visualizing technique is to concentrate on the image of a headache as contained in a glaring light bulb. Then, by using the full power of imagination, the light bulb is gradually dimmed. All such techniques require guided practice to start but, once mastered, frequently provide an effective way to control migraine and, at the same time, to break from a reliance on drugs.

Nowadays, more credence is given to the very real pain experienced by many migraine sufferers. If you have exhausted other possibilities and are unwilling to rely on drugs for relief, it might be worthwhile to enquire about a pain clinic at your nearest large hospital.

Non-prescription remedies
Over-the-counter preparations — acetaminophen (Panadol, Tylenol), or ASA (Aspirin, Anacin) — may be useful if taken immediately at onset and/or for mild migraines. Preparations containing codeine are not recommended because they are addictive and may cause nausea or vomiting.

Prescription remedies
Standard prescription drugs are ibuprofen (Amersol, Motrin) , requiring a prescription in Canada but not in the United States, or Tylenol or a form of ASA, which may be useful at onset. In about 50 per cent of cases, some forms of **ergotamine** tartrate (Ergomar, Gynergen), taken immediately at onset, ward off or shorten the migraine. Ergotamine is available in tablet form, in an inhaler, as a suppository, or by injection. Variations are ergot-and-caffeine (Cafergot), ergot-caffeine-belladonna-and-phenobarbital (Cafergot–P-B), and belladonna-ergot-and-phenobarbital (Bellergal and Bellergal Spacetabs). Frequent use of any ergot preparation is dangerous. Migraine sufferers who take ergot must remain under medical supervision to prevent over-use.

Migraines that occur more often than two or three times a month may be treated with preventative drugs. Propranolol (Inderal), a beta blocker used for hypertension or high blood pressure, is one such drug although it has been found to cause restless sleep with frequent awakenings. Another is **clonidine** (Dixarit or Catapres). Dixarit is usually prescribed for **hot flashes** but is also sometimes effective in preventing migraine. Another, pizytoline (Sandomigran) is structurally similar to a tricyclic antidepressant. Two others prescribed less frequently are naproxen (Anaprox), an antiprostaglandin often used for the relief of severe menstrual cramps, and methysergide maleate (Sansert). Each of these drugs has potential side-effects. None should be taken for more than a few months.

BURNING-MOUTH SYNDROME

Four years ago, in the middle of the afternoon, my mouth caught fire. And it remained that way for three years! For a few hours, I put it down to something I ate. After a few days, I became suspicious that it might be something more serious. After a few weeks, I saw my doctor.

Over the months since, I have seen many doctors — a family physician, dermatologist, allergist, and dentist. No one could diagnose the problem. To relieve it, I tried sucking on popsicles, ice cubes, mints, or chewing gum — anything wet or cold. A year later, I heard on the news that a mysterious disease had doctors baffled. Patients were complaining of a burning mouth and tongue. It was now recognized as a genuine disorder. I felt vindicated! The symptoms persisted for another year, but I took comfort in the fact that I was not alone.

Although we know that dry mouth can result from too much caffeine or too many antihistamines, burning-mouth syndrome is harder to treat. Sucking on ice cubes, drinking cold water, and sucking peppermint lozenges are the usual responses to this syndrome, but the only lasting relief has been found by massaging the gums. Because it is assumed that this condition is related to changes inside the vagina (the tissue involved is similar), studies have been done using **Vitamin E** oil or estrogen cream as a "massage agent." Both appear to be equally effective and it seems that it is the massage that makes the difference.

INDIGESTION, FLATUENCE, BLOAT

Gas problems have been an embarrassment for several years. I initially put the blame on irregular hours, eating habits, diet, what have you. I tried eliminating certain foods and adding others. Meat seemed to be hard to digest so I tried some papaya tablets. When the papaya helped somewhat, I got a stronger complex which included "Betain HCL." It solved my problem with flatulence completely.

During middle age, many persons (men and women) develop lactose intolerance and find milk and milk products —with the exception of yoghurt— difficult to digest. For some, garlic, green pepper, or cucumber may suddenly create problems. Foods high in fat often cause heartburn. All of this is very common and undoubtedly is related more to ageing than to menopause. However, it often shows up for the first time during the menopausal years. Perhaps you should make notes of foods you eat so that you can do some detective work.

If you notice excess gas after drinking milk or eating cheese, you may want to buy a lactase enzyme. These products are sold in drugstores and health-food stores, in liquid or tablet form. When added to milk, which must then sit for a few hours, it predigests the lactose. You can then have the benefit of the calcium in the milk without the problem of indigestion. Yoghurt, although technically a milk product, is often easier to digest than milk or cheese and may help the body to deal with other foods high in lactose.

In addition, foods high in potassium — bananas, apricots, and tomato or orange juice — may relieve excess gas (and may also help to reduce the risk of stroke!). Papaya tablets or charcoal tablets (both available at health-food stores) also help that terribly windy feeling.

SLEEP PROBLEMS

Room-darkening shades or blindfolds (the kind handed out by airlines during overnight flights) often make a difference. A glass of warm milk will provide tryptophan, an amino acid that has been found to be an effective and mild sleep-inducer. You can buy tryptophan tablets over the counter in the United States, but they require a prescription in Canada. If you are already on medication, be careful of taking tryptophan since it may interact with other drugs. If you are unsure, better check with your physician.

Regular exercise helps the quality of sleep. Many women find that a walk after dinner will allow them to fall asleep more easily. Practitioners of yoga can teach their bodies to relax since deep breathing invites sleep. Some women find progressive relaxation helpful. Audiotapes that give instructions in this technique are available from sleep clinics, clinical psychologists, or through advertisements in magazines such as *Psychology Today*. Because many of us wake up early no matter what time we go to sleep, we learn to go to bed earlier and to use the hours before breakfast for quiet chores or reading.

Prescription remedies
Although sleep **apnea** is more common among men, if you awaken frequently gasping for breath, or if you begin to snore very loudly, you

may want to be checked. Some hospitals have special sleep clinics. Some experimental psychologists are doing work on this condition. It may be worth making a telephone call to the psychology department of your local university.

If sleeplessness as a result of hot flashes or night sweats leads to intolerable fatigue, a short course of estrogen may help. Some studies have suggested that ERT may contribute to more restful sleep and, in particular, more dream sleep. Sleeping pills, on the other hand, reduce the amount of dream sleep. You should consider the quality of your sleep as well as the number of hours since an optimum amount of dream sleep is required for a sense of well-being. If you cannot or *will* not take estrogen and depression is *not* a problem, you may want to ask for a prescription for a mild tranquillizer. Tranquillizers are not as soporific as sleeping pills and do not cause a "drugged" feeling the next morning. However, tranquillizers are depressants and can be addictive. Don't use them unless you know that it will be a "sometime" thing — once every ten days or two weeks. If you know that you have addictive tendencies, don't use them. If you find you are using them more often, flush them away.

WEIGHT GAIN

Even when one is aware of the benefits to bones and the alleviation of hot flashes, it is hard to decide to live with a weight gain of ten to fifteen pounds. If weight soars beyond this extra cushion of fat — to 20 per cent more than ideal weight, the threshold of obesity — one is inviting a host of medical problems. The only solution to permanent weight loss is a long period of sensible eating and a loss of no more than two pounds a week. Prolonged diets have the advantage of inducing new eating habits, including a sharp cutback in alcoholic beverages. Weight gain is discussed more fully in Chapter 10.

MISCELLANEOUS AILMENTS

Be alert to newly developed sensitivities and allergies. I have found that my eyes run when the wind is cold — a form of rhinitis (inflammation of the nose) that may have something to do with big-city pollution, but which certainly started during my menopause. Other women have found that they react badly to cigarette smoke where they could tolerate it before. Some women have found that certain foods — wheat, for instance — add to a sense of fatigue.

If you experience one of the more unusual ailments — tachycardia (rapid heart beat), mysterious bruises, attacks of dizziness, "rubber legs," etc., keep track of when and where you experience it. Did something happen beforehand that might account for it? Have you had any similar experiences in the past? What have you done to try to make yourself feel better? Your complaint may or may not be taken seriously, but a conscientious doctor will order tests to rule out conditions that might cause the same or similar complaints. You may have to do without the firm professional assurance that it is related to menopause, but you may be relieved to find that you are generally healthy.

One of the most common remedies offered to menopausal women is the tranquillizer, a drug that is both addictive and a depressant. With the sole exception of sleeplessness, which may be *occasionally* relieved by the infrequent use of a mild tranquillizer, none of the physical ailments discussed in this chapter call for a prescription for lorazepam (Ativan) or diazepam (Valium). Doctors may offer a prescription not because they feel that it will alleviate a particular complaint, but because they know that patients *expect* to leave with a prescription. It is the concluding ritual of the appointment and a way of validating the patient's complaint. If your doctor can suggest only tranquillizers, you may want to find another physician or to consult with another kind of health practitioner.

CHAPTER 4

·

Psychological and Sexual Effects

THIS CHAPTER DEALS WITH psychological and sexual effects of **menopause** separately from other ailments not because they are any less important than physical ailments, but because they require a different approach. Many women who freely admit to **hot flashes** turn suddenly shy when talking about panic attacks or loss of sexual desire. The causes of each of these may be similar — a temporary biochemical disturbance — but less is known about the psychology and sexuality of menopause. Because the precise hormonal interactions are so poorly understood, no standard diagnosis or treatment has been formulated.

Physicians are thus often ill-equipped to handle discussions of mood swings, anxiety, panic attacks, and depression. When they refer their patients to a psychologist or psychiatrist, the patient feels that her problem is being redefined as "emotional" or "mental" when *she* feels, and often rightly, that it is the result of stress on the *body*.

In the same way, sexual problems involve not only the physical responses of the woman, but also the whole complex of attitudes and feelings of the woman and her partner. If physicians are ill-equipped to handle psychological complaints, they are often ill at ease with sexual questions. It helps to know that although some psychological and sexual effects require medical expertise, others may be solved through increased self-knowledge and better communication, both often facilitated by a qualified therapist.

PSYCHOLOGICAL PROBLEMS AT MENOPAUSE

Memory lapses
Menopausal forgetfulness is not something that most doctors care to discuss, nor do most women wish to bring it up. Many of us joke, a trifle uneasily, about the onset of Alzheimer's disease, although Alzheimer's victims apparently don't notice their failing memories. However, *we* feel the lack and, for many women, part of the pain is having this faltering memory brought to their attention. Women have traditionally

remembered the birthdays, the items needed at the store, the names of casual acquaintances. Now we feel we are letting others down.

Of all the psychological effects of menopause, forgetfulness is probably the most common. We are told that this is caused by ageing, that we have too much on our minds, that it is the result of stress and that men have it, too. We are also directed to articles that teach us how to remember — mnemonic exercises to help us remember names or items on a list.

•

> Last year, I could go to the supermarket and remember ten items without a list. This year, I walk upstairs to get *one* thing and forget why I went upstairs. Last year, I knew the first names of all the wives of my husband's club members whom I see once every six months; this year, I remembered the names of two. Yesterday, I put the bread in the freezer and the ice cubes in the breadbox. Today, I'm buying another notebook to keep yet more lists.

Some nutritionists believe that memory lapses are partly due to a deficiency of a particular kind of lecithin (a phospholipid found in eggs and seeds); other experts say that the body manufactures all the lecithin we need. Many post-menopausal women say that their memories improve. Perhaps, unlike male memory, female memory takes a sudden nose-dive at menopause and then levels off again.

Anxiety

Many women find that the onset of menopause makes them more anxious. Chores that were once routine become fraught with worry. A teacher is suddenly self-conscious in front of her class; an executive worries about a presentation to a client; a hostess worries herself sick about a run-of-the-mill dinner party. Such women are victims of "free-floating anxiety," which seems to afflict many women as they enter menopause. The anxiety does not seem linked to any particular event; it is simply there. What was once considered new and fun becomes worrisome and even frightening. It seems important to force oneself to take on new challenges, although there is a compensating sympathy for women who subside into routine in order to avoid the unknown. Like many other facets of menopause, these flurries of anxiety — particularly over being faced with the new and untried — are likely to be temporary. It may be some comfort to think about the countless menopausal women lying in bed at night, self-consciously reviewing their stupidities of that day — an activity they had meant to give up at age fifteen!

One problem with anxiety is that it is so relative. Some women are anxious all the time and, although probably thought of as highly-strung, appear to function adequately if not serenely. The borderline that distinguishes normal (we're all neurotic about something) and abnormal neuroticism is one of degree and duration. Anxiety becomes debilitating when it seriously hampers one's ability to handle regular activities over a long period of time. Persons who make radical changes to established routine in order to avoid stressful situations, and who maintain this avoidance behaviour for months, are going beyond ordinary anxiety. If the disorder persists, it may become "phobic" and professional help should be sought. This occurs only rarely.

For most of us, it is comforting to know that the sense of anxiety is shared, that many other women are feeling the same way, and that, like our physical woes, it will go away in time. Meanwhile, perhaps we should order our nearest and dearest to refrain from expressions like, "Don't worry," "Just relax," or (the one I hate), "Lighten up, will you?" We will stop worrying and start relaxing when we are no longer feeling so anxious. And we will let the Pollyannas around us know when this happens!

Irritability

Irritability is even more visible than anxiety. We may get angry about things that never bothered us before. We may shake with rage over a trifling matter. The puzzlement we feel about our own behaviour is often echoed by puzzled looks on the faces of close friends, co-workers, or family members. It is worth considering whether irritability is more of a problem for you (the woman) or for those close to you. Many women are more concerned about the effect they have on others than they are about themselves. This leads to a situation where a woman takes pills for the benefit of those who tell her that she is not "herself." Unwilling to ask others to adjust to this newly wilful person, the woman may accept some sort of chemical help (usually a tranquillizer) to restore her amiability.

While it is true that menopausal women can be unusually "bitchy," they can also be unusually assertive and self-protective. It is *not* that a particular incident now irritates when it never did before. It's just that we are not willing to put up with that particular incident one more time. It may be that we're not feeling as well (and therefore it irritates more); it may be that something has always been vexing and it is now time to speak out about it. Because menopause makes us sharply conscious of ageing, we are more aware of the life we have left to live, and often super-conscious of the annoying traits of those around us. We may never have mentioned it before, but the prospect of living with it (whatever "it" is) for the rest of our days may be just too much.

Looked at in another way, many women come into their own at menopause. They have put others' needs first for years. Menopause may be the trigger that makes women demand their fair share for the first time. Sometimes this newly-found assertiveness is channelled into a new enterprise, whether hobby or work. The sense of impatience, of too much to do and not enough time, persuades women to return to school, to take up new challenges, to give up chores and responsibilities that have chafed or bored. There are many positive aspects to this "irritability."

■

In order to survive, I needed blocks of unfractured time and private space. Our children usually have rooms of their own; our parents have living space of their own. We, mothers and wives, may lay partial claim to a "master bedroom" (and hear what I am saying because we use words without thinking). A woman I spoke to not long ago said that what she wants is to find a dark closet somewhere and get some peace. I suggested a more daring approach — her own room in the house! And not a sewing room or a corner of the living-room either!

When I found myself sighing and sometimes crying in the bathroom (often after having waited to get in), I knew I was in deep trouble. We sorted this out during our family's weekly informal meetings.

The standard "remedy" for anxiety and irritability is a tranquillizer. If you accept a prescription, be sure that you do so for your *own* benefit and not merely to pacify those around you. Be aware also that it is potentially addictive and a depressant. If you are already feeling depressed, as well as anxious and irritable (a common situation), the tranquillizer will make you feel *more* depressed.

Panic attacks

■

After turning fifty, I suddenly found myself drenched in perspiration while out shopping, experiencing some very nasty dizzy spells and feelings of unreality, and I began to dread the daily trips to the supermarket. After a while, I began dropping my purchases and making a beeline for the nearest exit and home. The *worst* thing I could have done, of course, as counselling has since taught me! But try telling that to a person having a bad panic attack. They wouldn't stay around long enough to listen to you, yet alone heed your good advice!

Frankly, I am convinced that the chemical and hormonal imbalance that menopause brings about *does* play a very large part in upsetting our equilibrium. Some of us manage to muddle through somehow without falling apart at the seams. Others become so afraid that they become housebound.

Panic attacks are a more focused form of anxiety and involve the body as well as the mind. During a panic attack, adrenaline rushes into the bloodstream, the heart pounds, the palms of the hands sweat, and breathing becomes quick and shallow. Although the attack is undoubtedly caused by some sudden hormonal upset, the mind seems to seize on some*one* or some*thing* as a cause. Suddenly, out of nowhere, we imagine a terrible accident about to happen to a loved one, or something unspeakably stupid that we are about to do (like faint or fall over). It is only after the panic abates that we realize that the pounding heart and quick breathing came *first*, that the situation itself did not *cause* the panic attack.

Many menopausal women deal with panic attacks by breathing slowly and carefully, and by counting, singing, whistling, or reciting nursery rhymes (anything that keeps away negative thoughts). Some women carry a small brown-paper bag to breathe into; this often wards off hyperventilation — abnormally quick, shallow breathing. If the panic attacks are very severe or the recurrence is restricting activity in any way, it is time to get help. This is how **agoraphobia** starts but a psychotherapist can provide the tools to enable you to get past this kind of block.

It would be nice to have an explanation for these bizarre menopausal effects but, so far, no one has been able to trace the effects of brain chemistry on specific behaviours such as these. Menopause, by itself, may be a source of stress for the body, and this stress often adds to existing stress — stress imposed by the burden of commitments in the roles of wife, daughter, mother, housekeeper, worker, friend, etc. In other words, it may not be menopause itself that induces the anxiety (or the irritability, or the panic attacks) but rather the extra, added stress, which is just too much to handle at present.

■

I have come to the conclusion that the mind tries to give a name or substance to its fears when attempting to deal with free-floating anxiety, and that just about anything will do. I am now fifty-six and panic far more easily than I ever did before middle age and the onset of "the change." To be honest, in the past few years, I find myself panicking over so many stupid little things that, in earlier years, I would have never given a second thought to.

I also experience spells of great sadness at times and weep for no good reason. Sometimes there just seems to be an awful feeling of doom, as if something dreadful were about to happen. Just as quickly as these feelings come, they disappear.

Depression

Of all the psychological effects of menopause, the most dreaded is undoubtedly depression. Despite the fact that menopausal women are *less* likely to suffer from clinically diagnosed depression than are much younger women (particularly mothers of young children), depression continues to be a bugaboo. Not only are women frightened about being depressed but they're ashamed to admit that they are depressed. It somehow doesn't seem fitting for a "mature" woman in her forties or fifties. There is also the stigma of depression: depressed women have traditionally been treated as if they were personally responsible for their condition. They "didn't have enough to do" or "thought about themselves too much." Although these destructive attitudes still hang on — it's called "blaming the victim" — more and more we see that *some* women, for no known reason, *do* get depressed at menopause. This is much more likely to happen if the menopause is surgically induced, or if the woman has experienced a depression at some other point in her life, but it also happens to women who, by their own reckoning, have absolutely no reason to feel depressed. Menopause affects brain chemistry, depression results from a temporary imbalance in brain chemistry, and depression is self-limiting. In other words, a depression will go away whether you seek help or not. For most of us, the biggest struggle is to acknowledge depression — either in oneself or in a friend.

Menopausal depression is *not* "manic or bipolar" — a depression followed by a period of manic activity and energy and widely recognized as a genuine mental illness. It is rather a depression characterized by fatigue and an absence of a sense of purpose or of worth. According to the *Diagnostic and Statistical Manual of Mental Disorders*, 3rd edition (known as the *DSM-3*), this form of unipolar depression entails "gloominess, tearfulness, loss of enthusiasm, boredom, feeling worthless, listlessness, feeling mopey, loss of appetite, absence of sexual desire or enjoyment, feelings of apprehension or panic, brooding, irritability, disturbed or interrupted sleep, waking too early, restlessness, and (paradoxically) weight gain."

Menopausal depression has been found to be abnormally high among women who have had **hysterectomies** and **oophorectomies** (occurring in from 55 to 75 per cent of cases and peaking two years after the operation). However, a recent study tells us that depressed women are more likely to *report* severe menopausal ailments (to a clinic, or to their doctors), which may be why depression is so often thought of in connection with menopause. It is often hard to know which came first, the depression or the menopause.

■

I am forty-seven and was not going through menopause until hysterectomy completely devastated me a year ago. I knew nothing of menopause — had had no hot flashes nor depression. Now I can really relate to other women who are suffering these symptoms. I have had a terrible year. I find the depression worse than anything else. I wake up each morning with a silent prayer, "Please, God, let me have one good day so I can bear the rest." The odd good day keeps me going. I have wonderful friends and a husband who is loving and caring. If it were not for his tender understanding, I would never get through.

There is no real agreement about the cause of depression, but there are two main points of view. The first is that depression results from a reaction to the biological or social facts of being a woman. Women suffer from depression in numbers estimated to be from two to six times greater than the rate for men. Depression may be "rage turned inward": women may experience depression because they do not act out their anger in the way that men do. Instead of venting resentment or hostility in verbal or physical ways, women transform it into guilt, anxiety, or depression. (The old term for menopausal depression — "involutional melancholia" — means an inward-turning sadness.)

The depressed menopausal woman may be mourning — mourning the loss of reproductive ability, mourning (if she is childless) the babies she never had, mourning the opportunities missed, mourning her loss of attractiveness, etc. Or she may feel depressed because she has lost the socially valued role of mother (which often coincides with menopause) and must now confront the prospect of old age. Again, there is a mourning, but this is not so much a mourning for the loss of reproductive ability as for the loss of the social role that had defined that woman's place in her world. In her book *Women and Madness*, Phyllis Chesler says, "Women are in a continual state of mourning — for what they never had — or had too briefly, and for what they can't have in the present. . . ."

These explanations for depression at mid-life are all rooted in circumstances particular to the female. When we look at woman's role in this society, at the shockingly high rates of sexual and spousal abuse directed at females, we can understand how valid are women's deep-seated resentments, which may show themselves as depression.

There is also a biochemical basis for some kinds of depression. "Post-partum depression" (the kind of depression that follows childbirth, whether a temporary "blues" or a more long-standing condition) is assumed to be caused by an imbalance in **hormones** affecting brain chemistry (or brain chemistry that affects hormones). A woman who has just given birth moves into a high-risk category for depression as does the woman who has had a hysterectomy, whether or not the **ovaries** are left. No equivalent surgery (appendectomy, gall-bladder, etc.) produces the risk of depression that follows from the trauma (natural or induced) of the female reproductive organs. Logically then, menopause *may* (not *will*) induce depression in a minority of women as a result of some kind of biochemical effect. In real life, of course, it is often difficult to distinguish between a depression that is biochemically caused and one that is triggered by social experience, present or past.

Treatment for depression may involve exercise, counselling, drugs, or all three. Some women fight off depression with a combination of supplementary **Vitamin B$_6$** and a lot of exercise. Physical exertion has been found to change brain chemistry and to promote a more optimistic attitude.

If you need someone to talk to, the first step may be counselling. You may want to see a clinical psychologist, a psychotherapist, or a psychiatrist. Psychiatrists are medical doctors, can prescribe drugs, and are usually covered by both provincial and private health-care plans; psychologists and psychotherapists may or may not be covered. This may be worth checking. To see a psychiatrist in private practice, you will need a referral from your regular health professional. The alternative is to use the outpatient psychiatric services at your local hospital. Psychologists and many psychotherapists advertise; if you cannot (or will not) get suggestions or referrals from friends or other health professionals, you can check with your provincial Corporation of Psychologists regarding individual credentials and affiliations. Whether you are dealing with a psychiatrist, psychologist, or psychotherapist, you should have some positive feelings about his or her competence and personality during the first visit. If not, try someone else.

You may also be offered medication — by your regular doctor, by a psychologist (working with a medical doctor), or by a psychiatrist. Unfortunately, research shows that women are more likely to be of- fered tranquillizers (which will just make them more depressed) than anything else. Antidepressants are quite different from tranquillizers and are used in an effort to stimulate the brain to produce its own "feel-good" chemicals to induce a more positive state of mind. The antidepressants may be tricyclics (Anafranil, Aventyl, Surmontil, etc.), which help many people but which cause major side effects for some — dry mouth, constipation, urinary retention, etc. If tricyclics cannot be tolerated, monoamine oxidase (MAOIs) inhibitors (Nardil, Parnate, etc.) may be substituted. MAO inhibitors cause severe head- aches when taken with cheddar cheese, red wine, and a whole list of other foods, beverages, and drugs. If you accept a prescription for an antidepressant, make sure that you understand the anticipated effects of the medication, as well as the restrictions and possible side-effects. If you can't get the information from anyone else, discuss it with your pharmacist.

As mentioned earlier, depressions are self-limiting. Even if you choose *not* to accept medication, the counselling offered by a therapist may help you to sort out how much of the current situation is the result of menopause, and how much is caused by other events in your life. Much of the horror of depression is self-induced since many women in their late forties and early fifties feel that they don't *deserve* to be depressed. Rather than acknowledge the depression and deal with it, they stumble along — for six months or a year — hoping that it will just go away. It will, but it may be worthwhile to help it along a little!

SEXUAL FUNCTIONING

Since sexual function is linked to both physical and psychological states, it deserves a place of its own. It is often said that the important question to do with sex at menopause is not HOW OFTEN? but WITH WHOM? There are many women alone during menopause (divorced, widowed, or never married). For many, sexual functioning becomes merely a decision about whether or not to masturbate.

For those women who *do* have partners, menopause may have a number of effects: intensity of both desire and response, increased desire but a slower response, infrequent or absence of desire with normal response when aroused, or decreased desire and response. From a psychological standpoint, such variation can be accounted for in a number of ways. A woman may experience the loss of reproductive ability as sexual freedom: desire and response may intensify. Another woman finds sexual activity enhanced by the risk of pregnancy: without the risk, desire wanes, although she may still respond. Another woman has not enjoyed love-making in the past and is not looking forward to more. Unless there is more time spent in undisturbed love-making or there are other positive changes (such as a new partner), both desire and response may disappear. It has been found that depressed women are more likely to dream about sex; like sex fantasies, sex dreams often translate into heightened desire. The possibilities are many.

■

I have been separated for over four years (with no intimacy for years before that) and, in the intervening time, have married off three of the four children who had remained at home, had a hysterectomy and a period of mild hot flashes. During a particularly stressful period, I had even developed what the doctor termed "senile vaginitis." What a dreadful term for a young lady of fifty-two! And then it happened — a "date" after thirty-five years. The friendship with this man, seven years my senior, turned into a full-blown romance and I couldn't believe my body's response! My hormones were dancing in double quick time and I don't remember anything as exciting as this even before age thirty-five. Here's to sex after fifty-three — it's wonderful!

Many women enter menopause with healthy levels of desire and response but, as they move into their fifties, they start to view *themselves* as less desirable. They find their bodies lacking — too fat, too flabby, too wrinkled; this may be a psychological concern but it may also take into account a real change in physical appearance. Some women find that any kind of romantic caressing triggers a hot flash. This alone can diminish one's response to a sexual overture. Some find that they are suddenly extraordinarily sensitive to touch; rather than "turning them on," it causes them to flinch. This is very difficult to explain to a partner. Women who once anticipated many orgasms now find that they are satisfied with fewer, perhaps one or two, and that the orgasms are not so intense as they once were.

▪

I am fifty-one and ended my periods two years ago, have had hot sweats for five years but this is secondary to my real problem, which began two years ago. For some reason, it seems that this, the most devastating problem of my menopause — the abrupt end of any sexual pleasure — has received very little print. Although I had read several books, for some time I did not realize that my problem was mid-life–related. My innermost feeling is one of rage. I feel cheated and at times find it very difficult to deal with. I can now realize why marriages end. My own mate is also my best friend so we are O.K., but how I feel for women not so lucky!

Regular orgasm is known to be a pre-condition for a healthy **vagina**, and sexual activity (including masturbation) may help to prevent future problems, which, as already mentioned, include vaginal changes. The vagina tends to shorten and the walls grow thinner as menopause proceeds. Lubrication takes longer, requiring more foreplay. One menopause study tells us that one-quarter of menopausal women will experience discomfort during intercourse about 50 per cent of the time. Sexual activity is more likely to remain pleasurable when the woman has a measure of control over the depth of penetration (as, for instance, lying on or beside her partner) and the confidence to voice her needs.

Sex after surgery
Women who have surgery often have additional problems. Hysterectomized women may find that the quality of the orgasm changes, that

the deep, inside-the-body feeling produced by a throbbing **uterus** is lamentably absent. Recent research suggest that orgasmic response may result from pressure-sensitive nerves in the **cervix** that react to penile thrusting. In the absence of a cervix, the quality of the orgasm is bound to change. Many women who have lost uteruses and/or **ovaries** also report a complete absence of sexual arousal. Until recently, this was considered to be an individual and psychological response to surgery. Doctors assumed that women could only enjoy sex if they could make babies. It is now recognized that, in some cases, there is a basic physiological loss occurring during surgery, that the uterus itself may have important functions in *addition* to its acknowledged role as a "baby bag." It is important that women *know* that the amputation of sexual desire is neither intended nor foreseen. It is certainly not the woman's fault. This is just one more reason why hysterectomies should be performed only after long and careful deliberation.

•

I had a hysterectomy and partial oophorectomy at forty-three. The surgery left me a wreck. Although things were not great between my husband and me prior to the operation, the relationship took a nose-dive largely because of my ensuing depression. I was teary and felt out of control. It took about a year for me to regain most of my former well-being. The biggest physical effect of the surgery has been the loss of desire for sex. Since my operation, my sex drive has lessened enormously. My husband and I are at a loss as to what to do.

If sexual function has been affected by surgery, there are avenues to be explored. If the problem is painful intercourse ("dyspareunia"), most doctors are very happy to provide a prescription for estrogen cream. If the problem is absence of desire, your first problem may be to establish credibility with your surgeon. For too many years, women have been told that absence of desire, or loss of libido, was an individual problem related to underlying feelings about sex *prior* to the operation. This is a no-win situation for a woman because it is impossible to prove what one's "underlying" feelings are about *anything,* and it is hard to make a convincing case about how one used to feel or act in bed. (This is compellingly described in the provocative book *The Castrated Woman,* by Naomi Miller Stokes.) It has recently been found that the administration of male hormones may restore some or all of the missing sexual desire. The male hormone is variously described as an **androgen** or **testosterone**; both are called "male hormones" even though small amounts are produced in a normally functioning female. Your gynaecologist may be willing to read the relevant research and, if appropriate, prescribe for you. If the problem is the quality of the orgasm, or the need for a longer period of preparation (to aid lubrication), then a sex therapist might be a valuable ally.

Sex during natural menopause

If sexual function is problematic during a natural menopause, it is more likely to be a temporary situation. The traditional explanation is that women are mourning the loss of reproductive ability, and that this is unconsciously translated into a distaste for sex. This may be true for some women but certainly not for the vast majority. More likely, the capacity for both desire and response will be affected by energy levels and feelings of self-esteem. Many women report an inability to experience intense feelings of sexual response. Those who are not fit may find that unusual exertion or orgasm may bring on a muscle spasm. Sexual difficulties arise in long-term relationships when women permit themselves to draw invidious comparisons with "sex in the good old days," or when male partners — unwilling to admit that their own sex drive is not what it once was — blame lack of sexual activity on the women.

Women involved in *new* relationships report very few sexual problems during menopause; in fact, they often find it is better than ever. There are very few studies of lesbian relationships during menopause but those we do have tell us that sexuality rarely deteriorates at this time of life, because non-demanding sex play is possible and mutually enjoyable. This suggests that strong bonds of affection and clear communication are crucial to mutually satisfactory sexual relationships during menopause. We have lived through a period of time when sexuality in the elderly was viewed as unnatural, even obscene. We are now at a time when sexuality in the middle-aged is seen as merely the continuation of sexuality that marked the thirties and forties. This may not be the case. A fifty-year-old woman is not the same as a forty-year-old. There is very little research available on sex in the fifties. It may be that it is different in both quality and quantity from sexual activity among younger adults.

CHAPTER 5

.

Special Concerns:
Hormones and Osteoporosis

AS THEY APPROACH **menopause**, women worry about the hazards or benefits of **estrogen**, and the risks of **osteoporosis**, often without having a good understanding of the issues. There is controversy surrounding both the use of **hormones** at menopause and the dangers of osteoporosis after menopause. But much of this controversy is overlooked or minimized by articles in the popular press. This is because the pharmaceutical companies sponsor expensive public relations campaigns that stress the positive benefits of drugs. At the same time, the sales representatives of these companies (the "detail men") visit doctors to report on new and glowing uses for hormones.

Doctors have very little time to do research on the claims and counter-claims of different drug manufacturers. Some are bound to be influenced by the selection of articles offered to them. To counteract this, women's health activists publish information stressing the other side of the story — the side-effects and the possibility of long-term negative consequences of drug use. Little of this information gets into magazines and newspapers because the issues are too complex.

Complex or not, these are important concerns for women at mid-life and it is essential that they keep themselves informed.

THE QUESTION OF ESTROGEN

Although there is a great deal known about hormones in the body, there is still a great deal left to know. Hormones are produced primarily by **endocrine** (ductless) glands, which means that the hormones produced are pumped directly into the bloodstream. Doctors who specialize in the study of hormones are called **endocrinologists**. They are the first to acknowledge that the glands of the female reproductive system operate in an intricate manner that is still only partially understood.

When we talk about estrogen produced inside the body (endogenous estrogen), we usually mean a particular kind of estrogen from the ovaries called **estradiol**. This is not the only form of estrogen in the

Major Glands and Reproductive Organs

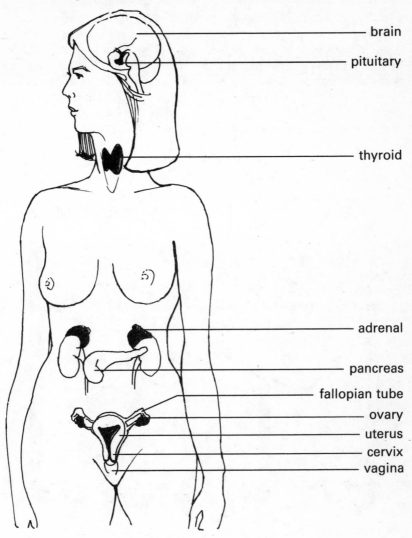

brain

pituitary

thyroid

adrenal

pancreas

fallopian tube

ovary

uterus

cervix

vagina

body. The **adrenal glands** (perched on the kidneys) produce substances that are converted to another form of estrogen called **estrone**. Estrone is produced in very small amounts during the reproductive years, but assumes more importance during menopause and **post-menopause**. A third kind of estrogen is also present — **estriol** — formed by the interaction of estradiol and estrone.

The process of estradiol production is initiated by the hypothalamus, a small gland in the brain. This gland, in turn, stimulates the nearby pituitary gland to produce FSH (follicle-stimulating hormone) and LH (luteinizing hormone), together known as gonadotropins. A **follicle** is the small vessel inside the **ovary** that contains an ovum, or egg. Stimulated by the FSH produced by the pituitary, the follicles begin to produce estradiol, the major estrogen of the menstruating years. The estrogen ensures a build-up of cells within the **uterus** (or womb), which will provide a safe environment for a fertilized egg. A high level of estradiol in the blood signals the pituitary to decrease FSH production and to send out LH instead.

Feedback System

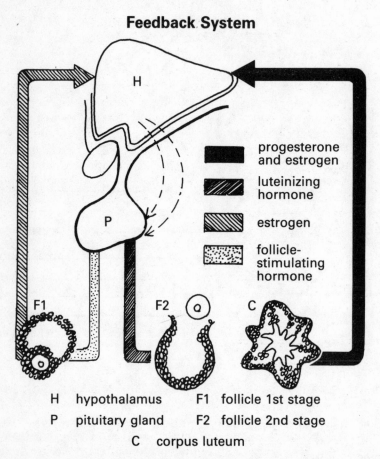

progesterone and estrogen

luteinizing hormone

estrogen

follicle-stimulating hormone

H	hypothalamus	F1 follicle 1st stage
P	pituitary gland	F2 follicle 2nd stage
	C corpus luteum	

LH causes a follicle to burst, producing an egg. This is ovulation. The egg travels into the **fallopian tube** while the spent follicle transforms itself into a "corpus luteum" (yellow body), which produces **progesterone**. Progesterone, the hormone that opposes or counteracts the effects of estrogen, takes over during the latter part of the menstrual cycle (the days between ovulation and menstruation) and, should the egg *not* be fertilized, ensures that the lining of the uterus (the endometrial tissue) is flushed out during menstruation.

As one approaches menopause, the follicle may take longer to rupture, requiring more FSH, a higher level of estrogen in the bloodstream, and a thicker layer of cells inside the uterus. As a result, menstruation may be late and may bring with it a heavier-than-normal menstrual flow. A high level of FSH in the blood is one indication of menopausal onset. Many women react to high levels of FSH by feeling "blue" and by temporarily losing interest in sex. This is also characteristic of the time just after childbirth, when high levels of FSH stimulate the first regular menstrual cycle after a long time with no periods.

It may take weeks, months, or years, but eventually the ovaries produce no more eggs and no more follicles. Estradiol production declines, but at the same time the production of estrone increases. Because estrone is formed in the fatty tissue of the body, women with a little bit more fat on their bones tend to be more efficient converters of estrone. This is why many experts now recommend weight gains of ten to fifteen pounds over "ideal weight" in order to help along this estrone production.

Most women complain of some menopausal effects during this "change-over" period. **Hot flashes** are the most common complaint and, although a surge of LH has been noted to occur at the same time as a hot flash, there doesn't seem to be any clear causal link. The hot flashes seem to occur at the same time as a *fall* in estrogen levels, suggesting that hot flashes may be more a result of sudden changes in estrogen levels than, as commonly believed, the lack of estrogen. Adding estrogen from outside the body may alleviate the hot flashes, but may also postpone adjustment to new levels and new kinds of estrogen from inside the body.

Synthetic hormones

Estrogen and progesterone were first isolated in 1923 and the first synthetic forms of these hormones were made available in the 1930s. During the years immediately following the Second World War, there was a slow but steady increase in the numbers of prescriptions of estrogen as "replacement therapy" during menopause. DES, a synthetic form of estrogen, was prescribed to millions of women worldwide in the 1940s, '50s, and '60s in the hope of preventing miscarriage. During this same time, there were enormous strides in the use and understanding of estrogen and progesterone in contraceptive pills. When the contraceptive pill was put on the market in the early 1960s, it was heralded as an historic breakthrough. Within a couple of years, **estrogen replacement therapy** (ERT) was being looked at in the same way. This was a decade of enormous faith in medical technology. There was very little questioning of side-effects or of long-term effects.

We are still living with the "fall-out" from that decade. There are many women who have been taking estrogen since the 1960s and who still firmly believe that it prolonged their youth, that it reduced wrinkles, helped them keep slim, and postponed greying of the hair. In fact, all these claims for estrogen — once widely believed — have been found to be false. Many older women have tried to stop taking estrogen but have found that the hot flashes return with renewed vengeance — at sixty-five, at seventy, at seventy-five. And we rarely hear from those women who took estrogen for a short period of time and gave up because of side-effects following the doctor's recommendation.

■

> I am fifty years old and had a total hysterectomy at the age of thirty-three. Since then I've been taking Premarin and have now discovered that, although the side-effects are worsening, I am unable to get along without it. The most unusual of these side-effects is a great sensation of heat on my left side. Besides this, my face and breasts swell, I'm continuously short of breath, and my legs ache. I attempted to go off Premarin for a month and, although the side-effects disappeared, I found myself getting terrible hot flashes and sinking into a terrible depression. I am now taking "nerve pills" prescribed by the doctor. Unfortunately, he has not been helpful in explaining how I could wean myself off the estrogen.

The form of estrogen first offered in estrogen replacement therapy — a synthetic estrogen called **ethynyl estradiol** — was similar to that used in the contraceptive pill but at a fraction of the potency. In later years, a new form of "conjugated estrogen" was made available; this estrogen is estrone, rather than estradiol. Because it is collected from animals rather than being made in the laboratory, it is often referred to as "natural" rather than "synthetic."

Effects of estrogen
From 1965 to 1975, estrogen was one of the four most commonly prescribed drugs in North America. The use of DES during pregnancy was not banned in North America until 1971 when it was found to be linked to cancer in the daughters of the women who had been given it. In 1975, the first study was published suggesting a link between the incidence of endometrial cancer (cancer of the lining of the uterus) and use of estrogen. Subsequent studies showed that estrogen users were from six to fourteen times more likely to develop this kind of cancer, with the risk increasing with strength of dose and number of

years taken. Recent research indicates that the increased risk remains for at least ten years after estrogen use is discontinued.

The problem with estrogen taken over time is that it continues to stimulate the cells of the uterus just as it does, naturally, to prepare the womb for the implantation of an egg. The rapid multiplication of endometrial cells sometimes paves the way for cancer, a slow-growing form of cancer that can be nipped if caught in time. Women on ERT should be checked every six months. Unusual cell growth can be scraped away during a **dilatation and curettage** (D&C) — a minor surgical procedure in which a spoon-shaped instrument is used to scoop out the excess cells lining the uterus — or a course of synthetic progesterone added to induce the kind of shedding of the **endometrium** that takes place at menstruation.

In order to forestall any build-up of cells, some doctors now prescribe a regular course of estrogen plus progesterone. When both drugs are prescribed, it is called **hormone replacement therapy** (HRT rather than ERT). Estrogen tablets are taken daily from Day 1 through Day 25 (or during weeks 1 to 3). Progesterone tablets are added from Day 12 to Day 25 (or during Week 3). Then both drugs are withdrawn from Day 25 through Day 30 (or during Week 4) so that a "**withdrawal bleed**" can take place. Although some doctors use the numbered days and others the numbered weeks, progesterone should be taken for a minimum of ten days and, ideally, thirteen days, to make sure the endometrial tissue is adequately shed. (Because this is an artificial period, the term "withdrawal bleed" is used to differentiate it from a menstrual period.)

Estrogen and progesterone, alone or separately, have profound effects on the body and it is not yet clear exactly how progesterone modifies the effects of estrogen. Estrogen levels in the bloodstream have been associated with a number of medical conditions although the precise relationship is not clearly understood. Gall-bladder disease, liver disease, migraine headaches, diabetes, high blood pressure (hypertension), and blood clots (**thromboembolisms** or **phlebitis**) are all affected by estrogen. Therefore, ERT is rarely given, or given with great caution, to menopausal women with any of these complaints. Uterine **fibroids** thrive in the presence of estrogen and women with large fibroids often experience a reduction in pain and discomfort with lowered levels of estrogen at menopause. Women with fibroids should avoid ERT if at all possible.

■

I had Premarin prescribed for a depression I was going through. At the same time, the gynecologist asked me if I knew that I had many large fibroids. I told him I *did* know and asked what their effect would be. He told me that they would cause erratic periods but made absolutely no mention of possible problems when taking hormones. Luckily, I had been on Premarin for only six weeks before I read that estrogen would enlarge the fibroids. I haven't taken estrogen since and find that exercise and vitamins do the job just as well.

Because obese women (that is, women who are more than 20 per cent over "ideal weight") already produce a lot of estrone, they are rarely put on ERT. Estrogen is involved with certain types of breast cancer but this is more likely to be a form of breast cancer in which estrogen-sensitive receptor sites act to stimulate tumour formation. This form of cancer is more typical of younger women who are still cycling regularly but there is a period of time in a woman's life when breast cancer could be either this type or the non–estrogen-dependent type of cancer more typical of post-menopause.

On the other hand, women on ERT appear to be more protected against some forms of heart disease and against the critical loss of bone mass that leads to osteoporosis. Estrogen also appears to relieve depression in some women (not all, by any means), helps to maintain a cushion of **collagen** under the outer layer of skin, and relieves **dry vagina**, the sensation of burning during urination (**cystitis**), and other complaints of the genito-urinary system.

When ERT becomes HRT with the addition of progesterone, some of the protection against heart disease may be lost; this will depend on the form of progesterone prescribed. "**Progestogen**" or "**progestin**" (names for synthetic progesterone) may also cause increased appetite, **bloat**, headaches, or swollen, tender breasts. Estrogen may also produce these side-effects and/or nausea, vomiting, cramps, dizziness, fluid retention, rashes, visual disturbances, depression, or changes in levels of sexual desire (libido). Estrogen may also cause **breakthrough bleeding** — bleeding between the expected times of withdrawal bleeds. This should be checked by a doctor.

·

A year and half ago, I had a hysterectomy and oophorectomy. I was started on estrogen and progesterone and had bowel failure. The estrogen was taken away and my bowels started to function. The gynaecologist I was seeing gave me hormone injections (estrogen plus testosterone) and another kind of synthetic estrogen over the course of about five months. I was then sent to an endocrinologist about the thirty-five pounds I had gained. His advice was to take a tranquillizer and stop worrying.

I went back to my family doctor really upset — I thought I was going off the deep end. I was having severe hot flashes, feeling depressed, suffering from severe anxiety, and had lost almost all interest in sex. He sent me to another endocrinologist who did a complete work-up and found elevated levels of testosterone. He put me back on estrogen tablets, which did not help.

Lately, I've stopped taking the estrogen and progesterone. My body is now readjusting and finally I feel in control of myself and of my body.

The controversy over estrogen (ERT) and estrogen-plus-progesterone (HRT) operates on a number of levels:

1. If menopause is viewed as a deficiency disease, or condition, as it is by some medical practitioners, then some kind of treatment will be viewed as beneficial to *all* women approaching menopause. If menopause is seen as a natural stage of biological development, estrogen will be seen as medication useful for those most seriously affected.
2. Some people feel that drugs were invented to cushion us from discomfort and stress, and that to spurn such relief is silly. Others feel that we swallow too many drugs without thinking of the consequences, and that sound nutrition and other changes in daily routine should be adopted before resorting to drugs. These differing attitudes influence many decisions about ERT.
3. The risk of endometrial cancer does not exist for women who have had hysterectomies (probably one woman in four or five). Those women who do have a uterus must look at the benefits of ERT — reduced risk of osteoporosis and heart disease, potential relief from hot flashes, etc. — and balance this against the increased risk of uterine cancer. With HRT, the protection against heart disease may disappear, there may be unwelcome side-effects, and there will be a monthly "withdrawal bleed." When a woman is prescribed ERT (or HRT), her doctor will usually insist on a check-up in three months, and then every six months thereafter. This means that women on ERT or HRT are *more* likely to have regular medical check-ups than women not receiving estrogen and, should any abnormality appear, it will be noticed immediately. Even for those women who see a doctor only once a year, uterine cancer is extremely slow-growing, and has a 97 per cent cure rate.
4. The long-term effects of ERT are not well understood. Some studies have linked ERT to breast cancer; other studies find ERT to be protective against breast cancer. The type of cancer and the age at which the cancer develops makes a difference. Moreover, the protective effect in relation to heart disease may mean a heightened vulnerability to stroke, since estrogen has complicated ef-

fects on blood chemistry. More research is needed in these areas.

5. Obese women are refused ERT because they are more vulnerable to many kinds of cancer, including breast cancer, because of the excess estrogen produced in their fatty tissue. Estrone is the "conjugated estrogen" used in ERT.

There is no test to decide who should take estrogen and who should not. Studies from the United States suggest that gynecologists are more likely to prescribe hormones than are family physicians, but it is often a very individual matter. Women active in the field of women's health are suspicious about long-term effects. The choice about whether to seek or to accept ERT has to be an individual one, based on quality of life and the many unknowns that still plague us.

OSTEOPOROSIS

The word "osteoporosis" means porous bone and was first named by a German pathologist in 1930. Although extensive studies were done on post-menopausal osteoporosis throughout the 1940s and 1950s, it did not reach the popular press or stir up public concern until a few years ago.

Osteoporosis is not a disease. It is the end result of many processes that lead to a state where bone mass is less than the needs of body mass. Bone may appear normal but, on close inspection, is found to be riddled with holes like a dry sponge. The bones of the forearm (near the wrist) and the thigh (at the hip) may become dangerously fragile, while bones in the spine threaten to collapse from the effort of holding up the body.

There are two different kinds of osteoporosis: primary and secondary. Primary osteoporosis is the form stressed in the articles appearing in popular magazines and develops as a consequence of natural ageing *in both men and women*. Secondary osteoporosis simply means that the condition is brought on, or worsened, as a result of other problems — prolonged bed rest, malfunctioning glands (thyroid, parathyroid, or adrenal), diabetes or other chronic illness, bone-marrow tumours, and/or as a side-effect of medication, such as **corticosteroids**, prescribed for other ailments. Only about 5 per cent of genuine osteoporotic cases are secondary.

Whether the form is primary or secondary, the osteoporotic woman is at risk for crush fractures of the lower and/or upper back (this latter is more evident as "dowager's hump"), for wrist fractures ("old lady's" or Colles' fracture), and for hip fractures. The immobility and complications resulting are said to be responsible for the deaths of 20 per cent of women suffering hip fractures, usually within four months of the accident.

Here are some other terms you may have heard or read about:

•**Osteopenia** — not as serious as osteoporosis but indicating a reduction in bone mass that may be a natural consequence of ageing.

•**Osteomalacia** — a disease characterized by softening of the bone, which may contribute to osteoporosis.

•**Osteoarthritis** — a non-inflammatory degenerative joint disease quite different from osteoporosis, although there appears to be some tendency for women with osteoarthritis to be prone to osteoporosis.

Bone is not only a framework for the body but also a storage organ for calcium and other minerals. In this latter function, bone is a dynamic and complex substance in which cells are constantly being formed, used, and sloughed off, much as we see happening on the outer layer of skin. The outer layer of bone sheds cells into the bloodstream. The cast-off cells are excreted. The vast majority of calcium in the body exists as bone or teeth, but there is a constant circulation of calcium in the bloodstream. It is the balance between the loss of bone cells ("resorption") and the formation of new cells ("absorption") that determines bone density and presumed durability of bone.

The effects of low bone density may depend on the type of bone affected. Cortical bone is the hard and shiny kind that makes up the outer surface. The inner part is called "trabecular" or "cancellous" and this more porous type of bone is characteristic of the major portion of the vertebrae of the spine. Trabecular bone is more vulnerable to osteoporosis than is cortical bone.

Calcium and estrogen therapy

During the growing years — that is, until the mid-thirties — the absorption of calcium into bone exceeds the resorption of calcium into the bloodstream, so bones get bigger and stronger. Although we inherit a tendency to strong or weak bones, the density of bone can also be affected by the amount of calcium in the diet and by the weight and activity of muscle pulling against it — the action involved in all movement. If there is a family tendency to dense, durable bone, and if this is complemented by good nutrition and exercise habits, a negative balance (that is, losing bone faster than it is formed) can be tolerated for some years. Men are generally heavier and more muscled than women and, until very recently, this difference was accentuated by men's wider participation in sports. This is the major reason why men in our society do not, as a rule, show evidence of osteoporosis until well into old age. Since the life expectancy of the male is considerably less than that of the female, the problem of osteoporosis is overwhelmingly a woman's health problem in this society. (Although there have been slight changes, the life expectancy of a woman is about six or seven years more than that of a man.)

Although we encourage growing children to drink lots of milk, it is not only the high level of calcium that acts to make new bone. Young bodies are geared to put calcium to work and, to do this, **Vitamin D** is used to extract the maximum calcium available on its way through the intestines. As we age, Vitamin D continues to provide this vital function, but it now appears that older people utilize Vitamin D less efficiently. Without enough Vitamin D, calcium may be ingested and excreted. (Paradoxically, when there is too much Vitamin D in the bloodstream, the positive effects on bone formation are reversed.)

Other substances also influence the use of calcium. For instance, sodium (whether in prepared foods or beverages, or in ordinary table salt) promotes excretion of calcium. So does phosphorus, found in red meat and soft drinks. Levels of magnesium and **calcitonin** (a hormone released by the thyroid gland) affect bone formation. Both caffeine and alcohol appear to inhibit use of calcium for bone, whereas the sex hormones (estrogen, progesterone, and testosterone) appear to stimulate bone formation.

Just how estrogen functions to increase bone formation is not thoroughly understood. However, we do know that:
- Women who have had a number of pregnancies (during which estrogen levels soar) are less vulnerable to osteoporosis.
- Women who have their ovaries removed begin to experience bone loss immediately after surgery, and this bone loss proceeds more swiftly than in naturally menopausal women.
- Women who are 10 to 15 per cent over "ideal body weight" are less prone to osteoporosis. (Some of this may be the result of the benefits of the extra weight putting stress on bone; some appears to result from higher production of estrone in the fatty tissue of the body.)

Estrogen appears to mediate the amount of calcium released by the bones into the bloodstream and the amount of calcium excreted by the kidneys. Therefore, estrogen levels during and after menopause affect the density of the bones.

Signs of osteoporosis
Osteoporisis is *not* a worldwide, female-only problem. It is more common in affluent, northern countries. Women who have had multiple pregnancies, who eat red meat infrequently, who do strenuous labour, and who are overweight (by our standards) are not likely to develop osteoporosis. These are the characteristics of the majority of

women in the world. Moreover, black women rarely suffer from osteo-porosis since their bones are genetically denser than those of white women. Orientals are, however, vulnerable, presumably because they tend to be small-boned and slim; because their genetic bone structure is not dense.

Surgical removal of the ovaries doubles the risk of osteoporosis. Since North America leads the world in numbers of hysterectomies performed and since many surgeons still routinely remove ovaries from any woman over forty, it is not hard to see how this contributes to high rates of osteoporosis. Other factors that contribute to high risk are corticosteroid use (for arthritis, asthma, etc.); use of anticonvulsants (to prevent seizures); glandular disorders (such as hypoglycemia, hypothyroidism, Cushing's syndrome, Addison's disease, or diabetes mellitus); habitual use of diuretics (to promote water loss) containing furosemide, or of antacid preparations containing aluminum; or kidney dialysis.

Among naturally menopausal women, approximately one-fourth are at risk. Women with fine, transparent skin seem more vulnerable; the decline in mineralized **collagen** (bone) is reflected in the absence of opaque collagen under the surface of the skin. This skin type is also characteristic of rheumatoid-arthritis sufferers, but what link exists between this and osteoporosis is not yet established. Periodontal dis-ease, which involves changes in the bones that hold the teeth in place or in the gum surrounding that bone, *may* be a sign of osteoporosis. One clue may be greater loss of bone in the upper jaw (which contains more trabecular bone) as compared to the lower.

Since the calcium that circulates in the blood helps to monitor muscle contraction, one early indication of osteoporosis may be knot-ting of the large muscles, particularly in the calf. (Low levels of potas-sium may also cause this kind of cramping, which can often be relieved simply by adding bananas to the diet.)

•

Seventeen years ago, I had my uterus and ovaries removed. I was taking estrogen for six years after that but finally decided to give it up as I dislike the idea of long-term dependency on a drug. Lately, I've been experienc-ing unbearable muscle spasms in my legs. My doctor is as stumped about this as I am. Even regular exercise has not helped.

A common symptom of more advanced osteoporosis (usually post-menopausal) is lower back pain, either as muscle spasm or dull ache. If the pain persists for some weeks and then goes away, it may signal the crushing of a vertebra. When bones are fragile, the smallest exertion — a sneeze or a hug — can cause a fracture.

Loss of height, particularly in the upper body, may be an indication of osteoporosis. Some loss of height occurs naturally as one ages — caused primarily by the contraction of the hip flexor muscles. But measurements of upper-torso size may be an indication of bone health. Some women measure themselves by wrapping a tape measure over the head and between the legs, then stretching as tall as they can and recording the measurement. This must be done again and again until a consistent result is obtained. An alternative is to use the "buddy system" and very carefully measure each other, particularly the upper body, making sure that you always stand in the same place in the same way. Arm span, the distance from fingertip to fingertip with the arms open wide, should equal total height. You should be measured every three months. Strive for accuracy because you will be looking for small losses in height that may indicate the beginnings of osteoporosis.

If you are exercising regularly, have ensured an adequate daily intake of calcium, and are *still* losing height, you should make an appointment to have your bone density checked. This may not be as easy as it sounds.

Diagnosis
One of the major problems with osteoporosis is that of diagnosis. Although all the diagnostic methods used are non-invasive, pain-free, and involve little discomfort, some are more effective than others. Routine X-rays show loss only when 20 to 30 per cent of bone is affected, often too late to take preventive action. CAT (computerized axial tomography) scans are available in large medical centres but must be specifically adapted and made available for osteoporosis. This often occurs only when the condition is so advanced that confirmation of diagnosis is sought. To have a CAT scan, the woman is placed on a cot, which is slid into a metal cylinder. The body is bombarded with rays that provide a computer print-out of bone density. The CAT scan, neutron-activation analysis (which is even more rare), and absorptiometry, all use radioactive materials but expose the patient to only a fraction of that used in standard X-rays. Dual photon absorptiometres (also called "densitometres"), which measure bone mass in the spine and arm and then calculate and display results on a computer screen, have been acquired by most teaching hospitals but many are used only for research. Single photon absorptiometres are half the price but measure only forearm bone and have not been as useful. **Ultrasound** is being used in some parts of the United States but few of these devices are available to the average woman.

However, more and more hospitals are making bone scans available to the general public and the Osteoporosis Society of Canada (see page 200) has been able to make arrangements with other hospitals to permit bone scanning of women who feel they are at risk for osteoporosis. If routine bone scans are not available at your local hospital, you might wish to contact the Society to see if arrangements have been made in a medical centre near you. If the answer is "yes," you will be asked to get permission from your doctor and then to make a donation to the Society. This donation will allow you to make an appointment for a bone scan (using a dual photon device).

The most telling symptom of osteoporosis is, of course, the broken bone. Once one fracture occurs, there is a tendency to break other bones: 95 per cent of osteoporotic women have at least five more fractures in the ten years following the first.

∎

> I am sixty-six years old and have been suffering from osteoporosis for two years. Last winter, I broke my hip in a fall and have since been extremely conscious of my calcium and Vitamin D intake. My doctor seems to feel, however, that if I begin to take estrogen now, the osteoporosis will decrease.

If osteoporosis is confirmed, either as a result of your own detective work or because of a fracture, and you are still menstruating (even if only erratically) or have stopped menstruating within the last six months, your doctor may suggest estrogen treatment to halt further loss of bone. If you are post-menopausal (that is, have not had a menstrual period in the previous twelve months), the worst damage has already been done. Estrogen will not strengthen existing bone, merely halt the accelerated loss that occurs around the time of the last menstrual period. Continue to exercise regularly and register with a doctor who specializes in or is interested in osteoporosis: there are many new developments in the treatment of this condition and you should have an advocate who will monitor these on your behalf.

Be aware, however, that a great deal of the information available to doctors about estrogen therapy and about osteoporosis is provided by the drug companies. Unless a practising physician has the time and motivation to read the vast numbers of research studies on the topic — hundreds of pages in more than twenty technical journals every month — he or she is likely to rely on summaries published and delivered by the local pharmaceuticals representative. Since most doctors have been trained to look for medical solutions (drugs or operations) to problems presented by patients, and since menopause is only fleetingly touched upon at medical school, most doctors do not think of adjustments in diet or changes in exercise patterns as solutions.

There are encouraging studies involving osteoporosis that look to electrotherapy (the use of a mild electric current to stimulate bone formation) or to full-spectrum lighting (which induces the body to use Vitamin D to lay down more calcium in the bone). Much of the current concern about osteoporosis is based on projections of the costs of caring for old ladies with broken hips. These projections are based on the present situation — an ageing population that has never been encouraged to eat bone-building foods or to exercise regularly — and ignores the possibility of alternative remedies, which may be less expensive and less risky.

Just now, estrogen provides relief for the worst effects of menopause but it may be at some cost. Meanwhile, there is very little research into alternative solutions for the relief of hot flashes that may have less far-reaching consequences. Women themselves need to understand and *manage* the conditions that may minimize their potential for dependence on ERT and maximize their resistance to osteoporosis. Keeping informed will enable us to make an educated choice.

CHAPTER 6

■

Menopause Under the Knife: Common Surgical Procedures

NONE OF THE SURGICAL PROCEDURES described in this chapter is unique to **menopause**, but they are procedures that the menopausal woman should have some knowledge about. This is particularly true of **hysterectomy** and **oophorectomy** (removal of the ovaries, sometimes known as ovariectomy), which may bring on an earlier-than-normal menopause and may strongly affect the quality of the menopause experience. If there is a possibility of surgery — often because of heavy or irregular bleeding — women tend to "want to get it over with" and, frightened to explore other avenues, may agree to an operation too readily. This may be one reason why such an unusual (and unequal) number of operations are performed on women. Of the ten most commonly performed operations in North America, four are performed exclusively on women.

DECIDING ABOUT SURGERY

It is no surprise that surgery is more likely to be proposed by a surgeon than by another type of physician. Gynaecologists are surgeons, and one of the strongest likelihoods of a high rate of surgery in a given geographical area is the number of surgeons. In England, where fewer surgeons are trained (as a proportion of all medical doctors), the rates for many standard surgical procedures are significantly lower. For instance only 11 per cent of English women have hysterectomies, as compared to 25 to 30 per cent in the United States. In fact, it is the discrepancy between rates of surgery from one country to another, from province to province, or from city to city, that has led medical-insurance companies to insist on a second opinion before agreeing to cover surgeons' fees. Those of us concerned with women's health recommend that you *always* get a second opinion. If you are contemplating major surgery, you may want a third opinion.

To get a second opinion, you should consult a doctor whose opinion is likely to be offered quite independently from the first opinion. This will involve finding a doctor with a different hospital affiliation, of a different age group, with offices in a different place, etc. You want someone who is *not* part of the same "old-boys' network." A good family physician or general practitioner is more likely to look at other options before recommending "the knife." No reputable surgeon will object to a second or third opinion and, if you feel you are being pressured into an operation, you should dig in your heels. The time you take to make decisions *before* surgery has a lot to do with your psychological well-being *after* surgery.

If your problem is unmanageable bleeding, whether regular (cyclical) or irregular, or an unbearable sensation of discomfort or pressure, and your doctor immediately recommends surgery (without providing an acceptable and clear rationale), you might be wise to switch to someone who will look at alternatives.

∎

Recently, I was hospitalized for severe abdominal pain with elevated temperature, pulse, and a drop in blood pressure. It was diagnosed as PID (Pelvic Inflammatory Disease) and my gynaecologist immediately recommended a hysterectomy. Uneasy about the idea of undergoing major surgery, I consulted a friend's doctor who instead suggested that, since it was the first flare-up, I try antibiotics. I was then treated with high doses of intravenous antibiotics and was released five days later. This happened four years ago this month and I've had no recurrence. I know now it pays to get a second opinion.

If you are post-menopausal and suddenly start to bleed, your doctor may be even more likely to recommend hysterectomy, suspecting cancer. According to the latest statistics, this kind of bleeding is caused by cancer in only 7 per cent of cases — not sufficient reason to consent to major surgery before other avenues are explored.

Some alternatives to surgery include use of antihistamines, medications that relieve congestion and may affect blood flow in and around the **uterus**. Although this is not a recommended use for this product, over-the-counter antihistamines have been found to relieve heavy menstrual bleeding in some women. Antiprostaglandins (Naproxen) have been found to control heavy menstrual bleeding for women who do *not* have **fibroids**; for women with fibroids, these products appear ineffective.

Hormonal treatments for heavy bleeding are **danazol** (Cyclomen), which is often prescribed to women with **endometriosis**, and the newer GnRH or gonadotropin-releasing hormone analog (Lupron), both of which are prescribed to still-menstruating women in order to induce a pseudo-menopause. This may be considered beneficial when endometriosis and/or fibroids cause heavy bleeding. Women who are no longer ovulating but who continue to bleed irregularly may be given **progesterone** (often **Provera**) to help flush out the uterus and tide them over until the last menstrual period. **Clomiphene citrate** (Clomid, the "fertility drug") is sometimes prescribed to re-establish ovulatory cycles. However, this drug stimulates growth of fibroids and should be avoided if at all possible. There are, of course, side-effects associated with any strong drug, so it is wise to inform yourself about these before you agree to treatment. If your doctor is reluctant to discuss side-effects, check the *Compendium of Pharmaceuticals and Specialties* at the library or ask to see your pharmacist's copy.

CONDITIONS OFTEN LEADING TO SURGERY

Fibroids
The most common reason for a hysterectomy is fibroids, dense and harmless growths inside, outside, or between the walls of the uterus or on a stalk attached to the uterus. Fibroids are tolerable until they grow so large that they exert pressure on the rectum, bladder, or **vagina** — or until they cause pain during menstruation as the uterus attempts to expel them.

Fibroids are not usually dangerous. Because they thrive on **estrogen**, they become more of a problem as estrogen levels dip and soar just prior to menopause. Some women don't know they have fibroids until they start on estrogen replacement therapy (ERT), which causes the fibroids to grow. Once the last menstrual period has passed (assuming there is no ERT), fibroids diminish and eventually disappear. For many women, the solution is to hold on for the last few years until menopause takes care of the situation. Should the fibroids become intolerable, a **myomectomy** (a procedure which removes the fibroids but not the uterus) may be indicated.

Very, very rarely a fibroid may become malignant (leiomyosarcoma) but this is estimated to occur to one woman in 150,000. Do not be frightened into having a hysterectomy "because it might turn cancerous."

■

Several years ago, my gynaecologist recommended a hysterectomy because of fibroid growth in my uterus. At the time he made no mention of alternative remedies, only that there seemed to be an increased risk of cancer if they were not removed. Terrified of even the thought of cancer, I underwent the surgery. Following the operation, I was told that he'd also removed both ovaries. When I asked why, he stated, "You're better off without them . . . you have no use for them anyway!" Now that I know this condition could have been alleviated by diet and greater information, it fills me with frustration and rage.

Recently there has been speculation about the relationship between fibroids and diets high in fat. It is known that fibroids are much more likely to occur in women who are overweight or obese, the risk increasing with each substantial weight gain. Anecdotal information, although scientifically suspect, exists to show that some women have reduced and eliminated fibroids by switching to a diet very low in fats — for example, a macrobiotic diet or the Pritikin Diet. (Low fats may also alleviate **fibrocystic** breast disease.)

Endometriosis

This condition accounts for about one-fifth of hysterectomies. For some unknown reason, cells of the lining of the uterus (the endometrium) migrate outside the uterus and lodge on the ovaries, **fallopian tubes**, bladder, rectum, etc. Slight endometriosis may go undetected since the cells are all-but-invisible in the early stages. However, larger clumps of cells tend to respond to the estrogen/progesterone of the normal menstrual cycle, swelling, bleeding and causing great pain because the blood cannot escape in the usual way. These clumps of cells eventually blacken and take on the appearance of burn sites inside the abdomen. Endometriosis is commonly found in women between thirty and forty, although it has been diagnosed in women of all ages. A woman may see a number of doctors before the condition is correctly diagnosed.

Since endometriosis disappears during pregnancy, drugs that induce a "false pregnancy" or "false menopause" may give some relief. Depending on age, a woman may be given oral contraceptives; danazol (Cyclomen), a drug which mimics a weak **androgen** (hormone produced by the **adrenal glands**); or GnRH, a gonadotropin-releasing hormone analog (Lupron). There are possible negative side-effects to any drug but it is worth pursuing drug therapy before resorting to surgery. At the same time, the doctor may use **laparoscopy** (a fibre-optic technique) to investigate the extent of the damage.

Like a D&C, laparoscopy may be either diagnostic or operative: if the diagnosis is confirmed, cauterization or lasers may be used to remove sites of errant cells. Sometimes a procedure related to laparoscopy, called laparotomy, is indicated. Laparoscopy requires an overnight stay in hospital and may be repeated with no untoward effects. Experiments are being conducted with other ways of controlling endometriosis — such as by cutting out parts of the peritoneum (the membrane lining the pelvic cavity), or by carefully washing down the pelvic cavity with a saline solution — but their effectiveness has yet to be established. None of these procedures cures the condition but they are used to "buy time," both for the woman wishing to conceive and for the woman nearing natural menopause.

.

I am thirty-six years old. Three weeks ago, I underwent surgery to remove a 10 cm cyst on my left ovary. This ovary was finally also removed as they discovered I had a severe case of endometriosis. Several cysts were also burned off the right ovary and my doctor says I now have a 50 per cent chance of reoccurrence, at which time my uterus, remaining ovary, and tubes will probably have to be removed — causing instant menopause.

According to the Endometriosis Association, hysterectomy is an effective remedy in only a minority of cases. After the operation, 85 per cent of women continue to have problems, even when ERT is withheld. (Many doctors suggest that ERT be introduced after an interval of a few months. This means that the patient may experience all the worst effects of menopause immediately after the operation.) If all else has failed, a hysterectomy and bilateral salpingo-oophorectomy (removal of the uterus, ovaries, and **fallopian tubes**) may be suggested. Even after this procedure, 5 per cent of endometriosis sufferers will experience a recurrence.

Adenomyosis

This condition is similar to endometriosis and also accounts for about one-fifth of all hysterectomies. In **adenomyosis**, endometrial cells move into the muscles of the uterus, causing the uterus to enlarge and harden. Menstruation becomes very heavy and very painful. However, adenomyosis remains undetected in about 30 per cent of cases and is discovered only when surgery is performed for another reason. Adenomyosis is most often found in women who have had more than one pregnancy and who are between the ages of forty and fifty. It is rare after menopause.

.

Two years ago, I began experiencing extremely heavy bleeding during my periods. They had always been fairly light and painless but gradually I became so incapacitated by the pain, I couldn't go to work for two days each month. I was also using about three or four more tampons every day. I consulted my doctor who suggested a D&C (dilatation and curettage). He suspected I had a condition called adenomyosis so I had a hysterectomy a month later. It turned out he was right. Although my recovery has been slow and difficult, I am now better able to function and no longer have to dread that "time of the month."

Prolapse

Most of us think of "uterus" when we hear the word "prolapse," although the word simply means the downward displacement of an organ or part, and it may affect the uterus, the bladder, the urethra, or the rectum.

Different Types of Prolapse

normal view

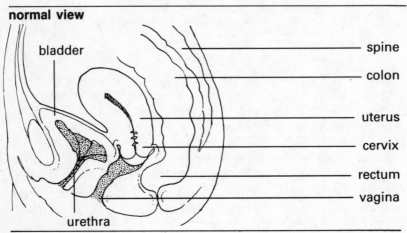

bladder

spine

colon

uterus

cervix

rectum

vagina

urethra

prolapse of uterus

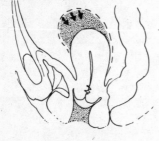

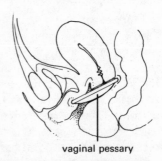

vaginal pessary

prolapse of bladder (cystocele)
prolapse of urethra (urethocele)

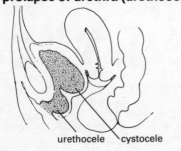

urethocele cystocele

prolapse of rectum (rectocele)

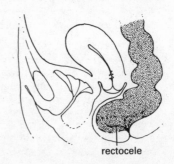

rectocele

84

According to one well-known English doctor, about one woman in five attending her clinic has some form of uterine prolapse. This means that the uterus begins to descend into the vagina but is *not* the same as a "tipped" uterus (which is more common than not). In extreme cases of prolapse, the uterus may protrude from the mouth of the vagina. Weakened pelvic muscles, resulting from childbirth or obesity, are often responsible.

The discomfort of an extreme uterine prolapse may be relieved by the insertion of a pessary, a device that lifts the uterus out of the vagina. While the pessary is in place, a strict and regular routine of Kegel exercises should be adopted (see page 38) and, if necessary, a weight-loss program. Some women have found that yoga exercises help, especially the shoulder stand. If this doesn't do the trick, a minor operation called a suspension may be performed, provided the muscles are in shape.

If a hysterectomy is warranted, it will usually be done through the vagina, using the **lithotomy position** but leaving the ovaries and fallopian tubes intact. This eliminates the worry of an incision but requires a "bottoms-up" operative position in which the patient is tipped toward a vertical position so that the surgeon may more easily see what he or she is doing. Since the table is tilted only after the patient is anaesthetized, many women wonder why they experience severe backache after the operation. Compared to an abdominal hysterectomy, this operation is more likely to incur damage to the bladder, ureters, or to the nerves affecting bowel and bladder function. This may lead to the involuntary passing of small amounts of urine. This form of urinary incontinence may be relieved by faithful repetitions of Kegel exercises or through a minor surgical procedure, a **colporrhaphy**, which tightens the support around the urethra (the tube that carries urine out of the body) and takes pressure off the vaginal wall.

Prolapse, whether of the uterus, bladder, urethra, or rectum, may also be relieved by exercise and diet, before a final decision about surgery is required. Doctors have noticed that the incidence of prolapse is decreasing, perhaps because women are having fewer children or perhaps because they are exercising more, keeping their muscles in better shape.

Cervical abnormalities

The **cervix**, or bottom third of the uterus, is prone to a number of conditions, which, if not watched closely or left untreated, may develop into something serious. **Cervicitis** is usually detected by means of an unusual discharge — unusual in colour, texture, or aroma — a signal to make an appointment with a doctor. Or you may be told of some abnormality as the result of a routine Pap test.

Depending on the results of your Pap test, you may be referred to a colposcopy clinic. A colposcope is a special microscope that permits magnification of the cervix ten to forty times. If there are suspicious-looking cells, samples are scraped for biopsy. The examination takes fifteen to twenty minutes and is uncomfortable but not painful. If the biopsy is not reassuring, more tissue will be needed. Cells on the cervix may be removed using a "punch" (very similar to the one used by the paperboy). The cervix has no nerves so this is uncomfortable but not terribly painful, although it may cause uterine cramps following the procedure. (Don't plan to go back to work!)

A more comprehensive sample of cells requires a "cone biopsy" entailing a general anaesthetic and hospital admission in order to remove a cone-shaped section of the cervix. This is so that cells deeper inside the cervix can be examined. Sometimes the cone is enough to arrest any abnormality. Although some cancers of the cervix have been halted using this procedure, **conization** is relatively rare these days. There is a tendency for the cervix to close up as a result of the procedure so the consequences of conization are more critical for women who wish to become pregnant. This effect may not be an issue for women approaching menopause. Results of the biopsy (punch or cone) may lead to cryosurgery or laser surgery. In cryosurgery, the cells on the surface of the cervix are frozen using a probe that directs a solution onto the surface of the cervix. This is uncomfortable but not painful. No anaesthetic is needed. The surface cells on the cervix are frozen and turn white. The process is certainly preferable to more drastic forms of surgery and results in a watery discharge for days or weeks afterwards, a discharge that can get unpleasantly smelly at times. But eventually the surface of the cervix grows new and normal cells. If you are booked for cryosurgery, make sure you bring your own sanitary napkin for use afterwards; otherwise, you may be supplied with one of those huge, bulky, maternity-ward pads!

There are some cervical conditions that may prompt remedial action, but very rarely is hysterectomy warranted. Even when a diagnosis of early **carcinoma in situ** (malignant cells confined to the surface) is made, steps can be taken to head off further trouble without resorting to hysterectomy. Choose your doctor carefully. You will want someone with a conservative approach — someone who views major surgery as a last resort.

Pelvic inflammatory disease (PID)

PID is a general term used to cover a variety of inflammations that may affect the pelvic cavity. Use of an intra-uterine device (IUD) for birth control, coupled with an increase in sexual activity (often with many partners) appear to have contributed to a higher incidence of PID. PID is often confused with sexually transmitted diseases (STD) — once known as venereal disease (VD) — but the causes of PID are more mysterious. It can happen to anyone. The symptoms may be pelvic pain with or without unusual bleeding but, unlike other conditions, there is often high fever during the acute phase. Most cases of PID respond to diligent treatment with antibiotics, but one episode of PID should be a signal for a woman to find and hold onto a good gynaecologist. PID can lead to a higher possibility of infertility or fertility problems, usually as a result of scarring of the fallopian tubes. If PID continues, it may require drastic surgery.

Endometrial abnormalities

Some women are frightened into having a hysterectomy as a result of a routine Pap test that indicates unusual cells within the uterus. When this happens, the cells may be identified as: (a) **hyperplasia** or hyperplastic; (b) cystic hyperplasia; (c) atypical adenomatous hyperplasia; or (d) carcinoma in situ.

"Hyperplasia" means an abnormal number of cells, the condition linked to prolonged and/or heavy use of estrogen without added progesterone. Each of these conditions is a step toward uterine cancer but none is serious enough to warrant an immediate hysterectomy. Even carcinoma in situ, frightening as it may sound, means cancerous cells restricted to one location. It may be possible to remove the cells without removing the uterus. (It is reckoned that the death rate from hysterectomy is higher than the death rate from endometrial cancer.) Endometrial cancer has a high cure rate because it is extremely slow-growing. Any condition described to you as "pre-cancerous" (or words of that kind) is unnecessarily alarming. After all, there's not one cell in your whole body that isn't "pre-cancerous."

There are a number of steps that can be taken to change the characteristics of the endometrial cells — a course of progesterone, a series of D&Cs, etc. Don't assume that you are simply postponing the inevitable and agree to an unnecessary operation. Always look at the alternatives to major surgery.

■

After two years without a menstrual period, I developed some vaginal bleeding. I had been on estrogen for about six years so my gynaecologist immediately stopped the hormones and told me to come back if there was any more "breakthrough bleeding" (as he called it) and he would do a D&C. I tried to ignore the slight bleeding for several months and then finally booked for a D&C. The results showed endometrial hyperplasia with atypical cells. According to the doctor, I now had several choices. One was to wait for more bleeding, then another D&C and, if cells had worsened, to have a hysterectomy. The second choice was to have a hysterectomy immediately. He recommended the second option.

After consulting several other doctors (including a young, recently graduated female gynaecologist) who all recommended the second option, I decided to go ahead with the surgery. I feel 100 per cent better than before surgery and would like to start losing weight, exercising and being generally more careful about my health. I would also like to stop taking estrogen, which I began again after surgery, but for now it is very necessary.

I went for a six-week check-up last week and everything has healed perfectly. When I asked if I should come back for a further check, the doctor said, "There's no need to come and see me; you have nothing for me to examine."

SURGICAL PROCEDURES

Dilatation and curettage (D&C)

This minor operation is often ordered to control extensive bleeding ("menorrhagia") when drug therapy has been unsuccessful. Dilatation opens up the uterus for inspection. The curette is a long-handled, spoon-like instrument used to scoop out the tissue lining the uterus.

A D&C may be warranted to better diagnose a problem as, for instance, following an abnormal Pap test or when adenomyosis (endometrial cells enlarging the uterus) is suspected. Sometimes a minor procedure such as this, or even a Pap test or punch biopsy, may prod the uterus into regulating itself. Aside from its diagnostic value, a D&C can also relieve uterine polyps (harmless, pod-shaped growths) or submucous fibroids. If the polyps or fibroids recur, a second or third D&C may eliminate the need for major surgery.

Dilatation and Curettage (D & C)

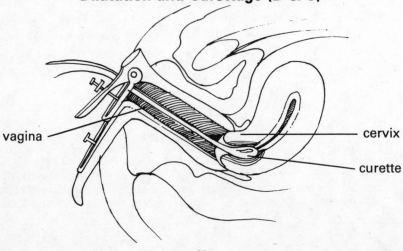

vagina — cervix

curette

Because the D&C is a minor procedure, it is sometimes done in an outpatient clinic. The patient reports early in the morning and is discharged that evening. When performed under general anaesthetic, there is an overnight stay. Scarring of the uterus may result and, for this reason, the D&C or a series of D&Cs may not be the best option for women wanting a child. However, for most menopausal women these consequences are not so important.

YAG (yttrium aluminum garnet) laser ablation

A newer alternative to a D&C is the YAG laser ablation of the endometrium, which may be effective when hormone treatment and/or D&Cs have been ineffective in halting severe bleeding. This procedure allows the surgeon to see the inside of the uterus and to destroy the deepest layer of the endometrium (lining of the uterus) so that it will not grow back. Preliminary results indicate a short recovery period (such as that for a D&C), no negative effects on sexual response (as compared to hysterectomy), and an encouraging success rate. It is assumed that the procedure induces sterility, but this is not yet confirmed.

This procedure will not be suitable for atypical cell changes inside the uterus (hyperplasia, etc.) or for pelvic inflammatory disease (PID). Because this is a fairly new procedure, it is available primarily in teaching hospitals. Some women may have to travel some distance to find a surgeon qualified to perform YAG laser treatment but it is an important alternative to hysterectomy.

Myomectomy

Myomectomy (or leiomyomectomy) is a procedure that is relatively rare in Canada, as opposed to England and Western Europe. A myomectomy is an operation that removes fibroids (benign tumours known as "myomas" or "leiomyomas") but leaves the uterus intact. The reason it is *not* more common in North America is that doctors have been trained to think of the uterus as an unnecessary organ (except for child-bearing), and most are not trained or practiced in the myomectomy procedure, which often requires more patience, time, and attention to detail than does a hysterectomy.

Fibroids are fairly common and come in different shapes and sizes. It is reckoned that 20 to 30 per cent of women harbour detectable fibroids, although only about one-third of these women will be bothered by them — experiencing abnormal bleeding, irregular menstrual periods, or feelings of pressure. Pathologists report that over 50 per cent of women have fibroids of some kind — some so tiny as to be almost invisible during autopsy.

Fibroids in and Around the Uterus

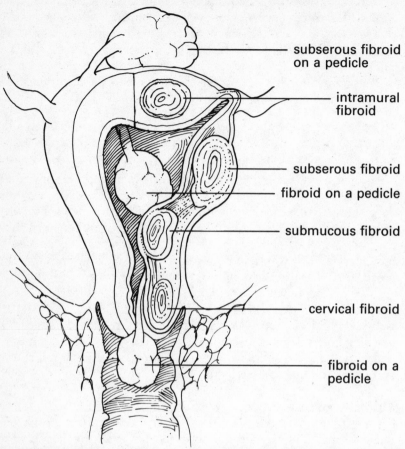

subserous fibroid on a pedicle

intramural fibroid

subserous fibroid

fibroid on a pedicle

submucous fibroid

cervical fibroid

fibroid on a pedicle

Surgeons who perform myomectomies remove an average of sixteen to twenty per operation, and the fibroids recur in a small minority (10 to 20 per cent) of cases. However, fibroids feed on estrogen and tend to diminish as one approaches menopause. If you are troubled with fibroids and wish to avoid the consequences of a hysterectomy, it may be worth your while to seek out a surgeon who will agree to perform a myomectomy.

■

I just received a letter from my sister in England. I had written to her about my upcoming surgery. Four months ago, my gynaecologist informed me that I have uterine fibroids and I am due to have a hysterectomy two weeks from tomorrow. Yet my sister seems to feel that a hysterectomy might be unnecessary. She sent me a newspaper clipping which states that there is an operation called "myomectomy" that involves removing only the fibroids and not the uterus. I've since spoken to two doctors. Neither had any information about or support for this procedure. I am outraged at their attitudes! They seem to feel that my uterus is of very little importance. I happen to care about it.

Hysterectomy

The word means "removal of the uterus" although it is often (and mistakenly) used to refer to removal of the ovaries as well as the uterus. When a doctor speaks about a "hysterectomy" or a "TAH" (total abdominal hysterectomy), he means removal of the uterus and cervix. A "partial hysterectomy" (rare in North America) removes the uterus and leaves a cervical "stump." A radical hysterectomy or "modified radical hysterectomy" involves lymph nodes outside the uterus and often entails a longer recovery with potentially more complications.

Hysterectomies are performed for a number of reasons, not all valid. When three women are hysterectomized in one area of the country for every two in another, it may be inferred that hysterectomies are still being used as the "easy" solution to a problem rather than as an operation of last resort. Some women continue to assume that, once their childbearing is finished, a hysterectomy is part of the routine. Misinformation or lack of information contributes to an inflated rate of hysterectomy in North America.

Some surgeons recommend a hysterectomy for heavy bleeding without attempting preliminary measures, or neglect to tell a woman that fibroids tend to diminish and disappear with menopause. There is often a significant difference between a male surgeon's view of your uterus and your own feelings about it. A striking example of this can be found in the hysterectomy rates in Switzerland, where female gynaecologists perform half as many hysterectomies as do their male counterparts. If you feel attached to your uterus (many of us do!) make this clear to your doctor. If he is the kind of doctor you want, he will be willing to discuss options other than surgery.

Despite the fact that medical texts and journals continue to document the adverse effects of hysterectomies, "women continue to be told that hysterectomy alone will not bring on menopause. They are told that oophorectomy will not alter their femininity; that drugs will replace their body's hormones; that recovery takes place within weeks; that sexual life will be unaffected or improved. In short, they are told they will be the same persons they have always been — only better" (*HERS Newsletter*, 2, Volume no 1, Winter 1984). Many more women are, unfortunately, told nothing at all.

Post-operative complications affect from 10 to 25 per cent of patients, particularly those who undergo radical hysterectomy. A signifi-

Different Types of Hysterectomy

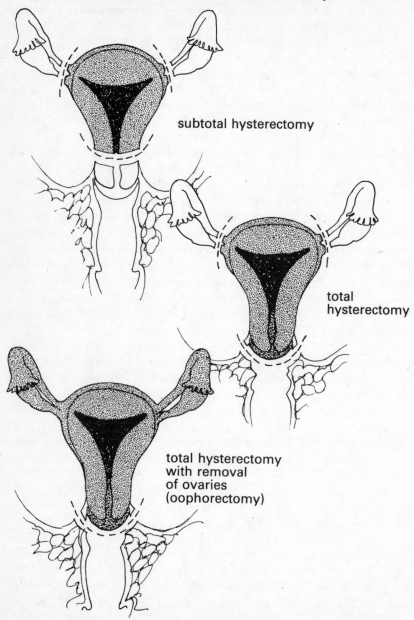

subtotal hysterectomy

total
hysterectomy

total hysterectomy
with removal
of ovaries
(oophorectomy)

cant number of those affected require re-hospitalization. Urinary-tract infections become much more common and, for pre-menopausal women, the prospect of premature menopause becomes a distinct possibility. Very few women know about this. Since the ovaries are moved inside the pelvic cavity, disrupting the blood flow carrying essential hormones, ovarian function is often affected. High levels of estrogen circulating in the bloodstream during the menstruating years help to protect against heart disease and **osteoporosis**. When ovaries falter as a result of hysterectomy, the risks of heart disease and osteoporosis climb.

Depression follows hysterectomy in from 30 to 50 per cent of cases; some studies say 70 per cent. Mostly this is minor (similar to depression after childbirth) but it is being recognized that there is a biochemical source for this depression. It is not due to the trauma of anaesthesia or surgery, since the effects are quite different from the experiences of women who have had appendectomies or cholecystectomies (gall-bladder surgery).

Hysterectomy may permanently diminish the experience of orgasm, not only because it removes the source of prostacyclin, a potent **vasodilator** produced in the uterus, but because it amputates the complementary throbbing of the uterus that often accompanies orgasm. Scar tissue at the end of the vagina may inhibit the ballooning characteristic of the vaginal barrel during orgasm; the woman may have to use a dilator to stretch the vagina and to plan, with her partner, sexual activity that will gradually make intercourse more pleasurable. (If the ovaries are removed at the time of hysterectomy, both sexual desire and the capacity for response may be seriously affected.)

Estrogen replacement therapy can never re-create the hormonal milieu, although it will work better for some women than others. (Women are told that drugs will "replace" lost estrogen but not about the high levels of FSH and LH that often follow surgery and may have unpredictable consequences.) It is impossible to predict how effective supplementary **hormones** will be for a particular patient. Most women find that it takes a full year to feel totally well, but some spend years trying different forms of replacement therapy in an unsuccessful effort to recapture the sensation of being well. Women are not likely to hear much of this from their surgeon.

If you decide to proceed with a hysterectomy, minimize the surprises by finding out as much as you can about the operation. Recovery is often longer and more difficult if the operation is scheduled during the two weeks prior to your menstrual period, so schedule it accordingly. If your doctor is not particularly forthcoming, this may be the time to think about switching doctors. Too many women are persuaded to stick with "experienced technicians" who are incapable of communicating effectively with their patients. Is that what you really want? Inquire about the tests required in advance, the types of anaesthetic used, the location of the incision, the pre-surgery routine (enema? shave?), and the post-surgery possibilities (catheter? IV [intravenous]? drains? lung-expansion exercises?). Examine the release forms you will be asked to sign and discuss contingencies with your doctors. When might you be expected to get up? to walk? to go home?

There are many, many women who find the quality of life much improved after a hysterectomy and who are very glad the decision was made. Research has shown that the outcome of a hysterectomy is favourable when the patient has had a few months to think over the situation and when she has a very clear idea of the reasons for, and techniques used, in the procedure itself; the post-surgery routine; and the detailed steps toward full recuperation. No self-respecting surgeon objects to a second opinion, or even a third, and each consultant is likely to contribute to a more accurate picture.

A woman who is in extreme discomfort or continual pain will not be dissuaded by this list of "things to think about," and rightly so. However, for every happy experience, there are many women confused and miserable after their operations. The rate of hysterectomy is much higher among poorly educated women with low-status jobs precisely *because* they have neither the opportunity nor the encouragement to look at other possibilities. It is for this reason that those interested in women's health urge caution and deliberation.

Oophorectomy (or ovariectomy)

These are the correct terms for removal of an ovary. When both ovaries are removed, it is a bilateral oophorectomy. When the fallopian tubes are also removed (as is often the case), this is a bilateral salpingectomy — often called a BSO (bilateral salpingo-oophorectomy) by doctors. Doctors refer to women who have had this operation as "castrates."

Removal of all ovarian tissue causes an immediate menopause, no matter what the age of the woman. Removal of most ovarian tissue is often followed by menopause, either as a result of the trauma (shock) of the surgery or because of a disturbance in the blood supply around the ovaries that carries the hormones produced by the ovaries. This interruption to the cycle often brings on premature menopause. Theoretically one small part of the ovary can produce hormones sufficient to keep the cycle regular until natural menopause. In practice, however, the outcome is unpredictable.

Many gynaecology textbooks still advocate the removal of healthy ovaries on any woman over forty. The shocking news is that this recommendation is based on a false statistic about ovarian cancer that has been repeated in textbook after textbook. Not too surprisingly, surgeons who graduated ten, twenty, or thirty years ago may still adhere to this recommendation; others routinely remove ovaries when performing a hysterectomy on a woman over forty-five. This is to avoid the possibility of ovarian cancer — a particularly lethal form of cancer that is difficult to detect and that, unlike uterine or endometrial cancer, takes hold very quickly. However, it is now recognized that removal of the ovaries prior to natural menopause significantly increases the risks of both heart disease and osteoporosis. And these risks are incurred for *every* woman who loses ovarian tissue in order to protect the *rare* woman who will develop ovarian cancer. It is ironic that the practice of removing the ovaries in any woman over forty has led to inflated rates of heart disease and osteoporosis among older women, who are then prescribed estrogen, a medical treatment, to alleviate a condition induced by the medical procedure. Recent studies suggest that for every seven hundred women who have their ovaries removed, perhaps *one* would have gone on to develop ovarian cancer. (This compares to about one in every hundred women in the general population.) Thus, the odds of developing ovarian cancer appear to be *reduced* in women who experience hysterectomy — perhaps because ovaries that are found to be healthy during surgery are likely to remain healthy. Removing one healthy ovary, or all but part of one ovary, are highly questionable practices since, so long as any ovarian tissue is present, the potential for ovarian cancer remains the same.

If the presence of an ovarian cyst requires investigative surgery, it should be understood — between the patient and her surgeon — that oophorectomy should not take place unless a malignancy is found. This will require a certain level of trust in the doctor.

Cancer of the prostate in men is about as common and about as lethal as cancer of the ovaries in women. However, prostectomies (the equivalent procedure for the male, which often results in impotence) are not routinely performed in order to protect them from prostate cancer. Women's health activists are protesting the practice of removing healthy ovaries.

Cholecystectomy (removal of the gall-bladder)

Most of the statistics that we read about hysterectomy tend to spill over from the United States, where more hysterectomies are performed (per 100,000 women) than in Canada. This leads us to expect higher rates of surgery across the board from the United States. Strangely enough, however, Canada can boast (if that's the word) a higher number of gall-bladder operations — more than half again as many as in the United States. In Canada, the numbers of women who undergo cholecystectomy are only slightly fewer than those undergoing hysterectomy, and it is an operation performed three times more often on women.

If you are overweight, over forty, and have had a number of child-ren, you are in a high-risk category. There are also certain ethnic groups more prone to gallstone problems (Spaniards and Swedes, for instance), although no one has figured out if this is a matter of heredi-ty or diet. Additional risk factors are diabetes, cirrhosis of the liver (from high alcohol consumption), and use of certain types of diuretics (Duretic, HydroDIURIL, or other thiazide derivatives).

Gallstones are hardened bits of cholesterol, calcium, and/or bile pigments, often detected only during other surgery (often hys-terectomy) or when ultrasound or CAT (computerized axial tomogra-phy) scans are used for some other purpose. CAT scans may, for in-stance, have been ordered for suspected osteoporosis.

Pathologists tell us that one woman in five has gallstones when she dies, although they may never have given her problems. These stones may be "silent" or asymptomatic (without symptoms); doctors treat these differently from quiescent gallstones, which *do* cause symptoms likely to recur.

The Occurrence of Gallstones

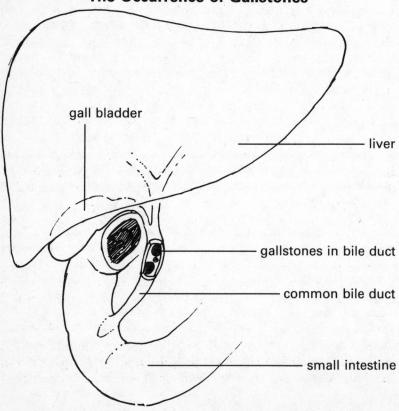

gall bladder

liver

gallstones in bile duct

common bile duct

small intestine

The gall-bladder is a storage facility for bile, the enzyme that is manufactured in the liver and directed toward the small intestine to help the breakdown of ingested fats. A gallstone may tumble into the biliary duct, which transports this bile, lodge there (causing great pain), or cause an infection. Women vulnerable to gall-bladder attacks are advised to stick to a low-fat diet to minimize the possibility of such an occurrence.

Because the risk of gallstones increases with use of oral contraceptives (particularly among very young women), estrogen replacement therapy is usually discouraged for women susceptible to gallstones. Obese women fall into this category since they already produce higher-than-normal amounts of **estrone**, a form of estrogen.

.

> I am writing to you because I want to share my experience with other women. Last month, I was told I had gallstones and surgery was advised. After having asked around a little, I discovered that the estrogen I've been taking to deal with menopause symptoms may very well have stimulated growth of the stones. I have stopped the estrogen and have gone on a low-fat diet. So far, all is well.

There are a number of non-surgical interventions for gallstones — pills that dissolve stones, drips that introduce a solvent directly into the gall-bladder, or shock waves intended to pulverize the stones (lithotripsy) — but some are more experimental than others and none is problem-free. The pills work well on cholesterol stones, but less well on other kinds of stones (and it is impossible to analyse the stones until they are *removed*). The drips must reach the precise site of the stones (a highly specialized manoeuvre) because it is toxic and could damage other organs. The shock waves (used more successfully on kidney stones) may harm nearby lung tissue and must be done under general anaesthetic.

There has been some speculation that increased rates of surgery may result from unnecessary medical intervention in asymptomatic gallstones. Recent reports suggest that both asymptomatic and quiescent stones require observation only, and that complications arise in only a very small minority of patients. In one study, where candidates with quiescent stones were followed very closely, the pain actually decreased after five years. Most doctors had assumed that it would get worse.

Some gall-bladder operations are recommended because of continuing flatulence (wind) and dyspepsia (heartburn/indigestion), which are presumed to be caused by gallstones. Studies have shown very little relationship between these symptoms and the presence of gallstones. When operations have been performed, the symptoms tend to reappear after the operation.

The best insurance against gall-bladder surgery appears to be a low-fat, high-fibre diet and strict monitoring of weight. Since gall-bladder problems appear to be related to a higher risk of heart attack, the low-fat diet advocated in Chapter 8 may help to reduce the risk of a number of diseases of mid-life — including fibroids, gallstones, and breast cancer.

The prospect of surgery is rarely pleasant and few of us are wheeled in, smiling, to the operating theatre. It helps if we have the support and counsel of someone we trust when making decisions about elective surgery. It helps, too, if the support comes from someone who understands how a woman feels about her body. Women's health organizations are doing a superb job of locating and circulating information about surgical procedures. Some are also attempting to provide an "advocate" for the frightened woman contemplating surgery — another woman who will sit in on discussions with the doctor, ask pertinent questions, bolster the morale and safeguard the rights of the woman faced with a decision. This is a role that each of us can play for the other.

CHAPTER 7

.

Increased Health Risks
at Menopause

FOR MANY OF US, **menopause** comes as a shock. We are forced to become
aware of our bodies and our health — things we often take for granted.
Because our bodies no longer respond, perform, acquiesce in the ways
that they once did, we are forced to recognize our age and our mortality.
For some, this is dreadful. But it does have its compensations.

Menopause, in a strange kind of way, reminds us to take stock of
our health and to initiate steps to withstand the threats to good health
that increase with age. It gives us the chance to decide whether we
will be sitting targets for diseases of old age or if we are willing to make
an effort to keep our health. This is not only for our own benefit, but
for the benefit of those who would have to take care of us.

Heart-related medical conditions — hardening of the arteries, high
blood pressure, heart disease, or stroke — account for more than half
of the disabling health problems on this continent. Before age sixty,
twice as many men are affected; after age sixty, women are as vulnerable as men. Menopause does not, of course, *cause* heart disease or
breast cancer, but after age fifty-five, women are more likely to have
high blood pressure than are men. Any book about menopause must
include the bad news: Menopause brings with it the increased risk of
heart disease, particularly for those who experience surgical menopause. Once a woman has had one heart attack, her chances of experiencing a second are greater than a man's. And women are less likely to
survive heart surgery.

We may not be aware of the heightened risks of cardio-vascular disease but many of us know, in some small, secret place, that we are also
moving into a high-risk category for breast cancer. In fact, 65 per cent
of new cases occur after the age of fifty.

BREAST HEALTH

Five out of ten women see their doctors, at some point in their lives,
about lumps, pain, swelling, or tenderness of the breasts. Pathologists
have discovered that 90 per cent of women show some evidence of the

kinds of cellular changes that have been called "**fibrocystic** breast disease." We are coming to realize that, if nine out of ten women experience lumps in the breast, it must not be a *disease* at all, but rather a normal part of being a woman. The fear of breast cancer can be alleviated to some degree when we recognize that lumps in the breast are part of life, and that there are many different kinds of lumps.

Breasts are very individual parts of the body and there are great variations in size and shape. In fact, the left breast is often larger than the right. The nipple may be inverted or not, large or small. The surrounding area (the **areola**) may be pale or dark, large or small. The internal structure is similar, however, made up of milk glands, forming

Structure of the Breast

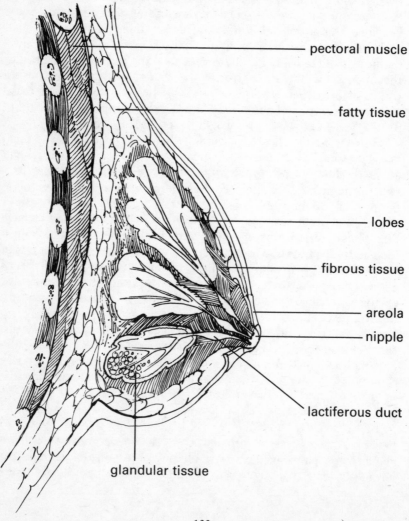

pectoral muscle

fatty tissue

lobes

fibrous tissue

areola

nipple

lactiferous duct

glandular tissue

lobes that converge on the nipple through a series of ducts. Fibrous bands hold the lobes apart and attach the breasts to the chest wall. The supporting fibres are responsible for the "lift," which is affected by body weight, breast size, pregnancy and breastfeeding. Age brings a thinning out of the fibres, with fatty tissue often filling up the spaces created.

Benign breast conditions

Although we tend to think of cancer whenever we notice anything unusual about our breasts, non-cancerous breast conditions are much more common. Benign breast conditions may involve changes in the fibrous tissue, changes in the cells of the milk ducts, or the formation of cysts. The most common of these is the formation of cysts (chronic **mastitis**), which affects some 30 per cent of women and which tends to be most bothersome between the ages of thirty and forty.

·

> At the age of thirty-eight, I discovered lumps in my breast. Convinced I had cancer, I rushed to my doctor and was given no reason to believe otherwise. My doctor suggested that the lumps were probably cancerous and made an appointment for a mammogram and biopsy. As it turned out, it was cystic mastitis. The cysts were drained and I am grateful that it wasn't worse. I've learned to do routine breast self-examination and I feel the importance of this cannot be stressed enough.

It is not known why cysts form, but there is apparently some relationship to the type of fibrous tissue, to diet, and to stimulation by cyclical **hormones**. Before menopause, fluctuations in estrogen tend to produce larger, more tender cysts before menstruation, with changes in size and sensation following the menstrual period. Generally cysts form hard, round nodes that can be moved easily and that are filled with fluid. There may be many small ones, a few medium-sized, or even one large one. When they are too large and too painful, they may be aspirated (drained) with a fine needle. A darkish fluid — yellow, green, or brown — will be withdrawn and sent for routine analysis. Cysts are rarely cancerous. Recent research suggests that the rare cancerous cyst may have more to do with the cyst lining, which is smooth when benign and irregular when malignant. Cysts often disappear spontaneously after menopause.

Methylxamine (found in coffee, tea, cola drinks, and chocolate) seems to aggravate formation of breast cysts. Nicotine may also be a factor, since smokers seem to have more trouble with cysts. Low-fat diets have helped some women to reduce the incidence and discomfort.

Evening primrose oil has been used by some women with promising results. Increased levels of **Vitamin A** (which is toxic in excess!), **Vitamin B₆** (50 mg daily), and **Vitamin E** (800 mg daily in four doses of 200 mg) have also been used with excellent results. (For more information about Vitamin E and some cautions about its use, see page 31.)

Changes in the fibrous tissue of the breasts can lead to a number of conditions. If a rubbery, painless tumour forms, this is a fibroadenoma. These tumours, which occur more commonly before age thirty-five, are not influenced by the menstrual cycle and move easily under the skin; they can usually be felt in the part of the breast closest to the armpit. A rare form of this condition may occur during menopause: **giant fibroadenoma** (also called cystosarcoma phyllodes or giant myxoma). I include all these terms in case you have a doctor who likes to bamboozle you with big words! If it is a case of giant fibroadenoma, the lump grows rapidly to a large size and must be surgically removed.

Another rare condition, which may also affect menopausal women, is **fibrosis** (not to be confused with fibrositis) or fibrous dysplasia. This consists of a firm, painless mass with no defined edges, making it difficult to feel where normal tissue stops and abnormal tissue starts. Nearly all of these fibrous-tissue abnormalities are benign.

Breast cancer is much more likely to stem from changes in the milk ducts although, even here, only a few conditions are viewed as pre-cancerous. **Adenosis** (which simply means "abnormal growth") is another form of breast lump that may occur inside the milk duct. A lump under the nipple or areola may be caused by **intraductal papillomas**, wart-like growths that may produce a discharge from the nipple. An inflammation of the milk ducts, which is more common among post-menopausal women, is **duct ectasia**, which may also produce nipple discharge.

It is estimated that up to 10 per cent of women may experience nipple discharge at one time or another. Some women will have a white discharge months after a baby is weaned. Others may notice a clear, or yellow, or reddy-brown discharge, either occurring spontaneously or when the nipple is squeezed. Any discharge should be investigated but it is not that unusual.

There are some serious forms of duct ectasia — plasma cell mastitis or comedomastitis. Occasionally the wart-like growths under the nipple are diagnosed as ductal papillomatosis and require intensive care. **Duct hyperplasia** (also known as hyperplastic disease) is a rare overgrowth of the lining of the milk ducts and is treated as a potential malignancy.

However, in addition to the four kinds of benign lumps already described — chronic mastitis, fibroadenoma, adenosis, and intraductal papillomas — a lump in the breast could be a **lipoma** (a fatty growth that can occur anywhere in the body) or fat **necrosis** (a hard lump resulting from a blow to the breast). Of all these kinds, textures and sizes of breast lumps, only 10 to 15 per cent will be malignant.

Breast self-examination (BSE)

Many of us shy away from **breast self-examination** despite the massive promotional efforts of the American and Canadian Cancer Societies. Unfortunately, the emphasis on BSE has been to *find lumps* rather than to be more familiar with a healthy part of the body. Most of us are very familiar with our neck and throat. We feel the neck as we adjust jewellery or fix our hair. We notice small changes — a gland swelling under the jawline, a funny bump behind the ear, a small bump, perhaps a mole, that we can feel but is out of sight in the mirror. We monitor the state of the neck regularly and quite unselfconsciously. Why can't we bring this same attitude to breast self-examination?

The steps involved are neither difficult nor time-consuming. Looking carefully at oneself in the mirror is easy. But the problem, for many of us, is the actual palpation — searching with the tips of the fingers for anything unusual. It is difficult to find anything unusual if one is not accustomed to the *usual*.

Many women have learned to examine their breasts while in the shower or in the tub, where soapy fingers or shower gel allow for more comfortable manipulation of breast tissue. (Baby oil also helps. You might ask your doctor to use baby oil to make breast examination more comfortable for you.) When we realize that the odds are very much in our favour — that we are likely to find everything normal or a harmless condition that can be easily treated — it is easier to stick to a resolution to examine the breasts at least once a month.

We don't have statistics on the numbers of benign breast conditions noticed, treated, and forgotten. But we do know that 85 to 90 per cent of breast cancers are initially reported by women doing BSE and that women who *do* examine their breasts regularly are able to notice lumps the size of the tip of a ballpoint pen, lumps such smaller than those found by experienced doctors.

■

In January last year I had a biopsy on my right breast which showed a carcinomic growth. To make a long story short, the cancer had spread to my spine and the blood tests showed it is a hormone-fed cancer. The clinic recommended cobalt radiation treatments to irradiate the ovaries.

Needless to say, I was fully into menopause literally overnight, with about twenty to thirty hot flushes daily. One thing I learned: If there is

Steps in Breast Self-Examination

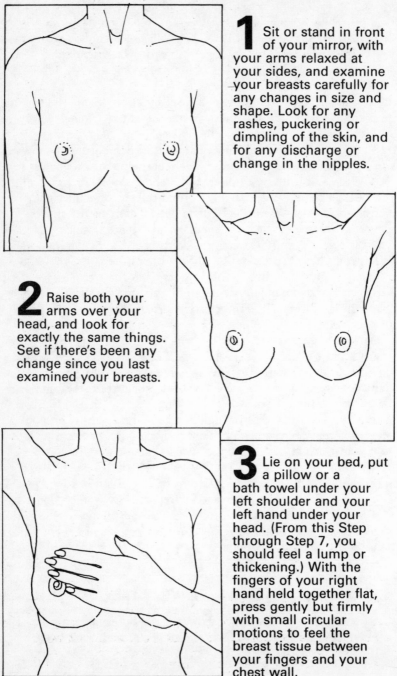

1 Sit or stand in front of your mirror, with your arms relaxed at your sides, and examine your breasts carefully for any changes in size and shape. Look for any rashes, puckering or dimpling of the skin, and for any discharge or change in the nipples.

2 Raise both your arms over your head, and look for exactly the same things. See if there's been any change since you last examined your breasts.

3 Lie on your bed, put a pillow or a bath towel under your left shoulder and your left hand under your head. (From this Step through Step 7, you should feel a lump or thickening.) With the fingers of your right hand held together flat, press gently but firmly with small circular motions to feel the breast tissue between your fingers and your chest wall.

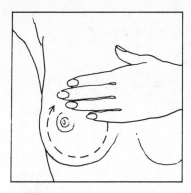

4 Start at the outside of your breast near your left armpit and feel slowly and carefully with small circular motions all the way around the rim of your breast. If your breasts are heavy they may fold over along the lower edge to form a firm ridge of tissue. This is quite normal.

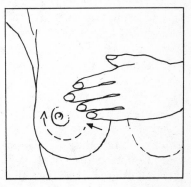

5 Now move your fingers in toward the nipple about 2 cms and feel all the way around again. Repeat this action as many times as necessary to be sure you have covered the entire breast, including the nipple.

6 Now bring your left arm down to your side and, still using the flat part of your fingers, feel under your armpit, since breast tissue is found there as well.

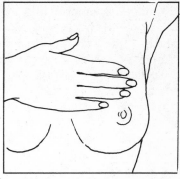

7 Repeat the entire procedure using your left hand on your right breast.

Examine your breasts every month — right after your period is best. If you are not menstruating, pick a special day, such as the first of the month or your birth date, to practise BSE. If you find any change in your breast, check it out with your doctor right away. Don't be frightened — most breast lumps or changes are not cancer, but why take the chance?

any visual change in your breasts — even if a lump cannot be found — get to a doctor immediately and keep going until you find a doctor who will listen to you. I had a dimple in my breast. I got worried when the doctor couldn't feel a lump. The dimple kept getting larger. Listen to your intuition because you know your body better than anyone else, including all doctors!

Diagnosis

Because of the increased risk of breast cancer in mid-life, many physicians now routinely send patients for a mammogram. The referral to the radiology department or clinic does *not* mean that anything unusual has been detected. If you have seen the doctor because of a lump, it may be biopsied in the doctor's office; if anything unusual shows up on the mammogram, you will be sent for a biopsy.

Rather than being over-dramatic about incipient cancer, we would be better off accepting mammograms and biopsies as routine procedures in the maintenance of good health. We don't get alarmed about standard blood tests or chest X-rays, although each could just as easily point to some kind of abnormal activity in the body. As we get older, it seems important to look at the biopsy procedure in the same way — just one more standard test that helps to confirm our continuing good health.

There are other ways to examine breast tissue without breaking the skin. **Thermography** uses heat sensitivity to map areas where there is rapid cell growth (assumed to be tumours) and to contrast this with normal tissue. However, a mild inflammation may produce heat and for this and other reasons, thermography has not been found to be sufficiently accurate. Transillumination (and a more recent offshoot of this, **diaphanography**) uses a bright light shining against the breast to show up darker masses of tissue. The accuracy of these methods depends on the density of the breast tissue. So far, they are useful only in conjunction with other methods. **Ultrasound**, which can differentiate fluid-filled cysts from solid masses, is less useful after menopause when the breast tissue changes (and when cysts tend to disappear anyway). Any or all of these methods may be used if the breast condition is judged to be benign and the patient is adamant about the radiation used in mammography.

Menopausal women have breasts that are better suited to mammography than are the breasts of younger women. At mid-life, breasts become less fibrous and more fatty, yielding the high contrasts needed for accurate diagnosis. Long-term effects of mammogram radiation are of concern to younger women but, by age fifty, we can afford to worry less; it is estimated that it would take thirty or forty years for the radiation effects to show up. Most experts recommend that a baseline mammogram be done at age fifty, followed by regular annual mammograms. If there is breast cancer in the immediate family, some experts recommend that examinations start at a younger age and be scheduled every six months.

The mammogram is usually conducted by a female technician in privacy and is a short and relatively painless procedure. Each breast is placed between two plates and pressure exerted to compress it as much as possible — once horizontally and once vertically. There are a lot of rumours about the pain of mammography but it is hard to find personal testimonials to this effect. Women with larger-than-normal breasts are likely to find it uncomfortable, and the sensation of cold steel against warm flesh is not a pleasant one. However, there are newer machines that use warmer substances and exert the final fractions of compression automatically at the time the technician steps into the booth. This means that the sensation of squeezing lasts only a second. If you do have the misfortune to run into an insensitive technician, make sure that you complain to the person in charge.

Because post-menopausal women do not have menstrual cycles to explain away the size or tenderness of breast lumps, any lump will be treated with suspicion. In addition, because the odds of breast cancer increase with age, doctors are on the alert for any abnormality. If you report finding a lump, your doctor may ask to do a quick, wide-needle biopsy in the office. This is done using a local anaesthetic, which freezes the area, and a second needle to draw out a sample of cells. Sometimes the procedure is done at the hospital's outpatient clinic.

Breast cancer
Despite the variety and frequency of benign breast conditions, the term "breast health," to most of us, means the avoidance of breast cancer. Because breasts are viewed in this culture primarily as symbols of femininity and sexuality (one reason why we may be reluctant to examine them), most of us harbour an irrational fear of breast cancer. We tell ourselves that we are not at risk, even though 70 to 80 per cent of new cancers are diagnosed in women who are *not* in a specific risk category. This is how fear gets in the way of sensible self-care.

If your mother or a sister has (or has had) breast cancer, you are at higher-than-normal risk. If you have never been pregnant, or had your first child after age thirty, or did not breastfeed, you are at slightly higher risk than average. If you had an early menarche (first menstrual period), and a late menopause, the risk is increased. And finally, if you are overweight, drink alcohol on a daily basis, and eat foods high in fats, your risk is higher. Some of these risk factors cannot be changed; some can be altered in your favour.

■

Some years ago I had my first mammogram and it was clear. This was because my left breast was inclined to be a bit fibrocystic so nothing could be seen. A year later, there was something there but in my right breast. You couldn't feel it though. It turned out to be malignant and, during a second operation to remove a quarter of my breast, lymph node involvement was found. I have presently had two bouts of chemotherapy with six to go. Four years ago, my sister (who is five years younger than me) had a mammogram which was clear. She was experiencing menopausal problems and her doctor prescribed estrogen. When they discovered that I had breast cancer, she asked for another mammogram and, sure enough, she had it, too! She, like me, had a lumpectomy and is presently undergoing radiation therapy. Both our tumours were less than 1 cm and the prognosis is good but I'm afraid I feel we would never have had these cancers if it weren't for estrogen. As soon as the cancer was diagnosed I was taken off estrogen and put on tamoxifen, which is an anti-estrogen. I was told the other day that my tumour has estrogen receptors. It makes me sick to think that for four years I was feeding the thing.

I should mention that my older sister has been on synthetic estrogen for about ten years and is fine. I guess not everyone is going to get cancer from taking estrogen, but I would not wish what I have been through on anyone. I think the risk is too great.

Some breast cancers are hormone-dependent, in which case treatment is directed toward reducing hormone levels in the body as quickly and as completely as possible. Other cancers do not react to hormones and still others appear to be a mixture of the two. There are contradictory reports about the long-term effects of oral contraceptives on breast cancer. Some say that long-term pill users are at decreased risk; some say the contrary. Synthetic **estrogen** in the form of diethylstilbestrol (DES) — once routinely administered to reduce the risk of miscarriage — is now suspected to be related to much higher-than-normal levels of breast cancer in the women who were given it. **Estrogen replacement therapy** (ERT) is suspected to cause an increase in breast cysts and fibrous lumps but we don't know enough about use of ERT in relation to breast cancer. (For more about this, see Chapter 5.)

Very rarely, a woman may notice that her nipple is itchy, red, and weeping. It may look and feel like a simple skin infection, but home remedies like salves and lotions won't help. Time to see a doctor. It could be Paget's disease, a rare form of cancer.

Because breast cancer is probably two or three different diseases (one of which may affect only women past menopause), there are many different treatments. If you know women who have breast cancer, you may find the difference in their treatments confusing. This does not necessarily reflect different attitudes of their doctors, but rather different types of cancer.

If you *do* find a lump in your breast and it *does* turn out to be malignant, the prospects for full recovery are better than they've ever been: 95 per cent of women with small, malignant breast lumps survive for at least twenty years after the operation. In such cases, most surgeons now lean to a lumpectomy (which removes the lump and leaves the breast virtually intact), coupled with adjuvant (drug) therapy and/or radiation treatments, rather than the traditional but disfiguring removal of the breast (mastectomy). This means that the odds of losing a breast, either with or without underlying muscle and/or underarm lymph nodes, have been markedly reduced. Some women, when faced with the prospect of drugs and radiation in addition to a lumpectomy, will decide on a mastectomy. Women should be given options. If you have a doctor who insists that you have the procedure *he* or *she* prefers, make sure you get a second opinion. (See Chapter 6 for how to go about getting a second opinion.)

When cancer is diagnosed, this is the time to find a strong friend to lean on. Discuss your options. Not only should you insist on a second opinion, but you should also insist on time. Women have, too often, been wheeled into an operating room not knowing whether they would emerge whole or not. It is generally conceded that, even in extreme cases, women should be permitted two separate procedures — first the biopsy and later, after advice and deliberation, a second operation. Most of all, women need support and friendship to resist hasty decisions.

The incidence of *never-discovered cancer* in women over age seventy (who have died of other causes) is nineteen times that of discovered (palpable) breast cancer. This means that, for every woman who has a breast lump diagnosed as malignant, there are nineteen women whose breast lumps never grow — lumps that appear and never grow larger or grow so slowly as never to be noticed. Some experts feel that these potentially cancerous lumps are with us from puberty onwards (when the breasts first develop), but how our immune system acts to stop these lumps from developing is still a mystery.

In other words, breast cancer may not be something "out there" that we catch like a cold or the flu. Environmental factors — pollutants, chemicals, diet, and even stress — may play a part. But the seeds of breast cancer are already sown in each of us and are as unpredictable and unexpected as all those other lumps — whether cysts, adenomas, adenosis, lipoma, or fat necrosis.

CARDIO-VASCULAR HEALTH

Until fairly recently, most of the studies that dealt with heart disease focused on men. This means that what was generally accepted to be true (in terms of those vulnerable to heart-related conditions) was based on information about males. For instance, heart disease was thought to be riskier for "Type A" personalities — tense, ambitious over-achievers. More often than not, this meant male, middle-class management-types. Among women, however, it is those on low wages, with low status, who are at greatest risk. These women are more likely to be blue-collar, working class, in low-paying jobs. We really know very little about *women's* vulnerability to diseases of the heart and blood vessels.

We all know people who have had heart attacks or strokes, who are taking pills or are on restricted diets for blood pressure or **angina**, or who are forced to tolerate varicose veins or hemorrhoids (piles). All of these are forms of cardio-vascular disease. But many of the words used to describe these conditions have been changed or become more specific. For instance, we used to hear about people who had "heart attacks" or a "massive coronary." Now we're likely to hear about "ischemic heart disease" or "myocardial infarction." This is confusing and makes it hard to understand medical problems that often affect friends and family.

The cardio-vascular system is made up of four basic components — the pump (or heart), the pipes (the veins and arteries), the control system (the nerves that cause the heart to beat, valves that ensure the one-way flow of blood, etc.), and the material moving through the system (the blood). Problems may be caused by: (a) clogging of the pump or pipes; (b) leaking or bursting of the pump or pipes; (c) some breakdown in the control system; or (d) changes in blood as it moves through the system. Some problems result from a single cause, but most arise from a combination. The major culprit is the clogging of the pump or pipes.

We are just beginning to understand something about the reasons for the clogging, which starts when elements carried along in the blood start to coat, invade, and then pile up on the inside of a blood vessel. The composition of the blood may be partly to blame, and the inner lining of the arteries may be roughened with wear, catching filaments as they flow by. But the particular pattern of the clogging and the location of the bottlenecks vary enormously from person to person. So far, no one knows exactly what causes a particular pattern to emerge. As the passage for the blood narrows, the heart must work harder to pump the blood into all the tissues. As the artery walls lose their elasticity, they may weaken and balloon out. This is an **aneurysm**. Should the aneurysm weaken and leak or burst, the consequences could be deadly.

In other cases, thrombi (blood clots) may hinder blood flow to the brain (cerebral thrombosis) or to the heart (coronary thrombosis). If the thrombosis is swept along to another site to block circulation of the blood, it is called an embolism. A pulmonary embolism is in the lungs; a cerebral embolism, in the brain.

When artery walls thicken and lose flexibility, the condition is known as **arteriosclerosis**. When the clogging is caused by deposits of certain kinds of fat (**atheromas**), the condition is known as **atherosclerosis**. In order to force blood past these obstructions in the arteries, the heart must do more work and the pressure of the blood in the arteries rises. This leads to high blood pressure or hypertension.

Hypertension

A blood-pressure reading is a normal part of every medical check-up. Blood pressure is charted according to the force of the heart pumping (the **systole**) over the force of the heart at rest (the **diastole**). Although the reading varies depending on amount of physical exertion, time of day, emotional state, etc., a consistent and acceptable reading is anything between 100 and 135 for the first number and between 50 and 85 for the second. A reading of 140 over 90 (written as 140/90) is considered "borderline."

Hypertension is known as "the silent killer" since you may have it and never know it. A person with high blood pressure is three times more likely to have a heart attack, eight times more likely to have a stroke, and five times more likely to experience heart failure. Hypertension may also lead to eye problems or kidney failure. It was once thought that blood pressure naturally got higher as one aged. Now it is known that blood pressure can be kept at a healthy level through diet, exercise, reducing salt intake, stopping smoking, careful weight watching, and adequate calcium in the diet.

■

I am a woman of fifty-three who has been experiencing menopausal problems for five years. I was always a workaholic, smoked a lot, and generally ignored my health. I refused to let menopause slow me down although my blood pressure was high and I suffered from insomnia. Two years ago, I had a heart attack. I've now changed my lifestyle completely: I've stopped smoking, I eat better and exercise regularly. My blood pressure is back to normal — thank God! — and I feel 100 per cent better.

When blood pressure climbs, a doctor has the option of prescribing medication (usually a diuretic) or enlisting patient co-operation to change bad habits. Diuretics promote the excretion of fluids including salt. Unpleasant side-effects are frequent urination and possible depletion of vital potassium. Strict anti-hypertensive drugs, however, often involve even more side-effects. One widely-used drug, reserpine, has been found to increase the risk of breast cancer; others lead to restless sleep and frequent awakenings. In addition, the benefits of hypertensive medication can be cancelled by the use of oral contraceptives, appetite depressants, or non-steroidal anti-inflammatory drugs (prescribed for arthritis).

More and more doctors recognize that a non-drug approach to controlling blood pressure may be as effective as medication, or more so. As much as one-third of the population is known to be sodium sensitive; for these people, sharp reduction in salt intake may stabilize borderline blood pressure, which may then be treated with commonsense precautions — no cigarettes, more exercise, and changes in diet.

Stroke

Leaking or clogging in the brain may lead to a major **stroke** (cerebrovascular accident, or CVA) or, if the leaking is intermittent and minor, to a transient ischemic attack (TIA). "Ischemic" means that the tissues are being starved of oxygen. If blood cannot reach brain cells, the starved cells will die. And, although some scientists now suspect that brain cells *may* have the capacity to regenerate, they really don't know how to promote this. This means that those particular cells may never be reactivated. If many cells are affected, the result may be paralysis, loss of speech, or other damage reflecting the part of the brain affected. Recovery is slow since new nerve pathways must be forged and old skills painfully relearned. If only a few brain cells are affected, the effects are more subtle — tingling in the extremities, momentary dizziness or weakness, etc. TIAs may be shrugged off as temporary inconveniences, but the cumulative effect of a series may be apparent in loss of brain function and even senility. At the end of a series of transient ischemic attacks, the patient may be hard to distinguish from someone suffering from Alzheimer's disease. One acetylsalicylic acid tablet (ASA) per day may reduce the threat of stroke. Coated tablets are available to those who find ASA upsetting to the stomach.

Heart attack

If leaking or clogging occurs in the coronary arteries, the diagnosis is coronary heart disease (CHD), or ischemic heart disease (IHD). The pain resulting from the heart's loss of its own blood supply is angina pectoris. The usual progression is atherosclerosis of the coronary arteries, followed by ischemic heart disease (which makes itself known by the pain of angina), and then a heart attack. The section of the heart fed by the clogged artery cannot last more than five minutes without an adequate blood supply. When heart muscle is damaged, this is myocardial infarction.

There are, of course, many other problems resulting from the leaking, clogging, and bursting of the heart and blood vessels. Some conditions are birth defects. Some result from scarring caused by disease (such as rheumatic fever). Some refer to bacterial infection or to conditions affecting specific parts of the heart or arteries.

Arrhythmia

Any disturbance to the natural rhythm of the heartbeat is **arrhythmia**, caused by a malfunction of the control system. The natural pacemaker of the heart functions inside the atrium, or upper chamber of the heart, and governs the regularity of the beat. When the heart begins to beat too fast (at about 180 beats per minute), this is **tachycardia**. If the heart speeds up even more, it may "flutter" at around 250 beats per minute, or flatten out completely during "fibrillation." (Remember the paramedics on those television shows who administer massive electric shocks to a heart no longer beating?)

A less dramatic but more common complaint during menopause is paroxysmal atrial tachycardia, which does *not* lead to flutter or fibrillation and may occur in otherwise normal, healthy persons. Occasionally it may be caused by migraine activity (see Chapter 2). It is estimated that one person in every hundred experiences "extra heartbeats" at some time or another. Tachycardia is very different from the more common **palpitations**, which is merely an unpleasant awareness of the heart beating and is often felt at times of anxiety or panic. The well-known heart specialist Dr. Michael DeBakey suggests that a person experiencing an episode of atrial tachycardia may be able to relieve it for herself either by gagging or by massaging the carotid sinus in the neck. The carotid sinus is the pulse in front of the ear and just below the jawbone.

If you do experience episodes of tachycardia, you should be referred to a cardiologist. When rapid heart rate results from the lower chamber of the heart, a more serious condition may be present.

Medication is often routinely administered to alleviate arrhythmia, but recent studies indicate that skipped beats, or a temporarily "racing heart," rarely have anything to do with heart disease. In fact, some studies suggest that the medication may cause more problems and that most people with heartbeat irregularities can expect to live as long and as healthily as anyone else.

The valves of the heart, arteries, and veins are a major part of the cardio-vascular control system since they make sure that the blood moves in the desired direction. Malfunction of the heart valves is not uncommon. When the **mitral valve** doesn't close properly after each beat, this can be heard through the stethoscope. In fact, prolapse of the mitral valve (Barlow's syndrome) is said to affect 15 per cent of women over the age of thirty. Echocardiography (a painless procedure that bounces sound waves into the chest cavity) can confirm the diagnosis, but there is relatively little risk. There may be a little chest pain, some palpitations, and some shortness of breath after exertion. Relief may sometimes be found by increasing magnesium intake — eating more fresh fruits and vegetables or experimenting with supplements. The greatest worry with mitral-valve prolapse is the risk of heart infection, which can follow from standard dental procedures. Women with mitral-valve prolapse are advised to keep a prescription for antibiotics on hand and to start ten days of treatment before any dental work (including teeth cleaning).

■

For the past year, I have suffered from severe heart palpitations and a very fast heartbeat. Cardiologists cannot find anything apart from a prolapse of the mitral valve, which apparently is of no concern. I'm sure I have a spine full of arthritis which causes pains in my neck, shoulders and arms, and which some days is just about more than I can bear. This all hit me within a year after a lifetime of being just fine. I'm only forty-three and when I mention to doctors that perhaps I could be starting my change of life, they laugh at me. Of course, they think I'm too young for that. I get dizzy spells and tire very easily. I have had all the tests to be had and everything appears normal. I'm on beta blockers to slow my heart down and I have side effects from this medication. So right now I feel like I have nowhere to turn. I know that I'm feeling like hell but the doctors apparently cannot or will not do anything for me.

Varicose veins

The venous valves, particularly those below the waist, are responsible for varicose veins, which may occur quite aside from any conditions affecting the arteries. One can have varicose veins without any worry about arteriosclerosis, or clogged arteries. Varicose veins are estimated to affect at least 20 per cent of women and perhaps 8 per cent of men, and they seem to run in families. They may show up as a visible network of enlarged veins in the legs, as a painful ache from the veins inside the legs, or as hemorrhoids. They may be aggravated by pregnancy, when veins swell to accommodate the enormous increase in circulating blood.

Although varicose veins are not attractive, they are rarely life-threatening. Superficial veins may require elastic stockings (either heavy-duty elastic or the less noticeable support hose), which should be put on first thing in the morning before getting out of bed. Restrictive garments — girdles, knee-high stockings, tight shoes or boots — and long periods of sitting or standing (especially if one is overweight) will make them worse. When sitting, the legs should be elevated as much as possible. A diet high in fibre and in Vitamin C has been found to be beneficial. Swollen surface veins can often be "stripped," forcing the blood to circulate through deeper veins. This is a relatively painless operation, usually covered by health plans. The major risk with varicose veins is the possibility of blood clots (thrombi) or **phlebitis**, inflammation in the deeper veins.

Phlebitis

Although thrombophlebitis also involves veins, it is more serious and indicates the presence of both blood clots and inflammation. The presence of varicose veins increases the risk of phlebitis, as does being on the contraceptive pill. Deep-vein phlebitis is more difficult to deal with. The inflammation (a dull ache and/or swelling) may signal the presence of a clot (the thrombus), which must be dissolved using anticoagulants and producing severe side-effects in about 5 per cent of patients. If the clot is not dissolved, it may loosen and move through the system to become a life-threatening embolism. The embolism itself may be signalled by chest pains or shortness of breath.

Blood clots may form after a blow to the legs, or a fall, or when blood flow is slowed down due to immobility, such as during illness or after surgery. Phlebitis is not common and is frequently misdiagnosed but new diagnostic tools (such as impedance plethysmography) are increasing medical know-how to deal with it. Women prone to phlebitis are advised to exercise regularly and to give up smoking. Bedridden patients should be carefully monitored and, where necessary, low-dose anti-coagulants used to increase blood flow.

RISK FACTORS FOR CARDIO-VASCULAR DISEASE

Most of the factors that lead to increased risk of cardio-vascular disease can be controlled. The exceptions are heredity, age, and sex. Let's deal with these first.

Heredity

Individuals may inherit a tendency to blood-chemistry conditions that put a strain on the heart, such as high cholesterol levels, or higher-than-normal white blood cell counts over an extended period of time. Black women in North America have higher rates of both heart disease and hypertension than do whites, despite the fact that blood-cholesterol levels are often lower. We may also inherit a tendency to obesity, to dark hair in and around the inner ear, or to a crease across the earlobe. Strange as it may seem, these are all indications of increased risk for cardio-vascular disease. On the other hand, some of us also inherit a tendency to high HDL (high density lipoprotein) levels (which are protective against heart disease), or to varicose veins (which pose a minor risk). With some detective work, most of us can discover our inherited tendencies and work to offset them.

Age

Age increases the risks for all forms of cardio-vascular diseases but women over thirty-five who take oral contraceptives are at substantially higher risk than women who use other forms of birth control. Studies indicate that women who have their ovaries removed before the age of forty-five are at much greater risk, and younger women who have had a **hysterectomy** (but who have retained their **ovaries**) may have a higher-than-normal tendency to develop heart disease. Women who are not on the pill and who have not had surgery enjoy greater protection from most cardio-vascular problems, as compared to men, until the late fifties, but are more prone to high blood pressure. (Although it has been assumed that it is high levels of **estrogen** that provide the extra margin of protection to women prior to menopause, estrogen administered to men results in more heart attacks. It may be the high level of **testosterone** in the male that makes him vulnerable and that the risk diminishes as testosterone levels fall with age.)

Diet

A high-fat diet, coupled with generous lashings of salt and lots of coffee, can significantly increase the risks of cardio-vascular disease. High salt consumption is a primary factor in hypertension. Recent studies also indicate a significantly higher risk of heart disease for those who average six or more cups of coffee a day. This appears to hold true whether or not you smoke.

   Cholesterol has acquired a bad reputation over the last few years, although many of us don't quite know why. It is an animal fat in many kinds of food (oils, meats, and eggs) but also manufactured by our bodies. The human liver can produce all the cholesterol we need. Excess cholesterol invades and clogs the arteries, contributing to hypertension and leading to heart disease. A woman with 265 mg of cholesterol per decilitre of blood is at twice the risk for heart disease as

116

a woman with 205 mg. A cholesterol level of 150 mg rarely leads to heart disease.

.

> I am one of those women who has a genetic tendency to high blood cholesterol. In my case, it is due to a deficiency in cholesterol receptors — a 50 per cent deficiency! I've had a dangerously high level of cholesterol for at least twenty years (260 mg/dl of blood) and, over these years, no amount of diet control has been able to lower the level significantly. Over the last six months, however, a new combination of drugs has lowered it dramatically. I now feel I can look forward to a healthy level of cholesterol and even a gracious old age!

Because cholesterol and other fats (called triglycerides) are not water-soluble, they must be bound to other molecules that act as "carriers" in order to circulate in the blood. The carrier molecules are called **lipoproteins**. Lipoproteins fit into four groups according to density. It now appears that low-density lipoproteins (LDLs), in combination with cholesterol, are responsible for the congestion of artery linings and create problems. High-density lipoproteins (HDLs), on the other hand, pick up stray bits of cholesterol and dispose of them, counteracting the dangerous effects of the LDL/cholesterol combination. Menstruating women tend to have higher levels of HDLs than do men, one reason why younger women enjoy prolonged protection from cardio-vascular disease. The concern with diet is to extend this protection past the menopausal years, so that women will not be at such increased risk for heart disease as they age.

A more complete explanation of the function of lipoproteins is included in the next chapter. However, most of what we know about the role of the various kinds of lipoproteins in relation to heart disease comes to us from large-scale studies done on men. It may be that women's blood chemistry has slightly different effects.

In addition to maximizing heart health by cutting down on dietary fats, you may want to use vitamin supplements in recommended amounts. **Vitamin C** has been reported to lower cholesterol levels. **Vitamin E** is said to decrease blood coagulation (which may prevent strokes). High calcium intake helps HDL levels and, along with exercise and **Vitamin D**, also protects against **osteoporosis**.

Alcohol
Low alcohol consumption is related to lower probability of heart disease, hypertension, and osteoporosis. Although recommendations

vary, the consensus seems to be that one to two ounces of alcohol per day is permissible.

Smoking
Inhaled nicotine constricts the peripheral blood vessels, increasing resistance and thus blood pressure. A smoker is six times more likely to develop high blood pressure. Nicotine interferes with the liver's ability to dispose of blood fats, allowing more cholesterol and trigly-cerides to circulate and to clog up the system. At the same time, carbon monoxide in the cigarette smoke permits cholesterol to more easily invade the artery lining and acts to reduce the oxygen-carrying capacity of the red blood cells. The risk of heart attack is directly related to the number of cigarettes smoked and women who smoke and also take a contraceptive pill increase the risk of heart attack by anywhere from two to forty times normal!

Stress
Risk of heart disease is also affected by stress. There is "good stress" and "bad stress." Stress produces a rush of epinephrine or adrenaline — chemicals that increase heart rate, blood pressure, and blood flow to the extremities. Evolution has programmed us to react swiftly to stress with heightened alertness and unusual physical strength. This enables us to run from the threat that produced the stress. We experience "good stress" when we rise to the occasion in a well-matched game of tennis or flog ourselves to swim another ten laps of the pool. However, if the chemicals are not dissipated through physical exertion, they can have damaging effects on the body. If these stressful episodes happen too frequently, or if any part of the cardio-vascular system is weakened or damaged, chronic high blood pressure may result.

Stress occurring in a situation of powerlessness may be even more damaging. There is an enormous difference between the stress generated by high-powered women who thrive in pressure-cooker situations, and the stress endured by those women exploited by others, whether in a dead-end job or a no-win relationship. It is women in the latter situation who run the greater risk of hypertension and heart disease.

Weight
A weight gain of 20 per cent over "ideal weight" is considered obesity and poses a significant risk. Women who are overweight appear to be at greater risk for cardio-vascular disease than are overweight men, particularly if the extra weight is carried on the abdomen. If the waist-line disappears and a "pot" develops, this is a warning sign. How the weight is distributed may be more important than sheer poundage. A

gain of 10 to 15 per cent over "ideal weight" (which may protect against osteoporosis and hot flashes) may be acceptable, provided the difference between waist and hip measurements remains roughly the same — e.g., instead of 26"/36" a change to 30"/40".

Lack of exercise

One of the best predictors of heart disease is a sedentary lifestyle. During exercise, the energy requirements for the muscles are chiefly provided by the blood. In order to provide increased oxygen during exercise, more blood pounds through the system as the heart speeds up, the rate of perspiration increases, and a larger amount of oxygen is extracted from the bloodstream by the organs and tissues. If the activity level is maintained, the arteries open up to increase the blood flow to working muscles. Exercise thus promotes the elasticity of the arteries, enhances blood flow, raises the level of HDLs in the blood, and reduces the probability of substantial weight gain. Regular aerobic exercise, which sustains heart rate at an optimum level for at least twenty minutes, is one of the best ways to prevent cardio-vascular problems. The next chapter explains how you can figure out for yourself if you are getting sufficient, regular aerobic activity.

Diabetes

Women with diabetes are five times more likely to develop heart disease.

Estrogen replacement therapy (ERT) is currently being promoted as a form of protection against cardio-vascular disease, although there are conflicting data. Many of the studies being reported in medical journals treat women undergoing a natural menopause as equivalent to hysterectomized and/or oophorectomized women. **Epidemiologists**, scientists who study the ways in which certain illnesses affect some people and not others, feel that the artificial menopause should be examined separately from natural menopause, and that the health risks for one group may not be the same as the health risks for the others. Moreover, women who are hysterectomized early may have a different profile than those who are hysterectomized later. To lump all these groups together and to average out the results just confuses the issue.

Studies that *have* found that ERT is protective against cardiovascular disease have differed in the types of estrogen used (synthetic or conjugated), in the dose administered, the way the doses were given, the length of time on estrogen, and the presence of supplementary hormones (**androgens** or **progesterone**). Some forms of ERT have been found to increase HDL levels (a cardio-vascular benefit) but, when certain forms of progesterone are added, the benefit is cancelled out. When ERT increased HDLs, it also increased triglyceride levels. Since triglycerides are suspected of increasing clot formation, protection from heart disease may be gained at the expense of increased risk of stroke. It is these fine distinctions between benefits conferred and potential problems that make decision-making difficult. If *you* had to choose, which would it be — a heart attack or a stroke?

There is a danger in jumping to hasty conclusions based solely on research done on males. Certainly the current picture suggests that cardio-vascular disease is more likely to strike someone with high LDL levels and low HDL levels. Some preliminary studies suggest that this may hold true for women prior to menopause, but that high triglyceride levels are more predictive of heart disease after menopause. The one thing we know for sure is that older women who exercise regularly and well maintain high HDL levels through the **post-menopause** years and have hearts and arteries characteristic of much younger women. More and more, we are recognizing that exercise may be the answer to a host of mid-life health problems.

CHAPTER 8

■

Preparing for Menopause: Nutrition and Exercise

THERE ARE A NUMBER of ways to experience an uneventful **menopause**. One way is to be born into a society where menopausal ailments are virtually unknown — a country such as Japan, for instance, where a word for "**hot flashes**" doesn't exist. We don't know whether this is due to culture, to race, or to diet. Another way to avoid menopausal distress would be to adhere to a well-balanced vegetarian diet; to eschew alcohol, caffeine, and cigarettes; and to be accustomed to regular physical exertion. There has been some speculation that multiple pregnancies and long periods of lactation might protect against severe menopause ailments. Perhaps the evolution of the female body does not tolerate well the recurring hormonal cycles typical of a society that practises efficient contraception.

We cannot change our personal or cultural history. If we want to minimize menopausal distress we should pay attention to nutrition and fitness before mid-life. We may also want to reconsider our attitudes toward menopause (and toward ageing). The sting of menopause may not derive so much from physiological effects as from the negative connotations that we have permitted. Now is the time to rid menopause of its mystique, to view it as just one more rung on the ladder of life. The view from the top of the ladder may be great, but you have to be fit enough to get there.

Your pre-menopausal years may be punctuated by a few bizarre and annoying changes that may send you to your doctor. One that bothered me, for instance, was a change in bowel movements — a change so startling that I made an appointment with the doctor and readily agreed to a barium enema. As I was forty-five, menopause never entered my mind. Since there had been no radical changes in what I regularly ate, it never occurred to me to experiment a little to see if my body had changed its way of processing certain foods. I knew nothing about menopause and I suspect my doctor knew very little about nutrition.

■

Prior to the onset of menopause, I found I was having problems with my digestion. I enjoyed red meat (loved roast beef!), lots of carbohydrates and spicy foods. All of a sudden, I realized that my all-time favourites were giving me heartburn, indigestion, diarrhoea, etc. It wasn't until my periods stopped that I made the connection. I've gradually altered my diet to include more vegetables, fruits, chicken, etc., and now have very few digestion problems.

Menopause reminds me of another similar change in my life — puberty! At thirteen or fourteen, I began to acquire a taste for foods which I had previously disliked. Now, at fifty-one, my tastes are changing again. And there's as much to look forward to with *this* change of life as there was with the last one!

Nutrition, on this continent, is basically preventive. As a small child during the Second World War, I was taught how *fortunate* I was to have the food on my plate. This attitude was reinforced by a nodding acquaintance with Canada's Food Rules, thanks to mandatory high school home-economics classes. Because North Americans ate better (and certainly more often) than most of the people on the planet, it was taken for granted that we were well fed in all senses of the term. It has only been in the last two or three decades that well-known writers on this subject (Adelle Davis, Carlton Fredericks, Earl Mindell, etc.) have challenged this complacency.

The basics of good nutrition are usually self-taught. Unless we have advanced training or have had a lifelong interest in diet, we probably don't know very much. We can't look to medical doctors for much information, since medical training tends to concentrate on pathological dietary deficiencies — **scurvy, rickets, kwashiorkor.** Few doctors think about diet when seeking solutions to a medical problem. Nutritionists, on the other hand, view proper nutrition as the sane approach to the prevention of a host of modern-day malaises, and recent cross-cultural data (gleaned by **epidemiologists**) have added weight to this perspective. Diet appears to be the major factor in the low incidence of breast cancer among Japanese women and the virtual absence of cardio-vascular disease among the Inuit.

If women of my generation knew very little about nutrition, we probably knew even less about exercise. Physical activity was something enforced at school and enjoyed outside school only as a way of being sociable. We tended to dabble in exercise as a way of keeping slim rather than of keeping fit. The concept of "participaction" seemed more appropriate for younger people until we discovered that regular exercise could reduce the risks of **osteoporosis** and the worst effects of depression. Women who experience severe **premenstrual**

syndrome (an ailment that may not *start* until menopause, whether artificial or natural) have found that diet and exercise combine to alleviate it. The case for the relationship between diet/exercise and maintenance of good health becomes more and more credible. If menopause is on *your* horizon and you want to handle it well, there is a great deal you can do to prepare for it.

NUTRITION IN THE MIDDLE YEARS

■

I have weighed between 130 and 135 lbs. since I was about twenty-five years old. I am now forty-nine. Two years ago, my weight soared — within a period of five months — to 170. Needless to say, I was devastated and set out to find an appropriate diet. Until six months ago, absolutely nothing helped. I literally tried every diet I could get my hands on. I spoke to two doctors both of whom said, "Menopause," but neither offered any help. They seemed to feel it was biologically inevitable and that I'd simply have to get used to weighing 35 lbs. more. Finally, I decided to see a nutritionist. This woman has taken the time to explain to me the various changes that are happening and she created a personalized diet for me, including my likes and dislikes, and making sure that I get the proper amounts of vitamins and other key nutrients. After four months on this diet, I've lost 15 lbs. and am feeling much better.

Caloric needs reduce by 2 per cent per decade after age twenty. This means that the average daily energy needs for a woman in her forties (height 5'4", weight 120 lbs.) is about 1,900 calories, and this will dwindle to 1,800 as she approaches fifty. Since we need fewer and fewer calories as we age, now is the time to learn about "nutrient-dense" foods and to evaluate our customary intake of foods rich in vitamins A, B, and C, as well as riboflavin and folic acid. This is particularly important if alcohol is part of our routine. Alcohol can inhibit the positive benefits of some vitamins and supply "empty calories."

Vitamins A, B, and C have been found to be inadequate in the diets of many menopausal women — diets that have probably been inadequate for some years.

Vitamin B_2 (riboflavin) and folic acid (from green, leafy vegetables) are related to optimum cognitive function. Since forgetfulness is a common aggravation during menopause, you can minimize the possibility by checking out your diet. Your need for iron is lessened as the reproductive years draw to a close (so you can forget about *ever* learning to like liver!) but you would be wise to train yourself to do without sugar in your decaffeinated coffee, and to reduce the amount of salt you use at the stove and at the table.

Caffeine may not keep you awake now, but many of us have belatedly discovered that it began to play a part in sleeplessness or early-morning awakening as we got older. Caffeine also blocks the absorption of calcium needed for healthy bones, of some B vitamins, of iron, and of Vitamin A. It is also suspected to have negative effects on serum (blood) **cholesterol** levels, a major indicator of potential heart disease. Caffeine may be responsible for a tendency to breast cysts and, as you get closer to the last menstrual period, often acts as a trigger for hot flashes. For diehard caffeine-addicts (I was one), the potency of the product is directly related to the pain of withdrawal. If you drink a lot of coffee, tea, and/or cola drinks, giving them up may bring on a severe and prolonged headache. This usually passes within a few days.

The good news is that there are many palatable decaffeinated beverages — decaffeinated espresso, brewed, or filtered coffees and delicious herbal teas. Those of us who have made the switch try to boycott restaurants that serve Sanka packets and a cup of hot water or, at least, to register a request for brewed decaffeinated. There are rumours about decaffeinated coffees being carcinogenic (cancer-causing) when treated with methylene chloride to remove the caffeine. The Swiss water process (used in Nescafé and Taster's Choice) and the use of ethyl acetate (Folger's) avoid this risk. Many restaurants also offer herbal teas. Some of these are caffeine-free and some aren't. You should ask to see the package.

Drinking black coffee (decaffeinated, that is) or clear tea (herbal, of course) requires three weeks of disciplined effort. After the taste buds are retrained, coffee or tea with sugar is like drinking maple syrup — fine over pancakes but too sweet as a beverage. Refined sugar contributes to the potential for high blood pressure, tends to block the benefits of some B vitamins (thiamine, riboflavin, choline, and niacin), and contributes to the incidence of non-specific vaginitis. Since we become more and more prone to vaginal infection as we near and pass the last menstrual period, the absence of refined sugar is a preventative against such infections, as well as against dental cavities and weight gain.

The use and over-use of salt is related to incipient high blood pressure — a condition that affects more women than men. Many women also find that it contributes to "**bloat**" — the unexpected and often grotesque swelling of the abdomen, which can cause extreme discomfort. Salt is an acquired taste and most prepared foods (packaged soups and fast foods) are heavily salted to suit the taste of North Americans.

Learning to do without extra salt is easier than it sounds. Lemon juice or combinations of herbs and spices are welcome substitutes.

The big breakthrough in nutritional research has to do with fat. Changes in our diet over the last half century have included enormous increases in the proportions of fats consumed as part of the so-called normal diet. It is now widely believed that a sharp reduction in the amounts and types of fat in our diet can have significant effects on our predisposition to many forms of cancer, as well as to coronary heart disease, **angina**, **stroke**, congestive heart failure, and hardening of the arteries.

Although many of us long ago switched from butter to margarine (at least at home) and reduced the consumption of eggs and fried foods in an effort to reduce dietary cholesterol, we are now told that this is either not enough or totally unnecessary (depending on whom you listen to). Many nutritionists would like us to cut down on meat (containing about 1 mg of cholesterol per gram) and eggs (containing about 250 mg each) to hold dietary cholesterol at from 250 to 300 mg per day. This can be compared to an intake of 400 mg of cholesterol per day in the average North American diet.

The information about cholesterol has been confusing because of the continuing debate about two key issues. One has to do with how cholesterol is processed by the body — how much of the cholesterol in the bloodstream is produced inside the body and how much is a result of cholesterol in the foods we eat. The other issue is the discovery that one-third to one-fifth of the population has a genetic tendency to high blood cholesterol. Until this condition was recognized, it was thought that *all* high cholesterol levels resulted from diet.

Nowadays, if a family tendency to high cholesterol levels is discovered (usually during routine medical checkups), potential problems can be offset, to some degree, by scrupulous attention to diet and carefully supervised medication.

The concern about the role of cholesterol has now broadened to include the issue of dietary fat. It is estimated that about 40 per cent of the average diet in this country consists of fat and that, to insure against a host of health risks, this should be reduced by at least 10 per cent — preferably more. Most of these fats come from meats, so a reduction in meat intake cuts back on cholesterol as well. Cholesterol circulates through the system, carried by fat molecules. Some of these fats, known as HDLs (or high-density **lipoproteins**) act to flush cholesterol out of the blood vessels. The ratio of HDLs to total cholesterol (expressed as TC/HDL) appears to be an accurate index of the probable risk of heart disease. A ratio of 3 is excellent (meaning that HDLs constitute one-third of blood cholesterol). The ratio for the average man in North America is 5 (or borderline); that of the average woman is 4.5.

Low-density lipoproteins (LDLs), another form of fat molecules, are potential trouble-makers. Once past a certain level, LDLs start to deposit cholesterol on the walls of the arteries, the first steps toward clogging circulation and forming clots — all precursors of hypertension, heart disease, and stroke.

Low levels of fat in the bloodstream (which is what happens when one follows a low-fat diet) are associated with lower-than-normal rates of various kinds of cancer — colorectal, prostate, breast, mouth, throat, larynx, and esophagal. The link between low fats and low rates of heart disease and cancer was first noticed in countries that habitually consume foods low in fat. It has been suggested that fats in the bloodstream become hazardous not only because of the deposits inside the arteries, but also because of the action of free radicals. Free radicals, which are thought to interfere with the body's defences against cancer, are molecules that can start a chain reaction, rupturing cell membranes and crippling the body's ability to marshal cancer-preventing nutrients.

■

I was diagnosed as having breast cancer three years ago. Since then, I've undergone surgery and radiation therapy. It appears the cancer is now in remission. Although I'm sure the radiation has had an impact on the cancer, diet has also played an important role in my situation. Immediately after my surgery, the doctor recommended I see a dietitian. I was told to keep track of which foods and how much I'd eaten for two weeks. I subsequently discovered that my diet was very high in fats and that this may have had some influence on the development of cancer.

In my case, the genetic tendency was strong (my mother died of breast cancer), but the importance of nutrition in decreasing the risks was brand new to me. I'm not only eating better now but, more important, I am extremely conscious of the role of diet in the (hopefully permanent) remission of this disease.

Free radicals are constantly being produced in the body, not only in response to certain foods but as a result of pollutants in the air and other environmental factors. We cannot eliminate free radicals but we can reduce them, and it is believed that the metabolism of fats produces the most damaging radicals. A reduction in fat intake allows the body's own defences to mobilize and take care of any threat posed by roaming free radicals.

Obviously, one cannot eliminate fats altogether, so it is helpful to know about various kinds of fat. It is recommended that saturated fats constitute no more than 10 per cent of daily calories and that polyunsaturated (or monounsaturated) fats constitute no more than 10 per cent. Saturated fats are butter, cheese, beef, veal, pork, and coconut and palm oils. Coconut and palm oil are often disguised as "vegetable oil" in prepared mixes, toppings, etc. Polyunsaturated fats — mayonnaise, margarine, corn oil, and sunflower and safflower oil — are fine at room temperature but, when heated, produce the free radicals thought to cause damage to artery walls. If you want to avoid both saturated fat and the dangers of free radicals released by hot polyunsaturates, use monounsaturated fats like olive oil or peanut oil. Or go for fat-free cooking in a Teflon pan. Holding the line at 10 per cent saturated plus 10 per cent poly- or monounsaturated may *appear* to permit only 20 per cent fats, but experts tell us that there is likely to be another hidden 10 per cent consumed daily.

The concern about fats and free radicals alters some previous advice. Eggs may be preferable to cheese, as a source of protein, because eggs are not as high in fats as is cheese. Butter, long suspect as a source of cholesterol, is now preferable to margarine when *heated*.

The dangers of red meat (as sources of both cholesterol and fat) are to be suspected if you've noticed the beef industry's recent and aggressive advertising to recapture favour. Unfortunately, the advertising doesn't respond to some basic concerns about current livestock practices. Many of us have read about the Puerto Rican children whose precocious sexual development has been traced to high levels of DES (a synthetic **estrogen**) fed to beef cattle. **Estradiol** (another form of estrogen), **progesterone**, and **testosterone** (the male hormone) are routinely fed to animals that we eat — as are antibiotics, plastic hay, newsprint and cardboard (for roughage), and oral larvicides. Given our ignorance about the long-term consequences of these chemicals in the food chain, it is not surprising that many of us choose to limit our intake of beef, pork, and veal. In other words, there is more than fat and cholesterol involved.

Vegetarians benefit from the absence of meat in their diets. Not only do they develop strong bones (vegetarians rarely suffer from osteoporosis), but the emphasis on fresh vegetables and fresh fruit provides the kind of fibre that keeps the stomach and intestinal tract healthy. High-fibre diets appear to be protective against heart disease, diverticulitis, and colon cancer, and help to avoid the kinds of problems with indigestion and constipation that are so often assumed to be caused by ageing.

Chicken and fish become more appealing as we age — perhaps an instance of "wisdom of the body." Since chicken fat resides on the skin, it is easily removed, and the oilier fishes appear now to confer hidden benefits in terms of heart-protecting fatty acids. I spent years pushing fish around my plate every Friday at dinner; now I order fish almost every time I eat out. I have found that fresh fish (and swift delivery from sea to market) makes an enormous difference — persuading me to forget an ancient grudge and to experiment with the wide range of fish available. And although I don't much like handling raw fish, it's one dish that cooks up evenly and quickly in a microwave.

It is hard to make sudden changes in diet because such changes often involve new ways of cooking and new recipes to replace dishes that can be made by heart. I, personally, find it virtually impossible to add up grams of fat or milligrams of calcium, not to mention caloric values. If your number memory is as poor as mine, it is helpful to check lists of foods and then to remember the *foods* you should be eating. The book *Nutriscore* by R. Fremes and Z. Sabry provides charts of the common nutrients in a wide variety of foods. Anne Lindsay's books, *Smart Cooking* and *The Lighthearted Cookbook*, provide recipes that follow the Canadian Heart Foundation and Cancer Society dietary guidelines. If you want to get serious about low-fat eating, the books consistently recommended are *Pritikin's Longevity Diet* or *The Pritikin Program for Diet and Exercise*. These books explain the benefits of low fats and provide basic recipes to get you started.

I have been meeting more and more people who have seen a nutritional consultant either in order to lose weight or just because they want to get a better "handle" on the subject. Athough the term "dietitian" and "nutritionist" are used almost interchangeably, there *can* be a difference. Provincial dietitians' associations and the Canadian Dietetic Association are pushing for the use of Registered Professional Dietitian (R.P.Dt.) as a way of recognizing valid credentials, i.e., someone with a recognized university degree plus an institutional internship. Those calling themselves "nutritionists" or "nutritional consultants" may or may not be adequately qualified — may not have training in food science, in biochemistry, in **naturopathy**, or it may mean they read publications that deal with diet (and also make available mail-order degrees in nutrition). If you want to get sound advice about what you eat and how it may affect your health, make sure you know whom you're dealing with.

Until you get interested enough to formulate your own rules, here are some basic guidelines that will help you to get healthy for menopause:
- •Reduce consumption of refined sugar, salt, and alcohol.
- •Eliminate caffeine.
- •Watch out for the tannin in tea and red wine.
- •Get in the habit of drinking water; aim for six to eight glasses a day.
- •Eat lots of whole-grain cereals and breads, and brown rice.

- Eat lots of fresh fruit and vegetables, preferably raw or very slightly cooked. (Store raw, cut vegetables in covered airtight containers.)
- Eat fish twice a week. Eat broiled chicken (skin removed) once a week.
- Explore meat substitutes (tofu, soya beans) or vegetarian dishes.
- Use small amounts of butter for frying; use peanut oil in wok cooking.
- Try low-fat dressings, dips, sauces (natural yoghurt instead of sour cream, etc.)
- Drink four cups of skim milk or equivalent daily (containing less than one-fifth the fat content of 2 per cent milk).
- Avoid bacon, cured or processed meats, and meat spreads. (Nitrites in these foods promote free radicals.)
- Ignore tempting advertising and chew sugar-free gum.

It would take a saint to make all of these changes at once and make them stick. However, taking a stab at a few is a good start. Like all good habits, healthy eating takes practice, backsliding, and more practice.

KEEPING FIT

Exercise is probably the most necessary and most overlooked prescription for a problem-free menopause. Exercise builds strong bones and tones up the cardio-vascular and respiratory systems, reducing the risks of osteoporosis, arthritis, **emphysema**, hypertension, heart disease, and stroke. Exercise has also been found effective in treating depression, constipation, and insomnia, and in guarding against the horrors of mid-life weight gain. (The *prospect* of gaining weight is horrible, but the actual experience isn't all that bad.)

Exercise appears to increase the body's capacity to sweat easily, and the ability to sweat appears to be related to the ability to tolerate fluctuations in temperature. This is a good way to prepare for hot flashes. Unless there are valid medical reasons *not* to exercise, we should all be enjoying regular physical activity. Why then do so few of us exercise?

For too many women, exercise is anything but routine. It is something that is added to the daily (or weekly) schedule when circumstances — time, money, relationships — permit. This means that any sustained good feelings derived from exercise are rarely experienced, or experienced for only a short time before being put aside in favour of other demands. Women over forty who have exercised regularly and well throughout their adult lives are hard to find. (Women over fifty are pearls!) I don't think that it is coincidental that many will have a hard time with menopause.

Recently an organization devoted to research in women's health conducted an informal survey of their membership to discover the reasons given for *not* being physically active. Over 90 per cent of the responses had to do with lack of time — either demanding jobs or overwhelming family responsibilities. But some women had more than one reason for not undertaking regular exercise. One woman in five was afraid that she wouldn't perform well; one in six cited a lack of encouragement from others or the influence of persons who felt that she shouldn't be athletic. One in ten was influenced by others who felt that she *couldn't* be athletic. Only a small minority were held back by the perceived cost involved. Far more were restrained by past or future opinions of others, whether real or anticipated. On the other hand, close to 20 per cent had *no* excuse for lack of physical activity.

■

I want to share my experience. When I hit menopause, I immediately gained 25 lbs. Weight gain was not unusual for me but this time it all went to my middle instead of clinging to my hips and thighs as it usually does. I realized that I was dealing with a different kind of animal and that I better do something. I checked out a few health clubs in my area but felt like too much of an old bat to join one. I'd never been athletic and got uncomfortable merely at the thought of how I'd look in a leotard! Finally, I watched a class at the local Y and found the class for me. It's a low-impact aerobic class given in the mid-afternoon. I have a part-time job (mornings only), so it's great. Apart from two or three young mothers who put us all to shame, the class is made up largely of women in their forties or fifties who are afflicted with the same kind of mid-life bulge as me. We laugh at ourselves and cheer each other on. Although I've only lost a few pounds, I've made some wonderful new friends and feel better than ever.

Despite the range of benefits that accrue to heart, lungs, blood vessels, bones, joints, brain, and self-image, regular exercise needs only three basic components — a warm-up, an aerobic period, and a cool-down.

The warm-up is a five- to ten-minute period of stretching that helps to ensure against damage during the more active part of the exercise. If you have ever taken part in a dance, fitness, or aerobics class, you will recognize the warm-up. But this warm-up should precede *every* kind of active exercise — before stepping onto the tennis or badminton court, or pushing off on your bicycle. If you swim, you can do stretching exercises in the shallow water before you start swimming laps. This preparation will ensure that your muscles are warm and supple. Many of the exercise programs that we learned years ago — limbering movements on first awakening, the first poses of a yoga class — fulfil this function. Vital as they are, however, they are not enough.

The core of regular physical activity is the aerobic exercise, a term that means the kind of strenuous exertion that carries oxygen into the system and gets your pulse beating at a sustained rate over a period of at least twenty minutes. Aerobic exercise may include dancing, jogging, skipping, cross-country skiing, cycling, rowing, or brisk walking — any exercise that is uninterrupted and pushes you to concentrated exertion. Most racquet sports are not particularly aerobic unless they're being played at championship level. Squash and handball are, for instance, much more aerobic than tennis or badminton. Swimming is aerobic only if the swimmer is going "all out" for a sustained period of time. Swimming laps may be relaxing and, to a degree, bone-strengthening, but it has debatable benefits for cardiovascular fitness. Brisk walking and cycling can be both aerobic and bone-building, but more beneficial to the legs than to the upper body. (Jogging and power or fitness walking require involvement of the arms as well.) Yoga or Tai Chi are anaerobic (*not* aerobic), although they increase flexibility and reduce stress.

It is the aerobic component of exercise that is directly beneficial to heart, lungs, and — if involving weight-bearing activity — the bones. It is the aerobic component that requires the most discipline, pushing oneself to breathe more efficiently (in through the nose, out through the mouth) and to perform better and longer, time after time. Because the aerobic component *is* demanding, it is recommended that every woman have a thorough physical examination before embarking on any program of aerobic activity.

To judge whether you have had a good work-out, you need to take your pulse. This can be done either in the standard way, using the wrist, or by placing your fingers under the jaw just below the ear. Count the number of beats over fifteen seconds and multiply by four. You should be aiming for a pulse rate of 220 minus your age times 0.75. (The 0.75 signifies 75 per cent of maximum heart rate.) In other words if you are forty-five, you would aim for a pulse rate of 131:

$$220 - 45 = 175 \times 0.75 = 131$$

If you are *beginning* aerobics and are over fifty, it is recommended that you look for a pulse rate of 60 per cent of maximum heart rate. Using the same formula as above, this would be:

$$220 - 50 = 170 \times 0.60 = 102$$

In time, the heart rate should be raised to around 126.

If you stop moving, the heart rate starts to plummet. If you want to monitor heart rate while exercising, slow down to a walk (don't stop), take a quick count for six seconds, and add a zero. Exceeding 80 per cent of maximum heart rate is not advised. Once you have been doing aerobic exercise for a few weeks, you should be able to get your pulse rate up to the desired level and hold it there for twenty minutes. A lower pulse rate means you're not working hard enough.

After the aerobic exercise, you need a short period of time to cool down. Wind down slowly. This is often the most overlooked aspect of an exercise program but a sudden stop is not good for the body. Walk around for a few minutes and allow your muscles to cool down. Then use a mat or folded blanket and stretch some more. Fitness instructors often add mat work to the cool-down, which may take twenty minutes or more of an hour-long class. However, the cool-down, like the warm-up, need last no more than five to ten minutes.

Experts suggest a minimum of three exercise sessions per week, with an optimum of five. Strenuous exercise every day of the week is not necessary and, in fact, may be more than is good for you.

Time of day is up to you, but you should avoid eating just before exercise. If you have trouble getting to sleep, a brisk walk in the early evening may alleviate the problem. If you have a nine-to-five job, you may want to schedule your exercise for early morning, during the lunch hour, or immediately after work. Investigate the kinds of facilities available in the area around work and home. In many centres, there are free-lance fitness instructors who will lead a class if you can organize a group and find a place. The new low-impact exercises avoid the strain on knees and ankles associated with high-impact aerobics and are also less noisy. If you work for a medium-to-large organization, you may be able to persuade those in charge of personnel to support such a venture, since regular exercise has been demonstrated to increase productivity and reduce vulnerability to illness.

If you find group exercise abhorrent, there are alternatives, but it requires dedication to get your heart rate up and keep it there. One idea is to get a pedometer and a Walkman (or a friend) and start a walking program. If you use a Walkman, make up your own tapes, starting off slowly (with stretching exercises, which you do at home), then warm-up walking, building up to a brisk pace that encourages you to pump your arms, and then slowing down again. If you walk with a friend, arrange to meet somewhere equidistant from your homes so that you can avoid the temptation to beg off during inclement weather.

■

In my city, there is a hiking organization which organizes hikes every Sunday in three categories: easy, medium, and difficult. Their fee is $5 for the day. I started by going on the easy hikes, afraid I wouldn't be able to make it. But it wasn't many months before I was going on the medium hikes. I wasn't first up the hill, but I got there! Then I met the man I married and we began going on our own hikes and climbs.

My husband is a member of the Alpine Club of Canada. He introduced me to rock climbing and the use of ropes. I enjoy it, but you don't have to rock climb in order to get exercise. A good hike up a mountain, taking small steps at a steady pace, and not stopping until you have gone for an hour (and then resting), is an excellent way to get uninterrupted exercise which pushes you to concentrated exertion. And not only that — all around you is the beauty of nature and you are breathing in fresh air, not car fumes. And when you get to the top, there is the view and out comes your lunch and thermos of herbal tea. What a feeling of satisfaction!

Many women feel they can get enough activity by following television exercise programs or videotaped work-outs. The problem is either that these are too short to bring the heart rate up for any sustained period of time or that they get boring very quickly, or both. The same can be said for exercycles and skipping in place. They may be adequate for highly disciplined types who will take the time to cycle, jog, or skip in place, but most of us don't have that kind of dedication.

Women who are "on the go" and who cope with heavy demands at work and at home are often (and understandably) reluctant to commit themselves to sessions of frantic aerobics and are more attracted to the relaxation of Hatha Yoga or Tai Chi. These are marvellous adjuncts to exercise, but they don't give your heart a work-out. If you are competitive by nature, you will find that the effort to keep up with a good aerobics instructor is just what you need to blank out your worries. Because you have to concentrate on the co-ordination of feet, arms, and breathing, you get a good forty minutes off from workaday worries.

Most of the articles and books about fitness and physical conditioning imply and sometimes even *promise* that exercise will restore or maintain a youthful body. This is misleading. You may or may not lose weight, but exercise has a value beyond any change in silhouette or dress size.

As we age, excess weight is deposited on different body parts. Through the thirties and forties, we fret about weight on the hips and thighs. As we enter the fifties, our waistlines and abdomens start to spread, chest size (and often bra size) may increase. The rib cage is at its broadest between the ages fifty-five and sixty-four. Most of these tendencies are inherited, so you probably know what to expect. Exercise may delay body changes caused by ageing, but there is no way that it can turn back the hands of the clock.

There is also a tendency to accumulate fat as we age. The body of a typical twenty-year-old woman consists of just over 25 per cent fat; in the thirties and forties this increases to 33 per cent, by the fifties, to over 40 per cent. Some increase in the proportion of body fat is bound to occur despite regular rigorous exercise. Even competitive women athletes (who can safely reduce body fat to no *less* than 12 per cent of body weight) find that it takes longer and harder work-outs to stay in shape. Physical activity will enhance a feeling of well-being for the average woman; it cannot obliterate the normal effects of age.

Nor is this all bad. As mentioned earlier, women who are ten to fifteen pounds over "ideal weight" suffer less from severe hot flashes. (And remember that hot flashes often start a year or two before the last menstrual period.) According to the Gerontology Research Center of the National Institute on Aging, weight gain is a normal result of ageing and mortality rates are *lower* for women who are slightly overweight according to standard weight/height charts.

To use their formula for calculating height and weight, divide height (in inches) by 66, multiply the result by itself, and then multiply this result by your age plus 100. Let's assume you are 45 and 5'4" tall:

$$64 \text{ (inches) divided by } 66 = 0.969$$
$$0.969 \times 0.969 = 0.939$$
$$0.939 \times 145 \text{ (age plus 100)} = 136 \text{ lbs.}$$

You can add or subtract nine pounds to allow for light or heavy bone structure, but this will give you a significantly higher weight than the conventional Metropolitan Life Insurance tables. The real point is that exercise may tone you up and trim away inches but may *not* trim away pounds. It will lead to cardio-vascular fitness, improved muscle tone, and a firmer body and it can help maintain body weight. What more do you want?

Those of us who have given up smoking recognize that added avoirdupois is the price one often pays for cleaner lungs and increased life expectancy. Ex-smokers who smoked fewer than ten cigarettes a day may gain about five pounds; those of us who smoked a pack or more a day may have to accept a heavier weight gain. This is not such a terrible price to pay for the health gains of *not* smoking, not to mention the comfort of once again being part of a majority!

There are so many groups available to help one stop smoking that it seems unnecessary to preach about smoking. We know that smokers are prone to high calcium loss (resulting in brittle bones), increased risks of heart disease and stroke, and earlier menopause. It is said that giving up smoking is worse than giving up heroin — I believe it! Now, having done without for close to seven years, I have nothing but sympathy and support for those who try to kick the habit.

Many of us have abused our bodies for some time — abused in the sense of imposing additional strains by smoking, consuming too much alcohol, perhaps relying on prescription drugs (tranquillizers or oral contraceptives) that deplete us of essential nutrients or inhibit optimum brain chemistry. We abuse our bodies when we don't get regular exercise and when we forgo sensible nutrition because we are too rushed, or too intent on taking care of others.

Our bodies can take a certain amount of abuse — more, if the first two decades of our lives provide a "cushion" of basic good health; less, if we have had to deal with major illness or surgery. As we look forward to the menopausal years, we should also look forward to ways in which to increase stamina, endurance, and peace of mind. With luck, none of these will be jeopardized by menopause but, if they are, a well-nourished and fit body will be added insurance against the worst.

CHAPTER 9

•

Relationships at Mid-Life

MENOPAUSE IS OFTEN MARKED BY a great deal of ambivalence about relationships. The physical changes, whether major or minor, often prompt a novel and giddy concentration on self. Aches, pains, fatigue, sleeplessness — all dictate time to get to know yourself again. Interruptions — demands from children, or husbands, or parents — are not welcome. For many of us, menopause signals the beginning of another period in our lives, and promises release from certain duties and responsibilities.

At the same time, a sense of connection resurfaces. When duty takes a back seat, when we no longer *have* to constantly do things for others, we are more free to recognize the web of relationships that connect us to family and friends. In a recognized study of the moral development of the female (Carol Gilligan's *In a Different Voice*), this need for connections to others was seen as the hallmark of woman. Certainly, the letters I receive illustrate the fact that, no matter how concerned with their own well-being, most women are also constantly monitoring the well-being of husband, children, parents, and friends. Perhaps menopause is significant as a point at which such attention is freely offered by the woman, rather than demanded of her.

FEMALE FRIENDSHIP

It's too bad that many of us have to wait until our forties or fifties to cherish the good sense and support that comes from our female friends. Our single friends may have learned to value their women friends, and many of the newly divorced or widowed quickly relearn the value of friends. But too many married women make room for female friendships only in the spaces not occupied by husbands and children. I'm sorry that I waited so long to find time for my friends — meeting for dinner, meeting for a weekend at a country inn, making impromptu long-distance calls just to keep in touch. Once upon a time, in our late teens and early twenties, those of us without dates on a Friday or Saturday night would congregate for an evening of talk about life and love. For many of us, that was the last real taste of woman-to-woman intimacy until the kitchen "kaffeeklatsches" where toddlers bounced against us as we chatted. Now we are rediscovering friendship as we experienced it when we were younger. And it is good.

It makes us wonder why it ever stopped. The biggest obstacle was often our own well-learned ethic: the man takes precedence. Being married and staying married pushed same-sex friendships aside. It's interesting to trace this ethic, this notion of woman as eternal competitor for the man. This is hardly the atmosphere that fosters cordial relations woman-to-woman.

Historically, women have found support, sympathy, and understanding from other women. Their common experience fostered a closeness quite different from the primarily economic ties to men. Written documents of earlier centuries reveal strong bonds uniting female relatives and friends, with common interests in domestic matters, the hazards of pregnancy and childbirth, and the aching suspense of nursing family members through illness. Because women's interests were sharply divided from men's, each sex was more likely to discuss matters of common interest with same-sex friends.

Also, there were more single women in those days, and widows and spinsters lived with the family, providing respite from childcare for the mother and support for each other. This situation changed as marriage assumed more importance. Marriage (as reflected in marriage rates) was, until very recently, more popular than at any time in known history. And this, of course, includes only registered marriages, not long-term arrangements or common-law marriages. It was the popularity of marriage, the idea that a woman had to be "completed" by marriage, that led women to see one another as competitors for a scarce resource. Social life marched two-by-two and "singles" were made to feel like third thumbs.

■

When I ran my first Mid-Life Workshop for Women in 1976, the energy generated by women sharing their life experiences could have illuminated the room. Throughout the workshop, women felt an intense closeness and bonding with each other and kept asking, "How come we've been so separated from each other all these years? Why have we each felt so isolated?"

Finally, someone said it: "Our men kept us apart. We were so afraid of losing our men to other women that we cut back on our female friendships!"

Women also looked for an ideal marriage relationship — a caring, supportive, understanding partner in whom to confide, on whom to rely, with whom to discuss and share everything. Very few marriages fulfil this ideal, and the high rates of divorce and separation over the last few decades are testimony to the disillusionment inherent in such an unrealistic expectation. But the majority of marriages endure and, because the illusion of an ideal marriage must be perpetuated, many married women continue to turn aside opportunities for friendship. Such women, by limiting their intimate friendships to one hetero-sexual relationship, are inviting spiritual **anorexia** — pointlessly starving themselves of friends.

Men often define a friend as someone to do things with. Women tend to define a friend as someone to talk to, to share feelings with. Women are more likely to recognize the connectedness of relation-ships; their decisions and actions take into account the effect on others, regardless of the absolute "right" or "wrong" of the situation. Where men see a hierarchy ("Who was in charge?" "Is that part of his job?"), women see a network ("Did everyone help out?" How did she feel?"). For men, power and control take precedence; friendship must bow to rules that separate employee from employer, member from non-member. Women are more likely to overlook status differences where mutual interests are recognized.

Given these differences in ways of seeing the world, it is easier to understand why women are open to the idea of intimate friendship and so lost without it, and why men, although open to the idea of friendship *in principle*, will often forgo it for the sake of a job, a title, the rules, or the team. Too often, we fail to recognize the deep-seated male envy of female friendships and, because we fail to recognize it, we participate in the trivialization of something that is important to us. Many of us who once found support and sympathy in hastily convened kitchen meetings have matured and now attend business meetings. We know that (aside from the constant interruption of children), we often solved more problems in those informal kaffeeklatsches than are solved by our high-minded committees.

The female definition of friendship is percolating into the business world. As women break into higher ranks of management, customs of informal socializing on the job are not only being tolerated, but are being encouraged because they contribute to higher productivity and morale. Seminars run by women bring groups of business people toge-ther to talk about attitudes or habits that are impediments to personal or professional progress. These seminars are not promoted as teaching "feminine" skills, but that is precisely what is going on.

No one should be without a friend. There are all sorts of opportu-nities in work (paid or volunteer), in educational or recreational set-tings, in social situations linked to work or club membership. Why, given all these opportunities, do some women still feel friendless? Part of it may be the low level of self-esteem that seems to follow from being housebound for years. Some of it is sheer lack of experience in nurturing friendship. Some of it comes from a misplaced reticence about "personal matters."

.

I learned very early in life that I couldn't trust my friends. Being a very sensitive child, it went pretty deep when I had been betrayed. Already a loner and middle child, it didn't take much for me to sort of abandon the human race and live a rather lonely life for many years. When I would occasionally long for a friend, of course there was nobody there.

In recent years, I have stretched out my hand more and more (if you want a friend, you have to be a friend) but it is hard work for me. A few times when I have reached out to a person with whom I felt I had something in common, I was rejected. I blamed it all on myself but have since learned that I shouldn't. (I've always been hard on myself.) Maybe I was just trying too hard. I envy those who have cultivated true friendships, but I haven't given up hope yet of acquiring the same for me.

It is difficult to become intimate with a woman who avoids self-disclosure. It is impossible to complain about one's own husband (inconsiderate lout!) to a woman who admits no flaw in her own, to express outrage about one's children (ungrateful wretches!) to a woman who appears to have perfect offspring, to mutter about the ceaseless demands of an ageing parent to a woman who is a Florence Nightingale. Perhaps such women feel that to admit to a problem would be to lower themselves in the eyes of others. Frankly, I find such attitudes a barrier to friendship. How marvellous to have a woman friend who makes no judgment calls, who allows you to unload all the anger, disappointment, and spite, and who is never surprised to find that, after all the anguish, you've forgiven and forgotten by the following day.

For many of us, female friendships grow sweeter as the years go by. Many of us are more free to spend time with friends, to linger over a glass of wine, to visit for weekends, to meet for all-day shopping binges, or to spend a few days enjoying shared interests. This is one of the bonuses of menopause. The pain and the puzzlement can be shared with our women friends. Menopause gives us an opportunity to strengthen old friendships or to forge new ones — friendships that will stand us in good stead in the years to come when many of the men in our lives will have passed on.

Women who have chosen to be single can teach us the value of friendship. Women abandoned by their partners, through death or divorce, find that female friends provide a safety net, a web of caring to keep them from hitting bottom. Our friends are companions in new adventures, sounding boards as we embark on a new stage of life. They share a range of experience that is unique to woman.

THE LONG-TERM RELATIONSHIP

∎

One evening after dinner, during my fifty-first year, I found myself pulling off my wedding ring and hurling it at my husband while I shrieked my intention of seeing a divorce lawyer. What had come over me? Too much wine, for one thing, and a great deal of emotional confusion. We didn't speak for the rest of that evening but we did climb into the same bed (every other bed being occupied that night). I woke up at 2:00 A.M., wondering whether I had finally lost my grip, and went downstairs to sit and think. Fortunately, my husband noticed my absence and came down to talk. We had had many, many emotional scenes in our twenty-seven years of marriage but we had *never* mentioned divorce before. And I had been the one to bring it up! I couldn't understand what was happening to us.

In long-term relationships that continue to work, there is an unspoken agreement. When *he* is feeling dejected and discouraged, *she* will be upbeat and optimistic. When *she* is feeling worn-out and useless, *he* will tell her she's one in a million. Marriage consists, in large part, of cheering each other up.

Then along comes menopause and mid-life. Frequently, both partners are consumed with their individual and very real problems and the unspoken agreement goes out the window. At least, that's my best guess at what happens.

Menopause often comes at a time when the husband (often just a few years older than the wife) is making a last-ditch effort to secure his place at work. The years just before retirement are the years that dictate the dollar value of his pension. They are also years when maintaining energy and dedication to the job may become more and more difficult. So, the man is often under strain.

If there are adolescent children in the house, this adds tension. Even the best-behaved teenager knows how to manipulate parents to get his or her way, and that manipulation often creates a divisive atmosphere. One parent views the other as too lax or as too strict. Even more havoc is caused by teenagers whose style of dress, taste in music, attitudes toward education or money (or both), become implicit or explicit threats to parental values. Such challenges to authority often arise at a time when Father is dealing with his own private insecurities, and when Mother is not feeling up to her usual role of mediator.

Where the children are older and away from the house, there are other strains. Sometimes men are winding down their jobs just as their wives, newly liberated from domestic responsibilities, are gearing up. Many women in their late forties or early fifties bravely return to school or to the workforce — or both — with the heady intention of now doing what *they* want to do. Women who have always been in the workforce may find renewed energy for their jobs, as household chores take a back seat. The husband who has been looking forward to spending more time with his wife (now that the children are gone) may find that his wife is rarely there. She is wrapped up in new and exciting interests that he cannot or will not share.

■

For many years, when the kids were small, my husband often went to bed for a nap right after supper. By the time he got up again, it was bedtime for the children. On days he didn't nap, there was a meeting, or a course to go to, or a work-out at the local YMCA. As a full-time homemaker, I cannot tell you how disappointed, frustrated, and angry I was when I didn't get the support I thought I needed — after having already spent all day alone with the little ones.

I felt I just *had* to get involved in the community in order to keep my sanity. Before long, I was into various things, which I very much enjoy but which keep me away from home some evenings. Since I'm still a full-time homemaker, with the kids at school and hardly anybody to talk to during the day, my contacts with these people in the evenings are my lifesavers. These groups have — in the absence of any relatives in North America — become my support system.

But now my husband is going through his own "change of life" as well. He demands more time, attention, ego-stroking, etc., and almost resents it when I'm out, sometimes a few evenings in a row. He stays home most evenings since he is feeling depressed and hasn't much energy. Doesn't that sound familiar? Now and then he says, "I don't seem to be too high on your list" or "Do I have to make an appointment with you?"

Not only have I got nothing to spare right now in the way of caregiving, but I also keep asking myself, "Where was *he* when *I* needed *him*?" Besides, I feel I have to have my own needs met for a change before I can be an effective caregiver again.

Responsibility for one's elderly parents also enters the picture. Sometimes the promised "togetherness" of mid-life marriage is usurped by the emotional and financial needs of older relatives — his, yours, or both.

Then there is the effect of menopause itself. It often brings on mood swings — emotional ups and downs that are difficult for the woman herself to understand or contend with, never mind her husband. As I have said before, there is something eerily reminiscent of adolescent emotionality in the yo-yo of menopausal moods. But this is not the whole story. It seems to me that there has been too much concentration on the moodiness of the menopausal woman and too little attention paid to the male half of the question.

It is *assumed* that the woman is being difficult during menopause. And she may be. But many men continue to think of themselves as the sweet, good-tempered souls they were at twenty-five or thirty. They forget about the invisible but unavoidable transfer of attitudes from work to home. If they have achieved any sort of authority on the job, that authority may also be exerted at home. The habits acquired when commanding others, when delegating chores, when minimizing complaints among subordinates, when problem-solving, may get in the way of the ability to listen, to sympathize, and to learn. This may be even more true of the man who has not been as successful as he had hoped. His need for admiration and respect may get in the way of the intimacy that his wife had expected from long-term marriage.

One of the greatest threats to good marriage at mid-life is the sense of vulnerability that many women feel. They look at their husbands and see people who are trudging through life at a steady pace, ageing slowly but often attractively, looking more prosperous and more confident than ever. In our society, the media present us with images of successful middle-aged men every day — in advertisements, in the news, in business appointments, in television shows. The greying, slightly corpulent middle-aged man often achieves an air of distinction denied to him at a younger age. And why *shouldn't* he look distinguished? Heaven knows, he's worked hard enough for it!

Then we look at ourselves. We see signs of ageing (weight gain, greying hair, aching joints) that arrive too quickly to be properly assimilated. Positive role models are few. There are middle-aged women in show business who continue to look thirty-five, and a few women in public life with airs of confidence and competence. But it is hard to find a woman to emulate, an image to aim for. In a society that celebrates youth, we judge ourselves as second rate — physical well-being unpredictable, confidence sagging. It's hard to talk about this to a husband. Why point out to him how fat you're getting if he hasn't noticed? Why tell him how miserable you're feeling when you know (and he knows) that there isn't any *reason* for you to feel so unsure of yourself? How many husbands have terminated a conversation in exasperation, "Why not see a doctor?" How many wives have given up trying to make him understand?

Many of us had already learned to "keep a cap on it" during the few days every month prior to our menstrual periods. At "that time of the month," we could easily turn a minor skirmish into a full-scale war so we learned (the hard way) to grit our teeth and keep quiet. It seems to me that menopause is often a prolonged premenstrual period. Instead of keeping a cap on it for two or three days, we may have to keep mum for two or three years. This is not easy to do (and we all break our good intentions and blurt out hurtful criticisms now and then), but at least we're trying. And we're trying because we have a very profound confidence in the viability (and durability) of the relationship.

It takes years to develop that kind of confidence: to know, at a gut level, that this is someone you want to spend your old age with, God willing. I know many women who don't feel that way. Some have decided to call it quits: the only common interest that had endured was the children. Others have decided to hang in: they are realists and recognize that they will never achieve the standard of living alone that they have become accustomed to as wives. I don't think men realize just how many women, smiling and compliant as they may appear, are living out these kinds of decisions.

I also know many women who have a great deal more in common with their husbands than they are willing to acknowledge. A divorced friend of mine refers to her ex-husband as her "history" — as much a part of her, after more than twenty-five years of marriage, as part of her own body. She does not regret her decision to divorce, but it took the divorce for her to recognize this shared past. Another friend made a different decision: after living apart from her husband for almost two years, she swallowed her pride and decided to go back. They have no more in common than they had when she left, but they appreciate each other more because of the separation. As this friend said, "Any habit is hard to break, and we had the habit of living together." Another friend is muddling through, as she says, by "reviving some of the customs of early married life." By this, she means being conscientiously *nice* — complimenting her husband when he does or says something positive, being more polite than usual, and, in general, being as considerate as she was at the beginning of married life. Her hope is that the marriage will evolve, as it did once before, into a comfortable relationship.

There are a lot of marriages that exist in the space between commitment (contented or working at it) and hostility (veiled or open). Some are jeopardized by sexual matters: wives who find sexual desire absent after surgery or who can no longer experience orgasm as they once did, husbands who disguise their own faltering sex drive by blaming their partners. Some relationships are fraught with the fear of disappointing, haunted by one partner's sense of never quite reaching the promise implied so many years ago. Some couples are so busy looking at the *little* differences that they never stop to recognize whole areas of their lives that offer mutual interest and delight. These are the marriages that could be enriched by a few sessions with a qualified marriage counsellor.

The challenges and rigours of menopause will never be well understood by a husband. Expecting much more than tolerance and forbearance may be expecting too much. Marriage at mid-life may not be too different from marriage at any other time — great, rotten, or somewhere in between — but it may be all of these things within the span of one day. This may be a time to cherish what you've got, to put it on "hold" as best you can, and to promise yourself to be good to him when you're feeling better.

MALE MENOPAUSE

∎

> For some time now I have felt that I, as well as my wife, am going through some bodily change. I feel on top of the world one day and just the opposite the next. I also don't have that "joie de vivre" that I was used to. What really concerns me is my sex drive, which at times just disappears. I am used to having a normal male sex drive and enjoy it very much; to suddenly find it evaporate for no reason was very hard to handle.

This letter conveys the essence of the so-called "male menopause" — the absence of sex drive. Actually, there is no such thing as "menopause" for the male because menopause requires a monthly menstrual period, but the term has been freely borrowed to describe two symptoms occasionally experienced by mid-life males — the absence of sexual desire and/or the inability to sustain an erection. Among other symptoms sometimes mentioned, these two assume paramount importance.

Male menopause is not the same thing as "mid-life crisis" — a term that has been in fairly common use for the last forty years but is applied nowadays mainly to men in the age range from thirty-five to forty-five. This is not because thirty-five to forty mark the real mid-point of an average man's life (although this is true), but rather because the fortieth year has gradually assumed great significance for men in our society, men who had intended to "make it" on the job. The crisis usually arises because he *hasn't made it, is not going* to make it — or *has* made it and wonders why it doesn't feel better.

Because the average adult male experiences a lengthy and very gradual reduction in the production of **androgens**, and particularly of **testosterone**, he is less likely to suffer from the kind of abrupt changes experienced by the average female at menopause. It seems likely, however, that *some* men (no one knows exactly how many) may be prone to sudden drops in **hormone** level at mid-life. The statistic that is frequently quoted is 15 per cent. (The figure comes from H.J. Ruebsaat and R. Hull's *The Male Climacteric*, but it is not substantiated.) Since middle-aged men are much less likely to visit their doctors with problems of any kind, it is impossible to estimate the incidence of "male menopause."

Hormone levels are also influenced by stress. Many men in their late forties and early fifties are dealing with tension on the job — tension stemming from unrelenting effort, from frustration, from apprehension, or from boredom and monotony. The tension may be compounded at home, particularly when there are adolescent children. The man may be consuming more food and more alcohol than is good for him. He may be experiencing new and annoying infirmities — a sore back, **bursitis**, inflamed or enlarged **prostate**. Any combination of these could lead to *secondary* testicular failure, or the temporary inability to produce adequate amounts of testosterone. This leads directly to loss of sexual desire.

Sexual performance is so intricately tied to a man's self-image that emotion often supplants reason. For many men, it is not so much the reduction in sex drive that is threatening, but the loss of what is seen as "manhood." To avoid dealing with it, he finds excuses. He may work late and come home exhausted; he may stay up to watch late-night television, allowing his wife to get to sleep first; he may pick arguments that enable him to go to bed mad. In some cases, the wife may be held responsible for his inability to "turn on" — she is not inviting, or enticing, or aggressive, or compliant, or available enough. In extreme cases, he may turn to another (and probably much younger) woman to see if novelty can stir up the desire he once took for granted.

The stress of feeling inadequate can lead to impotence, the inability to sustain an erection. Again, this type of impotence will be considered secondary since there is no functional block to potency. (One of the ways of deciding if impotence is primary or secondary is to look at the man's capacity for erection when waking in the morning, or during dream sleep. If he can have an erection at these times, then impotence is considered secondary.)

If it is felt that impotence is due to primary testicular failure, tests will be ordered to measure testosterone and **gonadotropin** levels. (Just as women secrete small amounts of testosterone, men secrete small amounts of FSH and LH.) However, the tests are not always accurate. As we know from female physiology, very small variations in hormone levels can produce remarkable effects. Unless the tests demonstrate a clear physical malfunction, most doctors will assume it is "secondary testicular deficiency" resulting from stress.

Doctors say that they are reluctant to experiment with HRT for males because about 25 per cent of men over the age of forty carry dormant cells that, if hormonally stimulated, could develop into prostate cancer. Physicians who *do* administer testosterone are warned that the dosage should be carefully individualized. Compare this to the 95 per cent of women who may carry dormant cells for breast cancer. We don't know how long these cells have been there (some experts say since puberty) nor do we know how hormonal stimulation affects them. However, the possibility of cancer has not seriously impeded the use of **hormone replacement therapy** — and in standardized (not individualized) doses — for females. Another double standard?

There are many middle-aged men who deserve our sympathy. We were all brought up to believe that our men, without exception, would be successful — that the virtues of hard work and thrift would provide a comfortable salary, perhaps by forty and certainly by fifty, and a secure old age. In the 1950s and 1960s, who could foresee being shunted into a dead-end job, being crowded into early retirement — or being asked to do the laundry? Men didn't count on mergers or redundancies, on the upheaval of new technology, or the demands of newly liberated wives or daughters. They went off to work and left us to raise their children. That's just how it was.

Now they envy the younger men who not only play with children, but cook for them, shop with them, *really* spend time with them. Many middle-aged men wish that they had spent more time with the children. The good news is that the discontents of men at this age will pass. Studies have shown that the need to control others or to drive themselves will pass as they reach the years of pre-retirement, when a more mellow outlook predominates.

THE EMPTY NEST

According to the *Second Barnard Dictionary of New English*, the "empty-nest syndrome" is a "form of depression supposedly common among women whose children have grown up and left home." The term was first used in a book published in 1952 but became common currency in the mid-1960s. The operative phrase is "supposedly common." For every woman suffering from empty-nest syndrome, there are several who feel guilty because they're so glad or anxious to have the children leave. The phrase is perpetuated, not by women, but by advertisers who push medication or new furniture as a cure for the temporary lull between stages of a woman's life.

The empty nest conjures up a picture of a woman alone in a house designed and furnished for a family. How applicable is this to women today? Not all women live in houses; not all are mothers with grown children; very few women spend their days at home. It assumes that women have neither the foresight nor the adaptability to take up new interests or activities as the children become more independent. It also assumes that the children have left for good.

Most of the women I hear from are not at all depressed by an empty nest. They find their ordered lives, their neater rooms, their freedom to come and go, quite marvellous. But they also apologize for being "unnatural mothers," not realizing that all available research findings agree: There is a very welcome rise in satisfaction with life after the departure of the last child — less concern about the children, more activities with husband and/or friends, and increased marital happiness.

■

> I can really relate to others who are saying goodby to their last child. Our youngest, who is now twenty-three, has just moved out for the last time. He has come home several times but we have now told him that this time he is on his own. We are hoping it will work out since he is now sharing a home with his sister. Guilt? None.
> It is great to know you can cook for two and only two will show up, and that there are times you can come home to a tidy and empty house. I really enjoy being able to go to bed at my early hour and have the house quiet enough to sleep. My husband works shifts so I'm often the only one home and I love it!

This is not to say that we don't experience strong feelings as the children leave. The "launching" of the last child marks the end of a period in our lives and forces us to acknowledge the passing of time. I remember crying when my eldest started first grade (I was expecting my fourth child at the time!) and when I was folding away the baby clothes after the last had outgrown them. Both events marked an end and a beginning, which is why I cried. But there was no yearning to go back. And so it is for most women when the last child leaves.

The woman to be concerned about is the rare woman whose empty nest brings on a real depression. This is a woman consumed by a ferocious rage, a rage that has turned inwards and is eating away at her. And what valid reasons for rage! This is a woman who married at a time when motherhood and homemaking were glorified as the consummate skills of the true woman. She had three or four children to fulfil that ideal and then was startled to find that, as the idea of limited population growth became popular, a family of more than two children invited criticism. (It is hard to grow up dreaming of three or four only to find yourself regarded as ecologically self-indulgent.) After ferrying the boys to hockey practice and the girls to ballet, she discovered that she was also guilty of sexist child-rearing. Then, just as the children got to the age where she could think about an "interesting" part-time job, the economy dried up. Not only were her academic qualifications inadequate when compared to those of younger women, but there were no jobs at all for middle-aged moms with no recent work experience. And, to top it off, all the young couples are determined to live close to their offices, her husband has become attached to their house in the suburbs, and now she must give up her dream of living downtown.

This is the story of many of my contemporaries. After inducing her to spend so many years as the "good mother," society now turns on her to ask, "And what do *you* do?" "Not much," she thinks.

The real emptiness that many of us dread is not tied to being a mother, but to intimacy and to some sense of control. Motherhood involves enormous power — a power that we acknowledge mostly in its negative form as child abuse, but power nonetheless. With the departure of the children, many women lose a sense of power and purpose that is denied to them in any other sphere. This loss is real and difficult to replace.

■

> I believe I have a classic case of empty nest. I have five children, the youngest now twenty-four and recently moved out on her own. For the last four or five years, I've been feeling guilty about actually wanting her to leave. My marriage has never been the greatest and I always hoped that extended periods of time alone would help the relationship between me and my husband. Unfortunately, I find myself feeling more alone than ever.
>
> My husband has never been a good communicator and he continues to shut me out of his life. My problem is one of conflicting emotions. On the one hand, I feel relieved that my children are gone but I also feel enormous guilt because I feel I may have pushed or prodded them out of the house. Now that they're gone, I miss the closeness and involvement in their daily lives, something I never get from my husband.

A more common concern than the empty nest, according to my correspondents, is the child who leaves, returns, and leaves again. Many women feel guilty that they don't miss their children more after they've left. Many feel guiltier still when the return of the child doesn't lift the heart, or lifts it only for a day or two! And yet, in these days of mounting tuition fees and escalating rents, many young adults *must* move home if they want to continue their education or get a leg up in the job market. And who is going to turf them out?

A researcher in England investigated parents' feelings about the empty nest. She found that mothers and fathers felt very differently about the departure of a child depending on the age of the child, where the child was going, the personality of the child, and the relationship with the parent or parents. This study highlights the complexity of a situation that has been simplistically exploited by the media. Women who talk to other women recognize that each situation — like each child — is unique, that the empty nest suggests much but describes very little.

THE SANDWICH GENERATION

Over the last few years, the phrase "sandwich generation" has become generally accepted as a way of describing mid-life women and men who are required to deal, at the same time, with the needs of the generations both older and younger — their parents and their children. More and more middle-aged women are experiencing the squeeze of the sandwich. Elaine Brody calls them "women in the middle," caught between the demands of the children (and often grandchildren) and the needs of ageing parents. Many are also caught between seething resentment and bouts of self-imposed guilt.

Our parents can expect to live longer these days. This is not necessarily a result of improved medical care (although this does play a part), but simply because of better education leading to improved hygiene and nutrition. There are also *more* old people relative to the population as a whole. As families have become smaller and as immigration has slowed, we have seen a steady increase in the proportion of elderly in our society. Those over sixty-five now constitute 10 per cent of the population; in another twenty-five years, they will make up 20 per cent. The aged are becoming more visible simply because there are more of them.

This has many effects. When the aged constitute a small proportion of the population, they are highly prized. They are the repositories of the oral history of a people, the witnesses to "the way we were." The child with a grandparent is special and is envied. As the aged population increases, veneration and respect for the individual yield to concern for and interest in the many. The study of the old (**gerontology**) and the care of the old (**geriatrics**) attract more interest and more tax dollars. Today researchers in the field no longer talk about the "old," but about the "young old" (aged fifty-five to seventy-five) and the "old-old" (aged seventy-five upwards.) The young-old are often the chief caretakers of the old-old.

One of the great ironies of the generation of women now dealing with menopause is that they often find themselves, after thirty years of hard work, better off than both their parents and their children. Most of us had expected to do better than our parents — this *is*, after all, the North American dream — and many of us did. But the dream has faded for our children, who form part of the first generation to be denied a standard of living higher than that of their parents. This means that many of us are caught between the demands of a younger generation with extended dependency needs, and an older generation embarrassed to ask for help.

We may be forced to acquire new skills. As parents, we must adopt a tactful and neutral silence when our grown children make silly mistakes — the kind of mistakes that *we* made when well out of the sight and hearing of Mom and Dad. At the same time, we are required to muster diplomatic skills in order to intervene in the best interests of parents. For the sandwich generation, the problem is how to "be there" for children and for parents — to help out when needed and to stand aside when appropriate. It is normal and natural to resent the encroachment on one's time. It is also normal and natural to feel apprehension at the prospect of years of caregiving to parents, particularly when the caregiving of children must go on.

∎

I feel like I am in a double-decker sandwich. I am, after twenty-five years of marriage, a single parent. I have a daughter twenty-two, and a son twenty, still living with me. I love them both dearly. I have been alone with them now for five years. They are adults but, because they are living with me, they still demand a great deal of my time, directly or indirectly. They contribute financially but emotionally, when you get three very strong-willed adults, there are bound to be waves from time to time.

Then there is my seventy-year-old mother, who is not well, and who is unable to do much for herself. I do her errands and many other things. At first, I was foolishly running myself off my feet and found this very draining. I finally woke up to the realization that my mother, who had never worked out of the home, just did not realize the demands she was making on me. I am employed full time and simply had to establish some priorities. Once she got to know when I would be coming over, that this would be regular and that she could count on it, there was no problem.

I don't think we should feel guilty if we put restrictions on our time. I think that what makes it difficult for the elderly is the uncertainty of their lives. Once they can rely on a regular routine (of visits, shopping, etc.), it is easier to cope.

Women reputed to be good managers can never rest on their laurels. The women who "cope" are the women who spring to mind when there is an unexpected need for someone to manage a crisis. Many events conspire to designate this "woman in the middle" — traditional attitudes about the roles and "innate" capabilities of women, experience with childhood crises, attention and sensitivity to family relationships. It is not justice that seeks her out, but rather her demonstrated ability to deal with one more family crisis.

This woman may still be the major caregiver for the children — those still at home and those who return. Chances are that she has always taken care of the weekly grocery order, the daily dinner, the clean sheets, and the "pick-it-up-and-put-it-away." Women seem to be stuck with this role. And even though many of us work outside the home, we are married to men who take it for granted that men's work is more important than women's, and that wives are biologically programmed to take care of the needs and niceties of "family" — extending invitations, remembering birthdays, sending gifts, offering services. We may chafe at this particular role now (although it may have been a shared expectation twenty years ago) but, by fulfilling it, we are perpetuating it.

The "woman in the middle" recognizes herself. She knows (and so do her brothers, sisters, and in-laws) that, when the time comes, she will be the one called upon. The story of the family where brothers and sisters spend equal amounts of time and effort amicably caring for ageing parents must be a fairy tale. (Just like the one where other members of the family *don't* tell you what to do about the adult children still underfoot!)

Women feel guilty about resenting adult children and they feel guilty about resenting the demands of ageing parents. One expert on ageing says that " . . . the most dominant and pervasive issue regarding inter-generational relationships is the subject of guilt. Often the adult offspring feel responsible for the general well-being of parents, [although they] frequently cannot improve their parents' general satisfaction with life" (P.K. Ragan, *Aging Parents*). This issue of guilt is an important one because it is guilt that leads dutiful daughters to say, "They took care of me as a child; it is my turn to take care of them now." But taking care of a child is done with the expectation that the child will become more independent and more self-sufficient; this kind of expectation is *not* realistic in relation to ageing parents.

What kinds of expectations *are* realistic? First of all, it may be *very* realistic to anticipate that you will do most of the worrying and most of the work. Sons tend to become caregivers only when they have no sisters and, even then, are more likely to call on their wives for "hands-on" help when dealing with their own parents. Sons may be marvellous for financial advice and for heavy work (lifting and carrying), but the women are almost always the primary caregivers. And the woman is typically a married, adult daughter (or daughter-in-law), a mother, and often a grandmother.

∎

Last week, Mom phoned every night, feeling terrible. I'd already taken time off (no pay) to take her to see two doctors and I had no car for two days. I finally phoned my brother and said, "You take Mom to the doctor's." "But, but . . . I'm busy," etc., etc. Finally I said, "You do it!" And he did. Hurray for persistence.

After Mom's second fall and hospitalization, I pulled over to the side of the road on the way home and had a good cry. I'm stressed but I can handle it. I have my man to complain to, my good friends, my workmates, and my daughters. Because I'm relating this situation to my own ageing, I'm learning. The guilt never goes but I will myself through it and God gives me patience and comfort to understand and try to help. I might be in my mother's place soon and I'm thankful that I have two daughters who will care for me.

It is *not* realistic to expect that gratitude for services rendered will smooth out rocky relations between the generations. If there is any kind of personality clash, it is likely to get worse, not better, as time goes on. Parents are always parents and they continue to feel and behave in parental ways. They are likely to stay the same, only more so, and their criticism or praise continues to have enormous influence on us, whether positive or negative. If they have no economic clout to wield, parents can still motivate us through flattery, gratitude, or guilt.

Nor is it realistic to expect that being surrounded by family will erase the void that the aged feel when confronted over and over again by the death of friends. Ageing parents need friends. Family members, no matter how well intentioned, cannot substitute for the sense of well-being provided by friendship and common interests. You can help your ageing parents to feel more comfortable but you may not be able to change their general level of satisfaction with life.

It may be wise to examine your intentions, however honourable, and your motivation in assuming care of ageing parents. Remind yourself that it is perfectly possible not to love a person and still care for him or her. Even if you feel genuine love for an ageing parent, there will be times when you find it hard to like him or her. Whether motivated by love, liking, duty, guilt, or a constantly changing mixture of all of these, there will be times when you feel squeezed beyond recognition.

When a parent or parents feel that they can no longer cope with a young adult child who is not working, seems unable to find a job, is doing badly at school, is planning to return home, seems not able to cope on his/her own, etc., most of us look for help. We turn to the resources that our tax dollars put in place. Academic advisors and trained counsellors are available in high schools, colleges, and universities; they can tap into job-retraining schemes, government bursaries, student-loan plans, employment opportunities, or psychological services. If there is genuine conflict over goals set by you, your husband, or your adult child, then family counselling may be recommended. Most parents are disposed to take advantage of such services, once they know about them, because it is for the child's ultimate benefit.

Unfortunately, many of us do not carry this attitude through when dealing with ageing parents. Guilt gets in the way and we view the use of community resources as an abandonment of responsibility. We see it as a personal failure if we are unable to fulfil the needs of our parents — although this is as unrealistic as expecting to fulfil *all* the needs of our children, needs that are beyond our expertise and cannot be foreseen.

Ideally, provision for care of ageing family members should take into account the opinions of the parent or parents. However, when ageing parents deny the encroaching limitations of old age ("I'm fine, dear; don't worry about me!"), this is no reason to postpone planning for the future. At the least, you can explore the facilities available in the community and have a better idea about what the future might be. If your parent(s) willingly participate in the discussion, so much the better.

Depending on income, time commitments, geographical location, etc., what responsibilities will be undertaken by other family members? What are your parents' financial resources, now and in the years to come? What kinds of alternative living arrangements might be acceptable to them, and what kinds of waiting lists do the "approved" facilities have? What kinds of community resources are available to help your parent(s) stay in their own home?

If a parent is seeing the doctor frequently, you may wish to find out if there is a geriatric-screening program available. This will permit a throrough and comprehensive examination without the necessity of making appointments with a number of specialists. The resulting report will give you and your parent(s) a clear idea of health status and may help to allay fears and/or lead to more constructive planning for the future.

Become familiar with the resources available in your parents' community. Family Services or Information and Referral Centres can inform you about services designed to make living at home easier — integrated homemaking care (which offers cleaning and shopping services), meals on wheels, telephone checks, special medical alarms (which can be easily tripped to elicit a return call and/or calls to a doctor, neighbour, near-by relative, or ambulance service), escort or transportation services, and help with home maintenance. You may be able to arrange for a public-health nurse, podiatrist, or hair stylist to visit. (Care of the hair gets more difficult for women as they age and care of the feet is particularly important if older people are to remain mobile and healthy.)

If you feel that a parent should not be left alone, you may be able to find sitting services. Some old age homes also offer "respite care" — short-term accommodation (from a few days to a few weeks) in a supervised setting so that the caregivers can have a weekend or a vacation. It is useful to familiarize yourself with all these services before you have to call on them.

Sometimes all the resources in the world cannot relieve the psychological stress of being responsible for family members. More and more community organizations are forming support groups for caretakers of the ageing. These groups may not be able to *change* the situation but they can offer the opportunity to meet with others in the same situation, to air grievances, anxieties, guilt feelings, and to ventilate the anger that accumulates. It may also help you to deal with the frustration at your inability to "make it all go away," to make things better for your parent(s) — an inability that we may recognize intellectually but that is emotionally difficult to accept.

The "woman in the middle" lives between the stress of competing "guilts." Braced for the accusation that she has never been as good a mother as she had intended to be, she accuses herself of not being the loving and dutiful daughter that her parents deserve. When the myth of the "good mother" is coupled with the myth of the "good daughter," it is powerful indeed. Women are tough meat in the sandwich.

Life often gets very complicated for the menopausal woman. If her body is being buffeted by wayward hormones, she wants a predictable routine, not too much stress, and the sympathetic support of her friends and her family. Too often, the man in her life is more exasperated than sympathetic and many women, resenting the lack of interest or concern, decide to keep their problems to themselves. But the man may also be dealing with his own demons — a nagging sense of "Is that all there is?", a diminishing sex drive, ambivalence about impending retirement, coupled with a determination to slug it out until the best possible pension is assured.

The menopausal mother may also be dealing with inconsiderate teenagers (Is there any other kind?) or with young adults who come and go, adding yet one more element of unpredictability to her life. Or she may be facing a home suddenly grown empty. There may be ageing parents who need her to run errands, to do shopping, to accompany them to the doctor. And today, on top of all this, she is more than likely holding down a full-time job.

If a woman is feeling well, these different demands can sometimes be juggled quite successfully. If she is not feeling well, the pressure can be overwhelming. It helps to know that it is happening to others. It helps to discuss it with warm and wonderful female friends because, by talking it over, you can often sort out which demands on your time should take priority and why. This, too, shall pass.

CHAPTER 10

•

Ageing and Appearance

Aging is much more a social judgment than a biological
eventuality. Far more extensive than the hard sense of
loss suffered during menopause . . . is the depression
about aging, which may or may not be set off by any real
event in a woman's life . . .

— Susan Sontag

DESPITE ALL THE PROTESTATIONS (and reassurances) that **menopause**
and middle age are two separate and separable events, the lived experience of women fuses them. For many women, menopause means
growing older, becoming invisible, losing one's power and one's credibility. Our higher intellectual functions may insist, "Not true! Not
true!" But our experience — as eyes glance off us, through us, by us —
make menopause and ageing indistinguishable.

A menopausal woman moves, quite suddenly and quite unexpectedly, from a category of "secondary person" (status based on sex)
to a category of "nonperson" (status based on age). This may sound
extreme, but let me explain. As a woman, one becomes accustomed
to throw-away lines that denigrate women: "She thinks like a man",
"Just like a woman!", etc. Some of us have learned to tune into these
kinds of remarks (many made quite unconsciously) and to counter
them. Those of us trained to examine and analyse social values may
feel some satisfaction in alerting others to these entrenched and sexist
attitudes and, in so doing, limping toward the goal of equality
between the sexes.

Then we run into agism. It is agist when a sales clerk insists on
serving everyone between the ages of twenty and forty before she con-
descends to serve the fifty-year-old woman who got there first. It is
agist when doctors spend time explaining options to younger patients
but then *tell* older patients what they must do. As compared to sexism,
agism is more difficult to combat for an ageing person: he or she must
attract attention in order to point it out. It is not ageing that is difficult. Much of the pain comes from banging against solid, unseen and
unexpected agist attitudes in this society.

Men appear to age at a fairly steady rate. The changes in hair
colour and texture, the alterations in girth and visual acuity, the

gradual decrease in energy level are incremental and barely notice-able. There are not many men who look thirty-five when they're close to fifty, and those who do will go to some pains to look their real age. The appearance of youth for a man is a disadvantage in a society run by middle-aged men.

Both the process and prospect of ageing are different for a woman. There are many, many women in their late forties who can easily pass for thirty-five. Because this knack of "not looking your age" is so ad-mired, many women deliberately try to look thirty-five forever. Some women just don't change that much — a few laugh lines, a bit of grey at the temples — in the years from thirty-five to fifty. This resistance to the effects of ageing, whether contrived or natural, sets the stage for what the French call *"un coup de vieux"* — ageing overnight. Many women in their early fifties are plunged into despair because time sud-denly catches up with them. At fifty-one or fifty-three, they look their age and, because they have looked thirty-five for so long, they appear to have aged fifteen years in five.

MAINTAINING OUR APPEARANCE

■

I feel that a valid role model for the middle-aged group is lacking. How can you call Joan Collins a role model when the principal reason she is lauded is because she is *not* typical? I am one of those women who is fortunate enough to look younger than her age. I find myself frequently telling people how old I am so that I can see the surprise register on their faces and get the inevitable reassuring compliments about how I cannot possibly be that old. And all this because it feels *good* to get the reassur-ance that I don't look like what I am.

I cannot feel good about myself when I am asking others to help me deny that I am what I inescapably am. I feel trapped by my looks. Trapped. When all I want to do is give up and be me.

Many middle-aged women have no clear idea of what it means to look one's age. Clothes, make-up, hair styles are all modelled for us on much younger women. By showing us that this is the way we are *sup-posed* to look, we are told, over and over, that age is an enemy to be conquered. This is to strengthen us for the battle but it also serves the purpose of emphasizing the horror of ageing — not only to women but to everyone else. It is implied that any middle-aged woman could look like this model, this actress, if only she *cared* enough. The truth is that the role models shown to us — ageing actresses or winners of cosmetic manufacturers' contests — are individuals who, by dint of exercise or cosmetic surgery or genetics (or all three), do not look their age.

Exercise is good. Each of us needs to have at least three hours of foot-pounding, arm-swinging exercise each week. This will enable our bones to remain strong, but this will not necessarily give us back the waistlines (and bustlines) of our youth. A dogged regimen of aerobics implies rewards and Jane Fonda's empire of videotapes and walking tapes implicitly promise a Jane Fonda shape. But Jane Fonda is built like Henry Fonda and *my* father (and probably yours) wasn't built at all like Henry Fonda! We must approach exercise in light of its real benefits and not in search of an impossible dream.

When I was taking my first course in word processing, I ran into a situation where the little flashing light (the "cursor") would not move. I had been typing away quite merrily when suddenly I couldn't get any more letters to jump onto the screen. I hit keys at random (there are many extra keys on the computer keyboard) and, when nothing happened, I appealed to the teacher. She glanced quickly at the screen and said, "But you have a closed field." She then explained that, since I hadn't given prior instructions to the computer, it wouldn't accept any additional information. It was not in the right "mode."

I've always thought that this was a perfect analogy to my situation at the time. I was learning to use a computer, with a view to perhaps launching a newsletter about menopause and mid-life. I was feeling very discouraged about myself — both in terms of appearance and frame of mind. My mother was urging me to tint my hair and I seemed to be moving into a larger dress size every few months. I had a clear idea of what kind of forty-ish woman I'd been and of the feisty old lady I intended to be, but I had absolutely no idea of what kind of person I'd be for the next fifteen years. I was so aware of my years that I lapsed into self-disparagement, referring to myself as "a tired old woman" or "your old mother." (I winced when I heard myself but I couldn't seem to stop it.) My field was "closed" — I couldn't find a realistic image of what I *could* be or what I *wanted* to be. I was suddenly confronting middle-age and I didn't like it.

From the letters I receive, I know that my own escalation from size eight to size twelve is not unusual. I agonized about too-tight clothes for months, telling myself that it was because I had quit smoking and had nothing to do with menopause. (This was, after all, what most of the books said.) I think now that stopping smoking helped me to gain weight but that the onset of menopause made sure that the weight stayed on. It took three years before I would look at myself, undressed, in a full-length mirror. Three years before I could begin to accept that the fat lady in the mirror was me.

Bodily changes

There is always a time lag when there is a physical change: the self-image (which is a purely mental construct) and the real image (what others see) may not jibe and it takes time for these two images to match. This is true for those who lose a limb, those who lose weight, and those who gain it. It takes time to get used to the new shape, and the adaptation period may not be particularly happy. Don't try to jam yourself into too-tight clothes; this just accentuates the weight gain. Pack away the clothes that don't fit (they may fit one day!) and start acquiring larger sizes. It helps if you have some kind of idea of what you look like, so ask a trusted friend to point out women who resemble you in terms of height and overall shape. Chances are you will be pleasantly surprised to find you are not as gargantuan as you had imagined!

■

> The problem I encountered with menopause was not so much the weight gain as the inability to shed those extra pounds. I weighed between 120 and 125 for most of my life and then, just as my periods started getting infrequent, I was up to 135! And it would *not* come off. I tried all the diets and I have finally accepted that this extra poundage is inevitable. I've gradually acquired a new wardrobe, have joined a fitness class and am truly feeling good about myself. I even think that the slight padding on my face makes me look better (but I don't know if everyone else agrees).

Remember that the extra pounds are providing extra **estrogen**, that the precursor for **estrone**, the most important estrogen post-menopausally, is converted *in your fatty tissue*, and that this process will not only defend you from **hot flashes**, but will get more efficient with time. Remind yourself that underweight women are more likely to suffer from **osteoporosis**. Better to gain weight at menopause than to suddenly lose weight.

How you move inside your body is often more important than shape. If you're discouraged by your new size, concentrate on keeping the body firm and flexible. If you already have the habit of regular exercise (as outlined in Chapter 8), you will be able to accommodate extra weight with grace. If you walk with a spring in your step, consciously adopting an air of confidence, others will react to you more positively. When I gained weight, I was frequently told how *well* I looked. I mourn my "lost" figure but the added pounds have taken away dark circles from under my eyes and added a certain roundness of cheek!

Nurturing the skin

If adolescence produces acne, then middle-age produces dry skin. Most of us can now indulge in bath oils, lotions, and moisturizers without having to lock them away from the reach of experimenting daughters. There are many, many products on the market: upscale products that feature models with flawless (and pore-less) skin; products aimed at "the wrinklies" (and marketed so successfully that our children buy us Oil of Olay for Christmas); and bins of products "on special" at the discount drugstore. The latter are probably as effective as any. Dermatologists recommend products containing **petrolatum** (Vaseline Lotion, Nivea Cream) or lanolin, and tell us to apply it while the skin is still damp. Rubbing Vaseline into the skin on your legs as you sit in a hot bath will be as effective as a high-priced body lotion. Buy soaps that have a minimal amount of detergent — clear soaps or Dove. Indulge yourself.

The skin changes in other ways. Many of us notice small red dots (cherry **angiomas**) appearing on the ribcage or stomach, or red thread-like marks (spider angiomas). Other marks appear, small reddish or purplish marks, or the suddenly observed tracery of small blood vessels under the skin. (When we see broken veins on the legs — our own or anyone else's — we often think of them as "varicose veins." This is often wrong; many of these broken veins can be removed quite easily through sclerotherapy.)

One of the most hated skin changes is the appearance of "liver spots" (**senile lentigos**), which have nothing to do with the liver at all but show up — on the back of the hands, on the arms, or on the face — and darken after exposure to the sun. Some women also notice patches of scaly, dark skin appearing on the chest or back. These "moles" feel oily and thick to the touch and are just one kind of mole that may appear. Others are flat, dark "beauty spots" or pale "skin tags" — light-coloured moles that hang away from the skin, usually at places that are constantly rubbed by bra straps, waistbands, etc. All of these are normal and most can be removed, if you wish, by a dermatologist.

∎

All my life I've looked on grey hair and liver spots as signs of old age. These two superficial (when you think about it) changes in appearance signified the "end of youth" for me. I was really upset when I noticed liver spots developing on the backs of my hands. I'd handled the grey hair by regular sessions with the wash-in hair colouring, but liver spots!! The only consolation I have is that, after a summer of carefree sunning, a couple of my friends started moaning about their liver spots. Misery does love company.

The skin changes that *should* worry us are forms of skin cancer. **Basal skin cancer** starts with a pink, hairless, waxy-looking growth, usually on the head or neck, and changes over time to a cluster of shiny white pimples and then to a deep, crusted sore. **Squamous cell cancer** starts as a small, hard, red pimple, and then becomes a crusted sore that refuses to heal — a sore with an irregular edge to it. Malignant melanoma (the cancer linked to imprudent and excessive exposure to the sun) starts as a slightly raised or bumpy, dark brown, black, or blue area of skin with irregular edges, usually more than six millimetres across, that changes in colour, shape, or size, and that may feel itchy or sore. These kinds of skin changes warrant an appointment with the doctor.

One of the most effective ways of encouraging healthy skin is to take more exercise. Many of us have found that the wintertime nuisance of dry, flaking skin on legs and arms can be noticeably modified by regular work-outs. If you can afford it, regular body massage is both comforting and nourishing to the skin. It's remarkable what gobs of lotion can be absorbed during a soothing massage.

Facial care

Wrinkling is caused, not by the outer layer of skin, but by changes in the connective tissue of the **epidermis**. With age, more and more of these connective fibres are produced and as you smile, frown, or grimace, the outer layer of skin creases to fit against the excess mass underneath. As you age, these creases get worn into the skin: the elasticity of youth is no longer there.

We can ensure premature wrinkles by smoking (which produces wrinkles fanning out from the lips or corners of the eyes) and, most of all, by sunbathing (which dries out the outer layer of skin prematurely). Cosmetic advertising would have us believe that the wrinkling process can be arrested. It can't. Most cosmetics that claim to "prevent wrinkles" contain a sunscreen. For many women, a sunscreen comes too late.

Almost all soaps dry the skin because they remove skin lipids (fats) and the skin's own moisturizing substances. There are all sorts of skin cleaners on the market but, if you need soap to feel clean, dermatologists recommend a mild soap followed by a moisturizer. Many suggest that the moisturizer be used on damp skin. Collagen-based cosmetics promise a restoration of the skin's *own* **collagen** (the protein that forms skin and bone) but the collagen actually comes from cows and the molecules are too large to get past the skin's outermost layer. Collagen injections can temporarily plump up skin and smooth out wrinkles, but this is a different matter entirely. If there is no adverse reaction to collagen (some women are allergic to it), the benefits will last from six to twelve months. The injections must be done by an experienced dermatologist or cosmetic surgeon.

Estrogen is often discussed as a "cure" for wrinkling. Women who are small-boned and very fair often develop the kind of transparent skin, particularly on the back of the hands, that shows every vein. This often signals a serious depletion of collagen — not only in the underlying layers of skin but also in bone. These are the kind of women most susceptible to **osteoporosis** and some forms of arthritis, and ERT is often prescribed to halt the loss of collagen or bone mass. Halting loss of collagen from the epidermis, the underlying layer of skin, does not affect the outermost layer, the **dermis**, which will still wrinkle.

(Ad)dressing the hair

The appearance of grey hair is, in our society, a marker of age. We envy those who are prematurely grey (seeing it as unusual and special) and those who retain their natural hair colour into old age. Most of us can expect to have 50 per cent of the hair on our head go grey by the age of fifty. And at least 50 per cent of fifty-year-old women will choose not to let this show, opting instead for at-home rinse-in "tints" or regular visits to the beauty salon for more lasting hair colouring.

There's no doubt that grey hair reinforces the image of middle-age. When I chose to go grey, the strongest argument I got against the idea was from my mother who did not want an obviously middle-aged daughter! However, I decided to let nature take its course because my hair was a natural auburn, which is almost impossible to reproduce, because it would take time and regular salon visits to keep it up, because the new grey hairs seemed softer and silkier than the natural red-brown "steel wool," and — most important of all — because I was afraid I wouldn't know when to *stop* dyeing my hair. Whenever I was out on the street, I would look for women who coloured their hair: I saw too many who *should* have had grey hair but who were sporting false and/or harsh colours they had chosen years before. Who, I wondered, would come up to me and say, "Excuse me, my dear, but your hair colour is so obviously false that you had better let your natural colour show"? Also, I have to admit, my husband went grey *first!*

All this to illustrate that the decision about whether or not to go grey is highly individual. And the decision often has to be made before there are significant grey hairs. Somehow the natural colour turns drab and lifeless just as the grey starts to creep in and, like it or not, you find yourself browsing the wash-in, non-peroxide products at the drugstore — looking for something to recapture the shine of healthy hair. Women who eat nutritious foods and exercise regularly may be less affected by this pre-menopausal drab hair but this is when most of us start thinking seriously about whether to use rinses or dyes.

Because grey hair is often finer (not always), the grey tide may also bring an unwelcome thinning, from about seven hundred hairs per square centimetre of scalp to five hundred. Tinting the hair coats the hair shaft and adds body if the problem is a minor one. Often there is a family tendency to thinning hair, and often this happens in families where hair tends to be fine in texture to start with. Some post-menopausal women are affected by "male pattern baldness" and find the hair thinning either at the temples or at the crown of the head. This is assumed to be caused by adrenal **hormones** that are no longer being counteracted by ovarian hormones. Until recently, nothing much could be done about this. A promising new product, originally developed to alleviate high blood pressure, is now being tested. It is expensive and must continue to be rubbed on the scalp indefinitely to be effective, but it may be available from your doctor. (If a woman suffers from patchy hair loss, this may be **alopecia areata**, a condition not linked to menopause.)

■

> My hair, although fine, has never been a problem. As a matter of fact, it has always been very healthy and certainly plentiful. In the last six months, it has been falling out at an alarming rate. My husband seems to think I'm over-reacting but I figure I know my hair best and this is really scaring me! It's not only that it's falling out, it's coming out in patches. In other words, I'm losing hair in places like around my temples. I'm beginning to wonder if this problem is related to menopause.

Beauticians suggest that hair colour should not mimic natural colour; in most cases, the colour chosen should be lighter. Ash blonde may be too drab; deep brunette is probably too harsh. You might take a tip from the "punkers" and their hair of many colours: experiment with some of the new brush-in colours that disappear after one shampoo. If you are trying a non-peroxide rinse, choose a shade close to your natural colour but warmer, and then gradually lighten the shade. (Since one of these rinses lasts for a few weeks, the gradual change will probably not even be noticed.) Keep your hair short — shoulder length at the longest — and use soft bangs or wisps of hair over the forehead and an uplift at the sides. Avoid backcombing, hair lacquer, or outdated "bouffant" styles. Hair mousse adds body without changing the colour and can be combed into the hair each morning, if necessary. Another way of adding body is the "body perm," which can be done at home, provided you use very large plastic rollers, larger than those supplied with the standard home-permanent kit.

It's unsettling to have these kinds of changes to deal with. My hair, which had once been very wavy, became quite unmanageable for a few years and I ended up having a series of curly perms because I was so awkward with a hair dryer or curling iron. Now that my hair is mostly grey, the wave has come back and I have gone back to finger combing it after a shampoo. In fact, in humid weather, my hair is wavier than it's been since I was a teenager. The analogy between menopause and adolescence holds, even for hair!

In addition to scalp hair, we must also deal with body hair and facial hair. Most of us notice a thinning of body hair — more and more infrequent shaving of the underarms, less need to shave the legs. On the other hand, the tweezers are needed more and more for stray chin hairs and, for women who tend to be dark and hairy ("hirsute") anyway, there may be the ominous shadow of a moustache. Of course, this whole idea of being hairless is a *learned* standard and quite silly when you think about it. There is no doubt that this society likes its women hairless to emphasize the childlike aspects of womanhood, whereas some societies find hairy women very sexy. Interesting how one can see this so plainly and yet feel compelled to banish all evidence of hair on the face, legs, and armpits!

Facial hairs seem to get worse during the menopause and then to ease up afterwards. I noticed that the whiskers appeared on a cyclical basis even after I stopped menstruating: for one week of the month, I would feel them, get rid of them, and worry that my face would one day be covered in stubble. Now I find the whiskers appear only rarely. So don't panic if you are tweezing whiskers regularly. It may resolve itself in time.

However, be aware that certain drugs — some hypertensive medications, diuretics, anti-depressants, and tranquillizers — encourage the growth of facial hair. Don't blame it all on menopause. **Estrogen replacement therapy** may diminish hair growth but should not be considered (or prescribed) for this reason alone. **Spironolactone**, an anti-androgen, has occasionally been prescribed in low doses to reduce growth of heavy facial hair, although it will take some time for the effects to be seen. Medication should be a last resort; spironolactone may also cause nausea, cramping, diarrhoea, drowsiness, headaches, etc.

If facial hair is fair, tweezing may be the simplest solution; you will need a good magnifying mirror in a place with a strong light. If the hair is fine but dark, you may want to invest in facial bleach. This is readily available at a drugstore and the instructions are easy to follow. If the hair is dark and sturdy, you may want to try a new depilatory for facial hair, or remove it (or have it removed) with wax; there are cold-wax and hot-wax methods. The most permanent solution is electrolysis, which kills individual follicles using an electric current. This needs to be done by a skilled operator but will require a number of sessions.

Dental tips

More and more of us are looking to dentists to improve our appearance. Some of this is involuntary as we all get "longer in the tooth" — literally as well as figuratively — and the periodontists get to work on our defective gums. Some dental work is optional and cosmetic. It is no longer strange to me to see women of forty or fifty wearing braces on their teeth, and orthodontists are attracting more middle-aged customers by offering sapphire braces, which are almost invisible, unlike metal braces. Even more numerous are those who have their teeth bonded to get rid of unsightly spots, the marks of old fillings, or to minimize small chips or gaps.

A friend who has spent some time living in Europe once remarked that the youth from North America could be picked out of a crowd because of the evenness and whiteness of their teeth. Perhaps the same will soon be said of North American women generally, as we all rush back to the dentist, periodontist, or orthodontist to get the teeth we always wanted to have!

Cosmetic surgery

■

> I resent those who react with a stiff neck to the idea of cosmetic surgery. It's no more artificial to extend the youthful appearance of the face with a facelift than it is to extend the elasticity of the vagina with an estrogen cream. I suspect a moral judgment at work here: vanity (self) is bad; sexual accessibility (other) is good. A love of beauty is by no means the worst part of us. I have supped of the notion that lines are an indication of character. Unless one is Lillian Hellman, lines are an indication of lines.

Not all of us are interested in cosmetic surgery; not all of us are candidates (a number of medical conditions dictate against it — hypertension, heart disease, diabetes, etc.); not all of us can afford it. When we think of cosmetic surgery, facelifts immediately come to mind. But more and more women are turning to cosmetic surgery for a "body lift."

"Body contouring," as it's euphemistically known, is not a substitute for dieting or exercise. In fact, it is not recommended for those whose weight tends to fluctuate. The ideal candidate for this operation has localized areas of excessive fat, an otherwise normal and fairly stable body weight, and good skin elasticity. Where skin has lost this elasticity (a natural effect of ageing), a complementary operation to remove excess skin (an **abdominoplasty** or "tummy tuck") may be performed — either at the same time or some weeks later.

Fat suction (also known as suction curettage, **lipectomy**, or lypolysis) is done under either local or general anaesthetic, depending on the extent and duration of surgery. Fat suction of the abdomen will require three incisions, one at each end of the pubic crease and another at the navel. For pads of fat under the breasts, on the sides of the waist, etc., additional incisions may be required. A long-handled looped instrument is inserted into each incision and moved around to break up the cells, then a miniature wand (similar to the extension on a vacuum cleaner but much smaller, of course) is inserted and moved about under the top layer of skin to suck out the fat.

After the fat has been vacuumed off, drains may be inserted and incisions closed with a suture. The drains are removed after twenty-four to forty-eight hours but the incisions are left open to allow for additional drainage. The patient is allowed to walk the evening after surgery and to shower forty-eight hours after the operation. The hospital or clinic stay will be for two to five days, with pressure dressings required for three weeks and, for older patients, an abdominal girdle of some kind for a week or two after that. Patients can usually resume normal activity in a week to ten days, and heavy exercise in three to four weeks. A change is noticeable within three weeks of the operation but, since damaged cells will continue to be sloughed off for some time, it may take a month or two for the full benefits to show.

Severe bruising follows from the operation but the extent and duration of the bruises will depend on age, colouring, etc. There is often a "rippling" effect on the skin — in other words, the skin does not necessarily go back to the smooth contours of youth. If the rippling is still unacceptable a month or two after the operation, a second procedure may be required. Potential side-effects are **necrosis** (death of clumps of cells), which may require additional surgery, and unexpected and disfiguring scars.

Fat suction may seem like any easy solution to abdominal padding, but there are disadvantages at menopause. The ethical plastic surgeon wants to operate on someone whose body weight is relatively stable and who will, therefore, derive a long-term benefit. For many menopausal women, the change in shape (whether it involves a weight change or not) is only part of the picture. Often there are fluctuations in energy levels or temporary feelings of anxiety, panic, or even depression. In such a state of flux, the trauma of anaesthesia combined with the shock of surgery may merely *add* to the physiological strain, putting *more* stress on a body already under siege. A well-known New York cosmetic surgeon has commented that such operations "buy time" for the woman not prepared to deal with the reality of ageing. My own feeling is that it is better to confront ageing and then, when you're feeling good about yourself, decide whether or not to reward yourself with smoother eyebrows or a flatter tummy.

It is estimated that about 10 per cent of cosmetic surgeries entail some unexpected and negative outcome. Surgeons are responsible for the conduct of the surgical procedure, but there is no guarantee of satisfactory results. For this reason, any woman seeking surgical treatment should be very wary.

Most of the books and articles we see about cosmetic surgery come from the United States and always advise us to look for a "board-certified" surgeon. This is because, in the United States, any licensed physician can legally perform any kind of surgery. To be board-certified, they must complete a two- to five-year residency in a surgical specialty and pass the qualifying examinations. In Canada, the equivalent to "board certification" is a fellowship in the Royal College of Physicians and Surgeons; no physician is allowed to do surgery without the credentials F.R.C.S.(C.), Fellow of the Royal College of Surgeons (Canada).

Some fellows of the Royal College of Surgeons have a certificate in plastic surgery (one of the recognized specialties of the college) but there is no such thing as a certificate in *cosmetic* surgery, and many plastic surgeons do not *do* cosmetic surgery. So, the "F.R.C.S.(C.)" after a name does not tell you how qualified one particular surgeon may be in the operation of your choice.

No matter what kind of operation you choose, you should look for a referral or recommendation from a family physician or from former patients who have had the same operation. If you are contemplating body contouring, you may want to check these names against the surgeons belonging to the Canadian Society of Plastic Surgeons or the Quebec Association of Plastic Surgeons. If you haven't any leads, you can telephone the hot line of the American Academy of Facial, Plastic and Reconstructive Surgeons (1-800-523-3223 in Canada; 1-800-322-3223 in the U.S.A.) for names of doctors in your area, and then check these names with the Accreditation Section of the Royal College of Physicians and Surgeons. If you are contemplating facial surgery, you might want to get in touch with the Canadian Institute of Facial Plastic Surgery. Members of this institute are initially trained in surgical techniques having to do with head and neck, or eyes, or skin, or jaws, and then take additional training in plastic surgery. If your doctor is affiliated with a hospital, you will know that he (or she) has also had to conform to certain hospital standards in order to use their facilities. If he practises in a private clinic, you may want to check to see if he *did*, at one time, have hospital privileges. If he has a university appointment, or is with a teaching hospital, this is usually considered a plus.

When you see the doctor, ask how many similar procedures he has performed and when. If he brushes you off ("Don't you worry about that; I know my business"), you can excuse yourself. Any surgeon should be willing to deal with this question frankly and honestly. If you don't know anyone who has experienced the same procedure, you can ask to see photographic results of other operations. If former patients are willing to be contacted, you may ask to get in touch with them. The more information you have, the better.

Before you start your investigation you should know that, because the surgery is for cosmetic purposes, it will not be covered by provincial (or private) health plans and can be very expensive. The exception is breast reduction, which is often covered.

.

> Last Spring I had a facelift. This was not common knowledge but my close friends knew about it and a couple of them came down hard on me for deciding to go ahead with it. It's funny because, although I had severe misgivings about "postponing" the ageing process, I feel I am benefiting from the operation.
>
> As women, we are continually reminded of the importance of our looks. It seems odd, then, that after years of emphasis on make-up and clothes, we're chided for trying to improve ourselves when we get to fifty or fifty-five. Granted, it's a drastic and costly step but I found it made a difference in my attitude to myself and, I think, in the attitude of my students toward me. I guess I look more "with it" now so they seem to pay more attention to what I have to say. Or maybe I'm just imagining it!

The ultimate solution to the spectre of ageing is, of course, the facelift. This procedure (**rhytidectomy**) requires a hospital or clinic stay of from one to three days, another week of isolation, and three more weeks before the swelling disappears completely. The effects last for five to eight years. An incision is made in the scalp behind the hair line at the temple, descending to the front of the ear and back up behind the ear. If neck tissue is to be removed, the incision will extend downwards from behind the ear and into the neck. Possible complications are hematomas (swellings containing blood) that occur in from 10 to 15 per cent of cases and must be drained. In addition, it is impossible to predict changes in skin pigmentation or the kind of scarring that may result. In very rare cases, injury may be caused to a facial nerve.

Chemical **face-peeling** is a procedure that burns off the top layer of skin and is often used to remove fine wrinkles about the mouth and eyes. It takes from four to twelve weeks for the skin to appear normal and you will have to stay out of the sun for a full year. Possible long-term effects are scarring or changes in skin colouring. **Dermabrasion** is often mentioned as an alternative to chemical face-peeling but is more useful for acne scars than for wrinkles.

For pouches under the eye or hooded eyelids, some women resort to the eyelift or **blepharoplasty**. The operation for the lower eyelid is more difficult and, if done improperly, may prevent the eye from closing properly. Eye surgery usually involves an overnight stay at a hospital or clinic and can be done under local anaesthetic. The patient must keep a compress on the eyes for at least ten hours, often longer, and this is usually the most intolerable part of the procedure. It takes about ten days to recover and two months before the final effect is achieved.

For bags under the eyes, which are primarily composed of fat, a newer technique uses an electrically heated needle to vaporize the fat. Done under local anaesthetic, this procedure takes about thirty minutes and heals in about a week. Plastic surgeons can use this same procedure to remove pads of fat under the chin. A non-surgical solution to hooded eyelids is a piece of medical adhesive, specially designed to hold up the kind of eyelids that fold right down to, or past, the eyelashes. This product can be used daily.

Make-up and fashion

Whether or not you choose to spend money and time on cosmetic surgery, you still want to look your best. When you start to notice a loss of lustre or colour in your hair (whether tinted or not), you will also notice changes in skin colour. If you continue to use the same make-up colours and techniques at fifty-five that you used at thirty-five, you are probably doing yourself a disservice. The experts say that, as you age, you should conscientiously try to be more deft, more subtle with make-up, matching foundation carefully to skin colour and abandoning rouge for a carefully dusted-on contouring powder.

Soft pencil can be used under the eye and along the upper lid, but it should be softened or smeared to avoid a hard line. Reddish-brown or pinkish-brown eye shadow is more natural than turquoise or blue. If you wear glasses, you can use more eye make-up; the glasses soften the effect.

For cracked or chapped lips, use a lip balm, wipe to remove dead skin, and use a lip primer to prevent "bleeding" of lipstick into lip creases. These primers are expensive but they last a very long time. A lip pencil will also help to keep the lipstick inside the lines. Also, as small wrinkles appear around the mouth, any lipline that does not follow the natural lipline appears more and more false. Softer lipstick shades are more flattering to the mid-life woman; they draw the eye away from the mouth and up toward the wise and worldly eyes!

Nowadays, many malls have boutiques that sell cosmetics and also offer free make-up sessions. I tried this once, with a friend, and received a lot of useful tips. Because these malls are bathed in artificial light, the amount of make-up applied is too garish (for my taste) during daylight hours, but it gave me confidence in making myself up for swank evening events (where you want to look your best and the lighting will tolerate a heavier hand). I bought some of the little brushes in return for this "free make-up session": a fair trade, I thought. For women committed to the natural look, the use of make-up just takes up time and money. But for those of us who like a touch of artifice, self-enhancement becomes a challenge.

We are fortunate in that fashion options are so wide these days. Despite the announcements that "waists are nipped" or "skirts are shorter," we can pick and choose in a way not available to mid-life women twenty or thirty years ago. Coping with bodily changes means more than buying the same old thing but in a larger size. A skirt hangs differently over a budding tummy and the waistband cuts during a temporary episode of "**bloat.**" It was strange to me to feel my pantyhose, panties, and skirts all clinging to different parts of my middle; my waist seemed to be everywhere and nowhere.

Not long ago, I read this remark from a fashion expert: "Middle-aged women will love the shorter skirts because the legs are the last to go." Despite the anger I felt at this woman's patronizing remark, I had to admit that there was a grain of truth. Few of us worry about gaining weight on our legs. There is a tendency for weight to accumulate around the waist, on the diaphragm, across the back — a different story from the heavy hips and thighs that are the usual problem areas at younger ages.

Mid-life women need elasticized waistbands, pleats that are stitched down to the hip or that fall from a yoke, big tops that sit easily on the hips or skim down to the old "three-quarter" length. We need bright touches of colour to cheer us up and to go with our changing hair and skin colour. How many of us tune into television shows like "The Golden Girls," not for the story line, but to get ideas for suitable clothes?

Women are motivated to seek adjustments to their appeearance for a number of reasons. Some are touched by the "now-or-never syndrome" — the same syndrome that incites a mid-life woman to leave a marriage or to start a business. These women will go in search of the straight teeth, the firm chin, the wide-open eyes that they have fantasized about for years. Other women find that their physical appearance just does not *fit* with their personalities; for them, worn wrappings do not fairly represent the up-to-date contents.

These may not be the women you think of in connection with cosmetic surgery, but they are as much a part of the picture as the common stereotype of the woman frightened of ageing, the woman who blindly seeks help from a surgeon rather than confronting her own nightmares. We rarely notice the surgical enhancement of the stable woman; what we remark on are the ageing women with the incongruously young faces. The tragedy of such women is that their movements and attitudes are so antiquated, so ageing, that the facelifts are merely grotesque.

Because the aged are devalued in this society, most of us find any evidence of ageing unwelcome. In one study of middle-agers, more than one-third voluntarily cited changes in physical appearance as a concern. There is no doubt that, for many women, menopause brings many changes; it's not easy to cope with a new shape and a new image. But, if we're realistic about it, we will acknowledge that it is not being fifty that bothers us, but rather the prospect of being viewed as "old." If menopause is on the doorstep of old age, then we have to confront our fear of ageing.

·

I'm very conscious of getting older. I don't really want to be old. I'd like to put the clock back to about forty and stop there because, although I enjoyed the children when they were little, at forty I was enjoying my job. I was on top of the world. I was full of bounce . . . I'm a bit afraid now that I'm over fifty. I can see sixty coming and I really feel that that is very old . . .

I can see retirement and, although my husband says we'll go around the world and all sorts of things, my fear is that by the time we're old enough to do these things, we won't be young enough to enjoy them. I'm afraid that I will deteriorate very quickly when I get older.

I'm afraid that tiredness is going to stay with me and, in fact, increase. That really frightens me. I can't bear to think of not being well. I don't mind being old so long as I'm well.

CONFRONTING OUR OWN AGEING

We live in a society that values women as decorative, sexual, and utilitarian. The first two are reserved for youth. Many of us find the third small comfort, although it helps us to be more understanding of the legions of middle-aged women who take over committee work at church or at hospitals. Feeling "useful" and "needed" become urgent when one is devalued in other ways.

For many of us, growing old means not being needed. We all want a little niche where our presence will be noted, appreciated, and, in our absence, missed. Many women's lives are unbalanced from being needed too much for too long, and then suddenly needed too little. One friend, who has been forced to move away from her grown children and back to the place where her husband wants to grow old, says it has put her "off balance." Not much wonder. It requires enormous resilience to cope with a social worth that can so quickly change from "essential" to "non-essential."

Years ago, I was pushing our baby carriage toward the house. In the carriage was my new baby girl and her seventeen-month-old brother. On a little chair fitted over the carriage sat my eldest, not quite three. Rain was threatening and I was about to break into a trot when a little old lady stopped me, peered into the carriage, and said sweetly, "Ah, my dear, these are the best years of your life!" I remember the rage I felt that anyone should label these the "best" years of my life — years of constant fatigue and incredible self-doubt. What a price to pay for being needed! (It made for a nice irony when, twenty-five years later, I was filmed for a National Film Board production entitled *The Best Time of My Life: Portraits of Women in Mid-Life*.) Is it possible to designate any years as the "best"?

There are different ways of being needed. We may fulfil basic needs (food, clothing, shelter, love) or we may fulfil secondary needs (advice, friendship, affection, touching). If we spend a large part of our lives dispensing love along with hot meals and clean clothes, we sometimes confuse them. We fear that when we are no longer needed to cook, shop, and "do" for others, we will no longer be needed. But we are needed to love them, as we have always done.

It is normal to feel a sense of loss when one role ends and another has yet to begin. The gap created may leave us "off balance" but not, I hope, too shy to reach out to others who need us — who need our advice, our friendship, our touch. We *can* make a place for ourselves at this age as at any age. The gap closes.

Closely allied to the fear of not being needed is the fear of having no central objective or purpose to one's life. Menopause often coincides with other major events in a woman's life — the end of "active" mothering, the awarding of the twenty-five-year pin to the faithful employee, the sudden and saddening loss of a parent or spouse, the growing awareness that one may be destined to spend old age alone. Those of us who thought that we would feel great satisfaction when we surveyed our grown children find, instead, that it is all a blur. These young adults, fine as they are, seem to have appeared out of nowhere. Now, married, separated, divorced, or widowed, we have to look for new means to achieve satisfaction, the sense of a job well done.

At the same time, there is often a sense of being very *tired*, too tired to undertake anything new or different. You may just want to be left alone. I believe that this fatigue has its reasons. The body is adapting to a new internal rhythm and you need time to rest and to think. Menopause allows time for the reactivation of old dreams, the challenges of new learning, the tentative acquisition of new skills. When your energy comes flowing back — as it will — you will have found a cause, an activity, a source of satisfaction that will give meaning to what you do for the next major stage in your life.

It is during this "pause," the real gift of middle-age, that we should take time to examine our fears of ageing. Today, confronted with new facts about the patterns and prevalence of Alzheimer's disease, we find ourselves making weak jokes about menopausal forgetfulness, dying brain cells, premature senility, but there is often a nervous and deadly serious edge to it. We fumble for names; lose objects, which turn up in the most mysterious places; notice that every stranger we meet looks like someone else (are we really that old?); and remember arcane bits of information from childhood. Psychologists tell us that this is a different kind of memory, no better and no worse than the memory of youth. They also tell us that women (who are usually held responsible for remembering the trivia of everyday life) worry far more about loss of memory than do men, although the changes in memory are similar. Victims of Alzheimer's rarely worry about loss of memory since one of the symptoms is an inability to realize that they have forgotten something.

Like the fear of forgetting, the fear of becoming dependent is often expressed as black humour — for instance, the T-shirts and bumper stickers sold in Florida: "Avenge yourself. Live long enough to be a burden to your children." No one wants to be dependent and one of the greatest fears of ageing is being physically and/or financially reliant on others. Most of us know old people so haunted by this fear that it can never be spoken. There are no discussions, no contingency plans.

If the financial fears dog you, take this time to examine your economic future. The government listings in the telephone book can guide you to information about pension plans, federal or provincial. If you have a pension plan at work, you should be getting regular statements of your pension status. You can discuss this with your local bank manager and augment it, if possible, with registered retirement savings plans (RRSP). If you are dependent on your husband's pension, make sure you know what the provisions are.

Many of us are frightened by the prospect of having to depend on others for routine help — shopping, driving, fixing things around the house. In our determination to take care of ourselves, we often forget the joy that others may get from giving. There is a time to give and a time to allow others to give to us. In the meantime, we can do our best to assure our independence by assiduous attention to healthy living. By taking good care of ourselves now, we may ease the minds of our children and lighten the burden of those who will have to take care of us in our old age.

Middle age gives us a marvellous opportunity to prepare for being old. We have time to dream about, and to plan for the future. Even if we are feeling under strain just now, we can anticipate years of good health and renewed energy that will enable us to get involved in new projects and new causes.

I am often asked about the *good* things about menopause. It isn't hard to find them. First of all is the sense of freedom. We are free to experiment with new kinds of foods, new kinds of activities. We are free from the necessity of stocking sanitary pads or tampons or of scheduling events around the ups and downs of the menstrual cycle. We are free to strike up a conversation with a stranger in a bus, or on a street corner, without being thought of as forward or seductive. We are free from the compulsion to work toward the thinner thighs, the twenty-four–inch waist, or the perfect fingernails that we once longed for, and we are free to realize that it was a pretty silly ambition anyway! We are free to adopt our own standards of dress and decorum, guided more by good sense and comfort than by, "What will people think?"

Then there is the sense of getting another chance. Because menopause often brings us up short, psychologically and physiologically, it gives us a rare opportunity to evaluate where we are coming from and where we want to go. Because of this enforced disruption, many of us have found that we were continuing to do things that we didn't really enjoy. It was part of the routine and we hadn't stopped to think about it. Every day, middle-aged women are giving up cooking to take up woodworking; are boycotting movies in order to save for trips to faraway places; are signing up for piano lessons, or computer science, or philosophy courses. Women are making changes that are not perhaps significant in themselves, but allow for the expression of very personal interests — interests that sometimes have been lurking under the surface for years.

Finally, menopause gives women an opportunity to make friends. Because so little is known about the causes and effects of menopause, the only real understanding of it comes from other women. Menopause provides the perfect excuse to reach out to other women — to revive old friendships and to forge new ones. We know that the nourishment of friendship is a vital ingredient to a happy old age. We know that women are much more likely to survive into old age than are men. Thanks to menopause, we can enrich our lives now and carry these riches with us into an active and satisfying future.

CHAPTER 11

·

Menopause Clinics, Seminars and Groups

THERE ARE MORE RESOURCES available for the menopausal woman compared to the situation ten or even five years ago. More general information on the subject of **menopause** is available in books, booklets, newspaper and magazine articles, films, and radio and television programs. There are also organizations that offer information on particular aspects of menopause. Many of these references and resources are listed in the References and Resources for each chapter with a more extensive list starting on page 192.

When you read one book, you may think you have found all that you need to know. If you read two, you are likely to find such diametrically opposed points of view that you will be compelled to read a third! If your local public or school library does not have a book you are looking for, it is worth making a request. Your library may be willing to order a book that you ask about, since menopause is a subject of interest to growing numbers of people.

In addition, many organizations produce printed materials dealing with the more general aspects of menopause, or with specific problems that may be more troublesome to you (migraine, **hysterectomy**, etc.) Much of this material is free or available at cost. You can obtain more information by writing to, or calling the particular organization, or you may wish to contact a local woman's health organization or women's centre. They will be glad to help you find resources to fit your needs.

MENOPAUSE CLINICS

Some hospitals, particularly teaching hospitals, have menopause clinics. When a woman calls me with a list of debilitating complaints and nowhere to go, I may suggest that she contact a local menopause clinic. It is not a suggestion I make lightly. First of all, most women will not need the medical support of a clinic if they are seeing a doctor regularly. What they *may* need is a more understanding doctor but, as

Cynthia Carver makes clear in her book *Patient Beware*, the time to shop for a good doctor is before you need one. If you are not satisfied with your current doctor and you are approaching menopause, it is a good idea to check around until you have the names of three likely doctors, and then go and see each in turn. If you are not experiencing any problems associated with menopause, you probably won't need to consult a doctor. But if you have a good doctor, you may not need a menopause clinic.

My basic quarrel with the menopause clinic is the confusion about its function. The main goal of a menopause clinic is *understood* by the general public to be the welfare and well-being of menopausal women. However, it seems that the basic goal of most menopause clinics is to provide data for menopausal research and the secondary function is to help menopoausal women. Menopause clinics are usually subsidized (and supplied) by pharmaceutical companies. This means that, whether you know it or not, the "solutions" found for you will be limited to those geared to the purpose of the research study. Most of these clinics have long waiting lists and, when you finally get an appointment you may find that you are given a certain type of drug in order that the doctor may report on its effectiveness or you may be told that you are to take a certain drug when, in fact, you have been given a **placebo** (a substance that looks like the product being tested but that will have no objective effects).

There is nothing inherently wrong in this. Because of the abysmally low priority given to research funds in this country, most hospitals must accept funding (and drugs) in order to continue their work. However, there is a difference between a menopause clinic and a menopause research project, and I believe this should be made clear to the women who attend. Many women go to a menopause clinic expecting individualized attention to their particular complaints, answers to their questions, and information about a range of possible treatments. This is an understandable expectation, given that their own doctors may be unprepared to deal with their concerns about menopause. What these women are likely to get is routine treatment as specified by the particular study underway — perhaps a general medical check-up, a short meeting with a psychologist, a short meeting with a dietitian, some medication and another appointment.

If medication is prescribed (or administered), this, too, will conform to whatever is being studied in this particular project. It may be an **estrogen-testosterone** injection, an estrogen patch, estrogen gel (to rub on the abdomen), an estrogen tablet, **progestogen** or **progestin** tablets, or a placebo masquerading as any of these. The research study will be geared toward a particular type of drug, so that treatment varies from clinic to clinic, because the study (and the particular drug involved) will be tied to the funding of one pharmaceutical company. In other words, the menopause clinic's solution to most menopausal ailments will be a **hormone** preparation.

Some clinics do get involved in studies to do with sexuality, or with psychological symptoms. If a woman is aware of the current research underway, she will find it easier to decide whether or not to participate and, if she does participate, to understand and co-operate with the process. She may also wish to ask for a copy, or copies, of the completed research papers.

Not all menopause clinics are this narrow, although I know of one that threw open its doors, welcomed patients until the study results were in, and then promptly closed. Potential patients were told that it had been too popular. The truth was that the research funds dried up.

There may be a menopause clinic available in your community that does *not* operate in this manner. Your best bet is to enquire about sources of funding and medication provided by the clinic before you enrol.

MENOPAUSE SEMINARS

Hospitals and service organizations (often in conjunction with hospitals) occasionally present one-time menopause seminars or information sessions. These sessions, however they are labelled, usually take place in a medium to large hall (often a hospital or university auditorium) and permit very limited questions and answers from the floor. Most (not all) will feature medical experts, usually a doctor or doctors (sometimes a psychiatrist), occasionally a physiotherapist and/ or dietitian.

The basic problem with these kinds of sessions is that they often ignore the great diversity of opinion within the medical profession and among non-medical researchers. What you get is one doctor's (or a few doctors') opinions about menopause, based on the women that they see and the research that they do. Because doctors are, by and large, faithful to a medical model of menopause (the model that views it as a "deficiency condition"), and because they rarely see healthy, menopausal women, what they have to say may or may not correspond with your own experience. Some women discover that specialists (gynaecologists) view menopause so differently that the women are better off with their family doctors. These sessions often bolster the image of gynaecologist as all-knowing and there is rarely opportunity for discussion of the very real concerns that most women bring to these events.

These kinds of sessions are popular with women who are reluctant to commit themselves to more than one day or one evening for learning about menopause. The problem is that they may leave more confused than when they went in. A better bet for those who may not wish to air their problems and who do not want to listen to the problems of others is the menopause workshop.

MENOPAUSE WORKSHOP

The menopause workshop may also be called a discussion group or seminar, or may appear as part of the course offerings of a continuing-education or adult-education section of a local school, college, or university. Whatever its name, the workshop is usually scheduled at a particular time and location, to take place for a specified number of sessions, in a neutral setting. Someone trained in group work is hired to facilitate the discussion, and "experts" may be invited to some sessions to explain particular aspects of menopause. Depending on the size of the group and the topics to be covered, there may or may not be ample opportunity to air individual concerns.

The atmosphere in this kind of group depends on the continuing presence of a core group, the duration of the sessions, the number of sessions, how the women interact with one another, and the skills of the facilitator in putting people at ease. It is difficult to predict how satisfying the workshop will be for the individual participant, but the increased demand for such workshops across the country is testimony to their success. (These kinds of workshops should not be confused with the one-shot workshop that is often held in conjunction with an all-day information session on women's health issues. Often, smaller groups "workshop" on particular topics as a follow-up to a more general information session in the morning.)

A good workshop offers both structured information and moral support — both contribute to the sense that one's menopausal experiences are *not* unique, that one *can* cope, and that menopause is but a temporary disruption. If the structure of an on-going workshop appeals to you, it may be worth your while to contact some likely agencies in your community (your church or synagogue, school boards, community college, women's organization, YWCA, etc.). Often a call is enough to get the ball rolling. (The Vancouver Women's Health Collective, for instance, sponsors workshops in and around Vancouver. There are five sessions, at a nominal fee and from fifteen to twenty women attend.)

Many women who have attended workshops or discussion groups become so involved with the whole process of group learning that they are inspired to become trained facilitators themselves. Many community women's organizations both encourage and enable their members to learn the skills of facilitating groups, either in courses that they develop themselves or through Family-Life–Education programs at local colleges or universities.

Some women live too far away from the kinds of institutions that are likely to sponsor menopause workshops. Some women like the idea of the moral support, but are not particularly interested in a review of the physiological processes of menopause and are daunted by the thought of a large group or a classroom. Some women live too far from a proposed workshop, or would rather attend sessions at a different time of day. These women may be interested in the more informal, and often more intimate self-help group (also known as a mutual-aid or support group).

SELF-HELP GROUPS

Self-help groups come together because the people in them are (or will be) experiencing something in common, and because they want to talk together to help themselves and help each other. Self-help groups are not a substitute for professional help (although they are often a valuable adjunct to it) and are not dependent on professional expertise. Self-help groups require a willingness to make the group work, and a commitment from each member of the group to attend the first three or four meetings. Anything else can be decided once the group gets underway.

There are various opinions about the optimum size for a self-help group but the consensus seems to be in the range of six to twelve. The smaller the group, the more reliant you will be on the commitment of the members to the group; at the same time, smaller groups often foster more intimacy more quickly. Some groups adopt an "open door" policy, encouraging new members to join the group at any time. Others prefer to encourage intimacy and trust by closing the group, either for a limited number of meetings or for the duration. If the decision is made to close the group, it will require a solid commitment of attendance from each member.

If you wish to start a self-help group, you have various options. You can enlist the help of friends or acquaintances to find likely members. In other words, from the beginning, you can *share* the job of finding members. If word of mouth is inadequate, you might consider advertising — putting a notice on a bulletin board, placing an ad in a community newspaper or a church bulletin, etc. Your doctor or your friends' doctors may be willing to help by mentioning the idea to likely patients. Sometimes self-help groups can be recruited within the context of a larger meeting. Perhaps an existing women's group will agree to show a film on menopause, or a local organization may be willing to sponsor a presentation about menopause. This provides an opportunity to ask women who attend to sign up if they're interested in a self-help group, or to circulate a "sign-in" sheet and then contact each woman by telephone to see if she (and/or a friend) would be interested in joining the group.

The decision about where to hold the meetings is often a difficult one. The first meeting should be in a "neutral" place — a school, library, community centre, church, etc. — some place convenient and accessible. It may be decided to hold subsequent meetings in one another's homes, but this will depend on the size of the group and the living situation of the members. In other words, the meeting places should be protected from interruption by telephone calls, unexpected callers, other family members, etc.

No matter how you get started, the first meeting is often taken up with organizational questions. Even when *you* have a clear idea of why you wanted to start a group, you will find that others may have different ideas. It helps if you can articulate and obtain agreement about the general purpose of the group (e.g., "to help us to feel more comfortable about and with menopause"), leaving the precise ways to achieve this to be decided by the group. If the word "menopause" gets in the way of forming a group, a more acceptable goal might be "the exploration of changes in mid-life" or something general and non-threatening. Widow-to-widow groups, or groups for divorced women in their forties or fifties may view menopause as part of a more global objective. Whatever the goal, each member will arrive with her own "hidden agenda" — needs that may or may not be fulfilled by this particular group. In other words, although there may be consensus about the general goal of the self-help group, each person's way of achieving this is likely to be different. This is where the group must look to specific objectives or tasks to be accomplished at each meeting.

Most self-help groups attempt to meet once a week, but you may find that meeting once every two weeks suits your members better. The meeting itself should run for at least two hours; some groups find that three hours are necessary to allow time for everyone. If coffee (decaffeinated) or herbal tea is served, this should be confined to a short period just before or after the meeting. Some groups like to set up an agenda in advance with specific topics slotted for a particular evening. They may also wish to limit the life of the group to a definite number of sessions. (Six is usually the minimum, but some groups aim for eight, or decide to keep it open-ended.) Other groups prefer to see how much can be covered in one meeting and to spend the last few minutes deciding on the topic for the next. This kind of group may endure for as long as the members feel a need for it.

There are a number of pitfalls that may beset groups — many of which are clearly explained in the handbook *Helping Ourselves: A Handbook for Women Starting Groups*, developed by the Women's Counselling, Referral, and Education Centre (WCREC) in Toronto.

One of the greatest benefits of a group is the new sense of intimacy with women who can empathize with your experience in a way usually impossible for others important to you. But self-help groups can do much more than offer their members a chance to express feelings to each other. They can choose to take action about behaviours that contribute, directly or indirectly, to each woman's well-being. Groups of mid-life women can get together to exercise, taking "power walks" as a group and then sitting down for a meeting afterwards. Or they can hire a fitness instructor and enjoy a jazzercise or aerobics class together. Some groups might be interested in learning more about nutrition and practising recipes based on low-fat or no-fat cooking. Groups like this might be formed as a way of fostering general good health, or as a way of coping when a family member suffers from some form of cardio-vascular disease. Women who house or care for dependent parents often need the aid and support of other women; a group formed around this issue may be of enormous help to other women who find themselves suddenly placed in the same situation. Together, group members can locate and evaluate doctors in the community — even if the need for doctors' services is not imminent. If a member of the group is apprehensive about a visit to the doctor, another member of the group may go along to offer moral support. There are all sorts of possibilities for a self-help group.

Many of us have grown up with the old maxim "the gods help those who help themselves," priding ourselves on our self-sufficiency and quite ignoring the possibility that the help might be maximized if it is shared. One of the exciting aspects of support groups is the increased energy and sense of direction that often animates individual members. Women who have participated in groups as mothers of young children are more open to the idea of group work when they become mothers of adolescents. In the context of commitment to the group process, members quickly move past the kind of petty bickering that besets less dedicated groups and find, within themselves, resources, strengths, and abilities that they never knew they had.

SELECTED REFERENCES AND RESOURCES

CHAPTER 1

Backstrom, C.T.; H. Boyle; and D.T. Baird. "Persistence of symptoms of premenstrual tension in hysterectomized women." *British Journal of Obstetrics and Gynecology*, 88 (May 1981): 530–36.

Cattanach, John. "Oestrogen deficiency after tubal ligation." *The Lancet*, 1 (April 1985): 847–49.

Coulson, C.J. "Premenstrual Syndrome: Are gonadotropins the cause of the condition?" *Medical Hypothesis*, 19 (1986): 243–55.

Dalton, Katharina. *The Premenstrual Syndrome and Progesterone Therapy*, 2nd ed. Chicago: Year Book Medical Publishers, 1984.

Greer, Germaine. "Letting Go." *Vogue*, May 1986, p. 141.

McKinlay, S.; M. Jeffreys; and B. Thompson. "An investigation of the age at menopause." *Journal of Biosocial Science*, 4 (1972): 161–73.

Riedel, H-H.; E. Lehmann-Willenbrock; and K. Semm. "Ovarian failure after hysterectomy." *The Journal of Reproductive Medicine*, 31 (1986): 597–600.

Siddle, N.; P. Sarrel; and M. Whitehead. "The effect of hysterectomy on the age at ovarian failure: Identification of a subgroup of women with premature loss of ovarian function and literature review." *Fertility and Sterility*, 47, no. 1 (January 1987).

Treloar, Allan. "Predicting the close of menstrual life" in A.M. Voda, M. Dinnerstein, and S.R. O'Donnell, eds., *Changing Perspectives on Menopause*. Austin, Texas: University of Texas Press, 1982.

CHAPTER 2

Ballinger, S.E. "A comparison of life stresses and symptomatology of menopause clinic patients and non-patients." Paper presented at the 4th International Congress on the Menopause, Buena Vista, Florida, 1984.

Carver, Cynthia. *Patient Beware*. Toronto: Prentice-Hall, 1984.

Dudley, R., and W. Rowland. *How to Find Relief from Migraine*. Toronto: Collins, 1982.

Feldman, B.M.; A.M. Voda; and E. Gronseth. "The prevalence of hot flash and associated variables among perimenopausal women." *Research in Nursing and Health*, 8 (1985): 261–68.

Gillespie, Larrian. *You Don't Have to Live with Cystitis*. New York: Rawson Associates, 1987.

Goldenberg, D. "Fibromyalgia Syndrome," *Jrnl. of Amer. Med. Assoc.*, 257, no. 20 (May 22–29, 1987): 2782–87.

Grushka, Miriam; Barry J. Sessle; and Rickey Miller. "Pain and personality profiles in burning mouth syndrome." *Journal of Pain*, 28, no. 2 (February 1987): 155–67.

Kronenberg, F.; L.J. Cote; and D.M. Linkie. "Menopausal hot flashes: Thermoregulatory, cardiovascular and circulating catecholamine and LH changes." *Maturitas*, 6, no. 1 (1984): 31–43.

Notelovitz, Morris, and Marsha Ware. *Stand Tall: The Informed Woman's Guide to Preventing Osteoporosis*. Gainesville: Triad Publishing, 1982.

Price, V.H. "Women and hair loss: Alopecia areata." *National Women's Health Report*, 3, no. 5 (May 1985).

Sacks, Oliver. *Migraine: Evolution of a Common Disorder*. London: Faber and Faber, 1970.

Voda, Ann M. "Menopausal hot flash," in A.M. Voda, M. Dinnerstein, and S.R. O'Donnell, eds., *Changing Perspectives on Menopause*. Austin, Texas: University of Texas Press, 1982.

Voda, A.M.; B.M. Feldman; and E. Gronseth. "Description of the hot flash: sensations, meaning and change in frequency across time." Paper presented at the 4th International Congress on the Menopause, Buena Vista, Florida, 1984.

Woods, Nancy Fugate. "Menopausal distress: A model for epidemiological investigation," in Voda, et al., eds., *Changing Perspectives on Menopause*.

CHAPTER 3

For an informational packet on osteoporosis ($5.50 in U.S. funds) write to Melpomene Institute for Women's Health Research, 2125 E. Hennepin Avenue, Minneapolis, MN 55413, U.S.A. Telephone: (612) 378-0545

For *Osteoporosis Update*, a periodic publication, write to the Osteoporosis Society of Canada (see page 200).

Ostop Ottawa, and two affiliated organizations, Ostop Regina and Ostop B.C., have a stronger self-help focus than the Osteoporosis Society but all of these organizations co-operate in providing information about osteoporosis and its prevention, as well as support for women with real or incipient osteoporotic conditions.

A self-help group called "Help for Incontinent People (HIP)" publishes a quarterly newsletter with tips about foods and products, which, as known bladder irritants, may contribute to urge or stress incontinence, and the latest news about treatments. Send a stamped (U.S. stamp if you have one), self-addressed envelope to HIP, Box 544, Union, South Carolina 29379, U.S.A. HIP also publishes a *Resource Guide of Continence Aids and Services*, available for $3.00 (U.S.).

The Migraine Foundation, 390 Brunswick Avenue, Toronto, Ontario M5R 2Z4. Telephone: (416) 920-4916. This organization will provide information about migraine, in all its forms, and names of neurologists who specialize in its diagnosis and treatment.

Interstitial Cystitis Association, P.O. Box 1553, Madison Sq. Station, New York, N.Y. 10159, provides educational information and publishes a quarterly newsletter called *ICA Update*.

...

Clarkes, Rebecca. *Directory of Health Care Practitioners*. Available for $2.95 from Alive Books, Box 67333, Vancouver, B.C. V5W 3T1. Telephone: (604) 321-4811

Cooperstock, R., and J. Hill. *The Effects of Tranquillization: Benzodiazepine Use in Canada* Ottawa: Health and Welfare, 1982. A booklet describing the high rates of tranquillizer use by women in Canada, and explaining how medical school teaches doctors to reach for a prescription pad instead of looking for more imaginative and health-giving treatments.

Gillespie, Larrian. *You Don't Have to Live With Cystitis*. New York: Rawson Associates, 1987.

Greenwood, Sadja. *Menopause Naturally: Preparing for the Second Half of Your Life* (2nd ed.). San Francisco: Volcano Press, 1988. Contains an excellent self-administered questionnaire to determine if hormone replacement therapy might be appropriate.

Seaman, Barbara, and Gideon Seaman. *Women and the Crisis in Sex Hormones*. New York: Rawson Associates, 1977. Always the most quoted work in the resistance to the profligate prescription of sex hormones for a "female complaint."

Voda, Ann M. *Menopause Me & You: A Personal Handbook for Women*. Sensible advice about coping with menopause. Available for $5.95 in U.S. funds from the author at the College of Nursing, University of Utah, 25 S. Medical Drive, Salt Lake City, Utah, 84112, U.S.A.

CHAPTER 4

Ballinger, S.E. "A comparison of life stresses and symptomatology of menopause clinic patients and non-patients." Paper presented at the 4th International Congress on the Menopause, Buena Vista, Florida, 1984.

Barbach, L., and L. Levine. *Shared Intimacies: Women's Sexual Experiences*. Toronto: Bantam Books, 1980.

Bart, Pauline B. "Depression in middle-aged women," in V.G. Gornick and B.K. Moran, eds., *Woman in Sexist Society*.

Channon, L.S., and S.E. Ballinger. "Some aspects of sexuality and vaginal symptoms during menopause and their relation to anxiety and depression." *British Journal of Medical Psychology*, 59 (1986): 173–80.

Chesler, Phyllis. *Women and Madness*. New York: Doubleday, 1972.

Johnson, Karen. "Women and depression." *Medical Self Care*, 28 (Spring 1985): 15.

Kitzinger, Sheila. *Woman's Experience of Sex*. New York: G.P. Putnam's Sons, 1983.

Lax, Ruth. "The expectable depressive climacteric reaction." *Bulletin of the Menninger Clinic*, 46, no. 2 (1982): 151–67.

Lewisohn, P.M., et al. "Age at first onset for nonbipolar depression." *Journal of Abnormal Psychology*, 95, no. 4 (1986): 378–83.

Luria, Zella, and R.G. Meade. "Sexuality and the middle-aged woman," in G. Baruch and J. Brooks-Gunn, eds., *Women in Midlife*. New York: Plenum Press, 1984.

Masters, W.; V. Johnson; and R. Kolodny. *Human Sexuality*, 2nd ed. Boston: Little Brown, 1985.

Scarf, Maggie. *Unfinished Business: Pressure Points in the Lives of Women*. New York: Doubleday, 1980.

Women and Psychotherapy: A Consumer Handbook. Available for $5.00 (U.S.) from the Federation of Organizations for Professional Women (FOPW), 2000 P Street NW, Suite 403, Washington, D.C. 20036, U.S.A.

CHAPTER 5

Back Association of Canada. "Osteoporosis: Prevention is the key." *Back to Back*, 4, no. 4 (December 1984).

DeFazio, J., and L. Speroff. "Estrogen Replacement Therapy: Current thinking and practice." *Geriatrics*, 40, no. 11 (November 1985).

Dejanikus, T. "Major drug manufacturer funds osteoporosis public education campaign." *The National Women's Health Network News*, May/June 1985.

"Estrogen Therapy: The dangerous road to Shangri-La." *Consumer Reports*, November 1976: 642–45.

Henig, Robin M. "Will estrogen keep you young?" *Woman's Day*: 64, April 30, 1985.

Jensen, J.; C. Christiansen; and P. Rodbro. "Cigarette smoking, serum estrogens and bone loss during hormone replacement therapy early after menopause." *The New England Journal of Medicine*, 313, no. 16 (October 17, 1985).

Kennedy, D.L., et al. "Noncontraceptive estrogens and progestins: use patterns over time." *Obstetrics and Gynecology*, 65, no. 3: 441–46.

Lindsay, R. "How calcium and estrogen combine to prevent osteoporosis." *Contemporary Obstetrics and Gynecology*, April 1986: 108–19.

Lucisano, A., et al. "Ovarian and peripheral androgen and estrogen levels in postmenopausal women: Correlations with ovarian histology." *Maturitas*, 8 (1986).

Osteoporosis Society of Canada. *Osteoporosis: How to Cope* and *Osteoporosis: Back to the Basics* (booklets that provide basic information about this condition. The address for the Osteoporosis Society can be found on page 200).

Reed, M.J., et al. "Estrogen production and metabolism in peri-menopausal women." *Maturitas*, 8 (1986).

Schiff, Isaac. "Estrogen replacement at menopause." *Harvard Medical School Health Letter*, 12, no. 1 (November 1986).

Shapiro, S., et al. "Risk of localized and widespread endometrial cancer in relation to recent and discontinued use of conjugated estrogens." *New England Journal of Medicine*, 313, no. 16 (October 17, 1985).

Sturtridge, W.C. "Osteoporosis: Its assessment, investigation, treatment and prevention." *Geriatric Medicine*, 1 (October 1985).

CHAPTER 6

Aitken, J.M., et al. "Osteoporosis after oophorectomy for non-malignant disease in premenopausal women." *British Medical Journal*, May 12, 1973.

"An alternative to hysterectomy?" *Healthfacts*, May 1986.

Amerikia, H., and T.N. Evans. "Ten-year review of hysterectomies: Trends, indications and risks." *American Journal of Obstet. Gynecol.*, 134 (1979): 431-37.

Cohen, S., and R. Soloway. "The epidemiology of gallstone disease." *Gallstones*. New York: Churchill Livingstone, 1985.

Curtis, L.R.; G.B. Curtis; and M.K. Beard. *My Body — My Decision: What You Should Know About the Most Common Female Surgeries*. Tucson, Arizona: The Body Press, 1986.

Endometriosis Association, P.O. Box 92187, Milwaukee, WI 53202, U.S.A. (See page 197).

"Gallstones: Are there alternatives to surgery?" *Harvard Medical School Health Letter*, 12, no. 10, August 1987.

HERS (Hysterectomy Educational Resources and Services), 422 Bryn Mawr Ave. Bala Cynwyd, PA 19004, U.S.A.

"Hysterectomy as Social Process." *Women & Health*, 10, no. 1, Spring 1985.

Krogh, Carmen M.E. *Compendium of Pharmaceuticals and Specialties*. Ottawa: Canadian Pharmaceutical Association, 1987.

McPherson, K., et al. "Regional variations in the use of common surgical procedures: within and between England and Wales, Canada and the United States of America." *Soc. Sci. Med.*, 15A (1981): 273–88.

Older, Julia. *Endometriosis: A Woman's Guide to a Common but Often Undetected Disease that Can Cause Infertility and Other Major Medical Problems*. New York: Scribner's, 1984.

Payer, Lynn. *How To Avoid a Hysterectomy: An Indispensable Guide to Exploring Your Options Before You Consent to a Hysterectomy*. New York: Pantheon, 1987.

Petersen, N., and B. Hasselbring, "Endometriosis Reconsidered." *Medical SelfCare*, 40 (May-June 1987): 30.

Reidel, H-H., et al. "Ovarian failure after hysterectomy." *Journal of Reproductive Medicine*, 31 (July 1986): 597–600.

Richards, D.H. "A post-hysterectomy syndrome." *The Lancet*, October 26, 1974.

Shainwald, Sybil. "A legal response to hysterectomy abuse." *The Network News*, May/June 1985.

Simon, J.A., and G.S. diZerega. "Physiologic estradiol replacement following oophorectomy: failure to maintain precastration gonadotropin levels." *Obstetrics and Gynecology*, 59, no. 4 (April 1982).

Stokes, Naomi Miller. *The Castrated Woman*. Toronto: Franklin Watts, 1986.

Tangedahl, T.N. "Therapeutic options for gallstones." *Postgraduate Medicine*, 81, no. 1 (January 1987).

Vayda, E.; M. Morison; and G.D. Anderson. "Surgical rates in the Canadian provinces, 1968 to 1972." *The Canadian Journal of Surgery*, May 1976.

Weinstein, Kate. *Living with Endometriosis: How to Cope with the Physical and Emotional Challenges*. Don Mills, Ont.: Addison-Wesley, 1987.

Weiss, N.S., and B.L. Harlow. "Why does hysterectomy without bilateral oophorectomy influence the subsequent incidence of ovarian cancer?" *American Journal of Epidemiology*, 124, no. 5 (November 1986).

CHAPTER 7

Alderson, J.W. "An indecent proposal." *Mother Jones*, May 1985.

Baines, Cornelia J. "Breast-cancer screening: Current evidence on mammography and implications for practice." *Canadian Family Physician*, 33 (April 1987).

Berkowitz, G.S., et al. "Estrogen replacement therapy and fibrocystic breast disease in postmenopausal women." *American Journal of Epidemiology*, 121, no. 2 (1985).

"Breast Self-Examination," "Breast Cancer," etc., leaflets available free of charge from the Canadian Cancer Society. See page 198.

Bush, T.L., and E. Barrett-Connor. "Noncontraceptive estrogen use and cardiovascular disease." *Epidemiologic Reviews*, The Johns Hopkins U. School of Hygiene and Public Health, 7 (1985): 80–104.

Canadian Heart Foundation, 1200-1 Nicholas Street, Ottawa, Ontario K2N 7B7. For a list of materials available from this organization, see page 198.

Cauley, J.A., et al. "The relationship of physical activity to high density lipoprotein cholesterol in post-menopausal women." *Journal of Chronic Disease*, 39, no. 9 (1986): 687–97.

Colditz, G.A., et al. "Menopause and the risk of coronary heart disease in women." *The New England Journal of Medicine*, 316, no. 18 (April 30, 1987).

"Coronary Risk Factors: A self-test," in R.M. Henig, *How a Woman Ages*. New York: Ballantine Books, 1985.

"Facts on Breast Cancer," a leaflet available from the Canadian Cancer Society.

Hasselbring, Bobbie. "New and improved breast self-examination.," *DES Action Voice*, #32 (Spring 1987).

Lapidus, L., et al. "Triglycerides — Main lipid risk factor for cardiovascular disease in women?" *Acta Med. Scand.*, 217 (1985): 481–89.

———. "Concentrations of sex-hormone binding globulin and corticosteroid binding globulin in serum in relation to cardiovascular risk factors and to 12-year incidence of cardiovascular disease and overall mortality in postmenopausal women." *Clinical Chemistry*, 32, no. 1 (1986): 146–52.

LaRosa, J.C. "Effect of estrogen replacement therapy on lipids: Implications for cardiovascular risk." *Journal of Reproductive Medicine*, 30, no. 10 (1985).

Lubin, F., et al. "Overweight and changes in weight throughout adult life in breast cancer etiology." *American Journal of Epidemiology*, 122, no. 4 (1985).

"New study questions breast cancer detection tests for young women but finds value to those over 50." *Healthfacts*, July 1987.

Pick, R. "Atherosclerosis: The risk factors for women." *The Female Patient*, 2 (1986): 60–71.

Sherman, B.; R. Wallace; and J. Bean. "Estrogen use and breast cancer: Interaction with body mass." *Cancer*, 51 (1983): 1527–31.

Silfverstolpe, G., and N. Crona. "Hormonal replacement therapy — cardiovascular disease." *Acta Obstet. Gynecol. Scand. Suppl.*, 134 (1986): 93–5.

Stampfer, et al. "A prospective study of postmenopausal estrogen therapy and coronary heart disease." *The New England Journal of Medicine*, October 24, 1985.

Vancouver Women's Health Collective, 1720 Grant St., 3rd floor, Vancouver, BC V5L 3Y2. *Breast Health Kit*. ($4.50 plus $1 postage and handling).

Wilson, P.W.F.; R.J. Garrison; and W.P. Castelli. "Postmenopausal estrogen use, cigarette smoking, and cardiovascular morbidity in women over 50: The Framingham Study." *The New England Journal of Medicine*, October 24, 1985.

Wingo, P.A., et al. "The risk of breast cancer in postmenopausal women who have used ERT." *Journal of the American Medical Association*, 257 (1987): 209–15.

CHAPTER 8

Brody, Jane E. "Exercise is the fountain of youth." *The New York Times*, June 10–11, 1986.

Davis, Adelle. *Let's Eat Right to Keep Fit*. New York: Harcourt Brace Jovanovich, 1970.

Dickinson, Annette. *Safety of Vitamins and Minerals: A Summary of the Findings of Key Reviews*. Council for Responsible Nutrition, Suite 602, 2100 M Street N.W., Washington, D.C. 20037, U.S.A.

"Focus on Physical Activity." *The Melpomene Report*, October 1985.

Fredericks, Carlton. *Dr. Carlton Fredericks' New and Complete Nutrition Handbook*, Major Books, 1978.

Fremes, R., and Z. Sabry. *NutriSCORE: The Rate Yourself Plan for Better Nutrition*, 2nd ed. Toronto: Methuen, 1981.

Lindsay, Anne. *Smart Cooking: Quick and Tasty Recipes for Healthy Eating*. Toronto: Macmillan of Canada, 1986.

Lindsay, Anne. *The Lighthearted Cookbook: Recipes for Healthy Heart Cooking*. Toronto: Key Porter Books, 1988.

Lock, Margaret, ed. "Anthropological approaches to menopause: Questioning received wisdom." Special issue of *Culture, Medicine and Psychiatry*, 10, no. 1 (March 1986).

Luce, Gay Gaer. "Exercises for vitality and flexibility," in *Your Second Life: Vitality and Growth in Middle and Later Years*. New York: Delta Books, 1979.

Mindell, Earl. *Vitamin Bible*. New York: Warner Books, 1979.

Pritikin, N., and P.M. McGrady, Jr. *The Pritikin Program for Diet and Exercise.* New York: Bantam Books, 1979.

Prudden, Bonnie. *Bonnie Prudden's After Fifty Fitness Guide.* New York: Ballantine Books, 1986.

Shephard, R.J. "Exercise and the aging process: Prescribing a programme." *Geriatric Medicine,* 1, October 1985.

Tufts University Diet and Nutrition Letter (see page 205).

CHAPTER 9

Brody, E.W., et al. "Women's changing roles and help to elderly parents: Attitudes of three generations of women." *Journal of Gerontology,* 38, no. 5 (September 1983).

Brown, Mackey. "Keeping marriage alive through middle age," in M.H. Huyck, ed., *Growing Older.* New York: Prentice-Hall, 1974.

Doering, C.H., et al. "A cycle of plasma testosterone in the human male." *Journal of Clinical and Endocrinological Metabolism,* 40 (1975): 492.

Donohugh, Donald L. *The Middle Years.* New York: Berkley Books, 1983.

Eichenbaum, Luise, and Susie Orbach. *What do Women Want?* New York: Coward-McCann Inc., 1983.

Gottlieb, Annie. "To Love, Honor and Respect." *McCall's,* April 1986.

Horowitz, A. "Sons and daughters as caregivers to older parents: Differences in role performance and consequences." *The Gerontologist,* 25, no. 6 (December 1985).

Irwin, Theodore. "Male 'menopause': crisis in the middle years." Public Affairs pamphlet #526 (381 Park Avenue South, New York, N.Y. 10016, U.S.A.).

Lang, A.M., and E.M. Brody. "Characteristics of middle-aged daughters and help to their elderly mothers." *Journal of Marriage and the Family,* 45, no. 1 (February 1983).

Lear, Martha Weinman. "Is there a male menopause?" *The New York Times Magazine,* January 28, 1973.

Levinson, D.J., et al. *The Seasons of a Man's Life.* New York: Alfred A. Knopf, 1978.

Lowenthal, M.F.; M. Thurnher; and D. Chiriboga. *Four Stages of Life: A Comparative Study of Men and Women Facing Transitions.* San Francisco: Jossey-Bass, 1977.

Montagnes, A. "When elderly parents need care." *Chatelaine,* September 1984.

Moss, M.S. "The quality of relationships between elderly parents and their out-of-town children." *The Gerontologist,* 25, no. 2 (April 1985).

Notman, M. "Is there a male menopause?" In L. Rose, ed., *The Menopause Book.* New York: Hawthorn Books, 1977.

Peterson, James A. "Marriage and love in the middle years." Public Affairs pamphlet #456 (381 Park Avenue South, New York, N.Y. 10016, U.S.A.).

Ragan, P.K., ed. *Aging Parents.* California: Ethel Percy Andrus Gerontology Center, U. of Cal. Press, 1979.

Rosenthal, C.J. "Family supports in later life: Does ethnicity make a difference?" *The Geronologist*, 26, no. 1 (February 1986).

Rubin, L.B. *Intimate Strangers: Men and Women Together.* New York: Harper & Row, 1983.

————. *Just Friends: The Role of Friendship in Our Lives.* New York: Harper & Row, 1985.

Sanford, Linda Tschirhart, and Mary Ellen Donovan. *Women and Self-Esteem.* New York: Anchor Press, 1984.

Sheehy, Gail. *Passages: Predictable Crises of Adult Life.* New York: Bantam Books, 1976.

Silver, V. "The other generation gap." *Homemaker's*, 1985.

CHAPTER 10

ADOCE (Association des opérés en chirurgie esthétique), P.O. Box 230, 5135 Jean Talon East, Montreal, PQ H1S 2Z4. A nonprofit agency established to inform, warn, and protect patients who are contemplating cosmetic surgery or who have undergone it. It provides documentation and advice upon request. Membership costs $25.

Association of Plastic Surgeons of Quebec, 2 Complexe Desjardins, #3000, Montreal, Quebec H5B 1G8. Telephone (514) 845-2474

Baruch, Grace, and Jeanne Brooks-Gunn, eds. *Women in Midlife.* New York: Plenum Press, 1984.

Beeson, W.H., and E.G. McCullough. *Aesthetic Surgery of the Aging Face.* St. Louis: C.V. Mosby, 1986.

Berkun, Cleo S. "Changing appearance for women in the mid-years of life: Trauma?" in E. Markson, ed., *Older Women.*

Canadian Society of Facial Plastic Surgeons (Dr. Peter Adamson), P.O. Box 47, Toronto-Dominion Centre, Toronto, Ont. M5K 1B7. Telephone (416) 363-1716

Canadian Society of Plastic Surgeons (Dr. Douglas, Secretary/Treasurer), Room 324, E.K. Jones Bldg., 160 Wellesley St. East, Toronto, Ontario M4Y 1J3. Telephone (416) 926-4890

Chernin, Kim. *The Obsession: Reflections on the Tyranny of Slenderness.* New York: Harper Colophon, 1981.

Cohen, Leah. *Small Expectations.* Toronto: McClelland and Stewart, 1984.

Fairhurst, Eileen. "Mutton dressed as lamb: The social construction of aging." Paper presented at the 1st International Conference on the Future of Adult Life, Noordwijkerhout, The Netherlands, April 1987.

Henig, Robin Marantz. *The Myth of Senility: The Truth about the Brain and Aging* (rev. ed.). Glenview, Ill.: Scott, Foresman, 1985.

Lapointe, Philippe. "Cosmetic Surgery." *Protect Yourself,* March 1986.

LeGuin, Ursula K. "On Menopause: The space crone." *Medical Self Care.* Winter 1981.

Melamed, Elissa. *Mirror, Mirror: The Terror of Not Being Young.* New York: Linden Press, 1983.

Novak, Mark. *Successful Aging: The Myths, Realities and Future of Aging in Canada.* Markham, Ontario: Penguin, 1985.

"Ready for a miracle?" *Canadian Living*, 9, no. 10 (November 5, 1984).

Rees, T.D., and D. Wood-Smith. *Cosmetic Facial Surgery.* Philadelphia: W.B. Saunders, 1973.

Royal College of Physicians and Surgeons of Canada, 74 Stanley Ave., Ottawa, Ont. K1M 1P4. Telephone (613) 746-8177

Rubin, L.B. *Women of a Certain Age: The Midlife Search for Self.* New York: Harper Colophon, 1979.

Sontag, Susan. "The double standard of aging." *Saturday Review*, September 23, 1972: 182–90.

Stehlin, Dale. "Erasing wrinkles: Easier said than done." *FDA Consumer*, July/August 1987.

Teimourian, Dr. B. *Suction Lipectomy and Body Contouring.* St. Louis, Mo.: C.V. Mosby, 1987.

RECOMMENDED RESOURCES

CHAPTER 11

1. General materials about women's health and/or menopause. Each is worth having as a ready reference or as a source of information for a workshop or self-help group.

Boston Women's Health Book Collective. *The New Our Bodies Ourselves.* New York: Simon and Schuster, 1984. The best-known reference on issues dealing with women's health.

Feltin, Marie, M.D. *A Woman's Guide to Good Health After 50.* Glenview, Ill.: Scott Foresman, 1987. Good all-around reference book.

Gannon, Linda R. *Menstrual Disorders and Menopause: Biological, Psychological and Cultural Research.* New York: Praeger Publishers, 1985. Heavily academic but a refreshing change from the purely medical view of woman's reproductive life.

Greenwood, Sadja. *Menopause Naturally: Preparing for the Second Half of Your Life*, 2nd ed. San Francisco: Volcano Press, 1988. Contains an excellent self-administered questionnaire to determine if hormone replacement therapy might be appropriate.

Henig, Robin Marantz. *How a Woman Ages: What to Expect and What You can do About It.* New York: Ballantine Books, 1985. This is the companion volume to *How a Man Ages* and both are good to have around the house.

McDonnell, Kathleen, and Mariana Valverde, eds. *The Healthsharing Book: Resources for Canadian Women.* Toronto: Women's Press, 1985.

Trien, Susan Flamholtz. *Change of Life: The Menopause Handbook.* New York: Fawcett, Columbine, 1986. A well-written account of all aspects of menopause.

Vancouver Women's Health Collective. *The Menopause Kit,* 1720 Grant St., 3rd floor, Vancouver, B.C. V5L 3Y2 ($4.50 plus $1 for postage and handling). Excellent material for use in a workshop; includes suggestions for organizing a menopause support group.

Voda, Ann M. *Menopause Me & You: A Personal Handbook for Women.* College of Nursing, University of Utah, 25 S. Medical Drive, Salt Lake City, Utah 48112, U.S.A. ($5.95 U.S.). Contains excellent advice and charts for monitoring and understanding hot flashes.

Woods, Nancy Fugate. "Menopausal distress: A model for epidemiological investigation," in Voda et al., eds., *Changing Perspectives on Menopause.* Austin, Texas: University of Texas Press, 1982. A summary of menopausal symptoms as derived from a review of many menopause research studies.

Weideger, Paula. *Menstruation and Menopause: The Physiology and Psychology, the Myth and the Reality.* New York: Alfred Knopf, 1976. Examines social attitudes toward menstruation and menopause: an early and thoughtful approach that has had an enormous influence on subsequent writers.

Weiss, Kay, ed. *Women's Health Care: A Guide to Alternatives.* Reston, Va.: Reston Publishing Co., 1984. There are other options and this book explores them for you.

2. Books or booklets that deal with specific issues of interest to individuals or groups.

Carver, Cynthia. *Patient Beware.* Toronto: Prentice-Hall, 1984. This book, written by a doctor, gives excellent advice on how to choose a doctor and what to expect when receiving medical care.

Cooperstock, R., and J. Hill. *The Effects of Tranquillization: Benzodiazepine Use in Canada.* Ottawa: Health and Welfare, 1982. A booklet describing the high rates of tranquillizer use by women in Canada, and explaining how medical school teaches doctors to reach for a prescription pad instead of looking for more imaginative and health-giving treatments. Available from your regional office of the Health Promotion Directorate, Health and Welfare Canada.

Corea, Gina. *Women's Health Care: The Hidden Malpractice.* New York: Wm. Morrow, 1977. An investigative report of the role of American medicine in the medical treatment of women, past and present.

Doress, Paula Brown, and Diana Laskin Siegal (and the Midlife and Older Women Book Project). *Ourselves Growing Older.* New York: Simon and Schuster, 1987. A book written in co-operation with the Boston Women's Health Book Collective and focusing on health and medical information for the older woman.

Dreifus, Claudia, ed. *Seizing Our Bodies: The Politics of Women's Health.* New York: Random House, Vintage Books, 1977. Since 93 per cent of gynaecologists are men, nearly every woman must deal with a masculine point of view at the most critical times of her life: when she needs contraception, when she gives birth, when she enters menopause. This explains why and how woman should regain control of their bodies.

Ehrenreich, Barbara, and Deirdre English. *Complaints and Disorders: The Sexual Politics of Sickness* (Glass Mountain Pamphlet No. 2). Brooklyn, N.Y.: Faculty Press, 1973. A review of the medical treatment of women from the late nineteenth century into the early part of the twentieth century.

Ehrenreich, Barbara, and Deirdre English. *For Her Own Good: 150 years of the experts' advice to women.* New York: Anchor Books, 1979. The title of the book tells it all. Fascinating.

Nellis, Muriel. *The Female Fix.* Pennsylvania: Penguin Books, 1980. An insightful discussion of women's drug and alcohol problems.

Payer, Lynn. *How to Avoid a Hysterectomy: An Indispensable Guide to Exploring All Your Options Before You Consent to a Hysterectomy.* Toronto: Random House, 1987. An invaluable book for the woman contemplating (or being pressured into) surgery.

Scully, Diana H. *Men Who Control Women's Health.* Boston: Houghton Mifflin, 1980. An inside look at the way gynaecologists are trained.

Seaman, Barbara, and Gideon Seaman. *Women and the Crisis in Sex Hormones.* New York: Rawson Associates, 1977. Always the most quoted work in the resistance to the profligate prescription of sex hormones for a "female complaint."

Vancouver Women's Health Collective. *Breast Health Kit.* 1720 Grant St., 3rd floor, Vancouver, B.C. V5L 3Y2 ($4.50 plus $1 postage and handling). Wide range of materials and easy to understand.

3. Materials useful for planning a series of workshops or for setting up a self-help group.

a. *Workshops*

Bolton, Valerie. *'Women Being Well' Training Guide: Facilitator Training and Organizational Skills for Women Establishing Mutual Aid Support Groups.* Women Being Well, P.O. Box 1405, Clinton, Ont. N0M 1L0

Lopez, Maria Cristina, et al. *Menopause: A Self-Care Manual.* Available for $5.00 (U.S.) from the Santa Fe Health Education Project, P.O. Box 577, Santa Fe, New Mexico 87502, U.S.A.

Thomson, Sidney. "Sharing the menopause experience." *Healthsharing,* Winter 1986: 10–13

b. *Self-Help Groups*

Hill, Karen. *Helping You Helps Me: A guide book for self-help groups.* Available free from Canadian Council on Social Development, P.O. Box 3505, Station C, Ottawa Ont. K1Y 4G1

Lopez, Maria Cristina, et al. *Menopause: A Self-Care Manual* (see listing above).

North Island Women's Services Society. *Working Together for Change: Women's self-help handbook and training manual.* A four-book set available from Ptarmigan Press, 1372 Island Highway, Campbell River, British Columbia V9Z 1X9, for $40 (U.S. funds) plus $3 for shipping and handling.

Romeder, Jean-Marie. *Self-help Groups in Canada.* Available free from Program Information Unit, Social Services Directorate, Health and Welfare Canada, 7th floor, Brooke Claxton Building, Ottawa, Ont. K1A 1B5

Vancouver Women's Health Collective. *Facilitating Self-Help Workshops: Workshop Kit and Guide.* Available for $4.50 (plus $1 postage and handling) from 1720 Grant St., 3rd floor, Vancouver, B.C. V5L 3Y2

Women's Counselling, Referral, and Education Centre (WCREC). *Helping Ourselves: A handbook for women starting groups.* Available from Women's Press, 229 College Street, #204, Toronto, Ont. M5T 1R4, for $8.95.

4. Films and videotapes useful for information and for attracting women to a discussion on menopause.

The Best Time of My Life: A portrait of women in mid-life. Patricia Watson, director (58 minutes). A look at women dealing with mid-life and menopause; the women reflect a range of family lifestyles, careers, and experiences. Available for sale or rent from the National Film Board. *

Brittle with Age: The unnecessary tragedy of osteoporosis. N.J. Hall and R.E. Foushee, directors (23 minutes). Focusing on the personal experiences of osteoporosis patients, this videotape (available in VHS, ¾ inch, and Beta) emphasizes the value of education as a preventative tool for this debilitating bone disease. Available for rent at $50 (U.S.), or $35 (U.S.) for non-profit organizations, from Melpomene Institute, Minneapolis (see listing under U.S. Organizations).

Brittle Bones (22 minutes). Film or videotape available from Visual Education Centre, 75 Horner Avenue, Unit 1, Toronto, Ont. M8Z 4X5. Telephone (416) 252-5907.

D.E.S.: An uncertain legacy. Bonnie Andrukaitis, director (54 minutes). A study of the development, marketing, and medical consequences of DES (diethylstilbestrol), a synthetic estrogen prescribed to millions of pregnant women between 1941 and 1971 to prevent miscarriage. Available for sale or rent from the National Film Board* or through your local DES Action chapter (see listing under Canadian Organizations).

Is It Hot in Here? Laura Alper and Haida Paul, directors (36 minutes). An informative and sometimes humorous look at menopause as revealed primarily through women's own experiences. Available for sale or rent from the National Film Board. *

The Menopause Story. Marilyn Belec, director (30 minutes). Film available from Mobius Productions, 188 Davenport Rd., Toronto, Ont. M5R 1J2. Telephone (416) 964-8484.

Stalking the Silent Thief: Osteoporosis (26 minutes), *Osteoporosis: What is it?* (14 minutes), *Exercise for Osteoporosis* (21 minutes), *Nutrition for Osteoporosis* (18 minutes), and *Coping with Osteoporosis* (16 minutes). Videotapes available in VHS, Beta, or ¾ inch. The first is $25 for Beta or VHS, and $40 for ¼ inch. The

---

* There are regional NFB offices in St. John's, Corner Brook, Charlottetown, Halifax, Sydney, Moncton, Saint John, Chicoutimi, Rimouski, Sherbrooke, Trois-Rivières, Rouyn, Quebec City, Montreal, Toronto, Hamilton, Kingston, Kitchener, London, North Bay, Thunder Bay, Ottawa, Winnipeg, Regina, Saskatoon, Calgary, Edmonton, Vancouver, Prince George, and Victoria. NFB films are also available in New York City.

others are $30 each in all formats, from the Osteoporosis Society of Canada, 76 St. Clair Ave. West, Suite 502, Toronto, Ont. M4V 1N2.

Tai Chi Instructional Video (58 minutes). An introduction to the history, purposes, and benefits of Tai Chi; a description of the positions and stances; and a demonstration of 108 movements. Available from James Houston, 750A Yonge St., Toronto, Ont. M4Y 2B6, for $59 plus $3 for shipping and handling.

Turning Fifty ("Demain la cinquantaine"). Hélène Roy, director (43 minutes). An attractive woman meets middle age; this fictional account stresses the new learning, new feelings, and changing relationships that often occur as women encounter menopause. Available in VHS, ¾ inch, or Beta from Vidéo Femmes, 56 St-Pierre, #203, Quebec City, PQ G1K 4A1.

Yes, You Can (30 minutes). A film about coping with osteoporosis and highlighting the story of Lindy Fraser, the founder of OSTOP Ottawa. Available from Audio-Visual Services, Health and Welfare Canada, Ottawa, Ont. Telephone (613) 993-6951.

5. Organizations dealing with women's health. Some publish a newsletter, some provide information, some are local organizations that run workshops or sponsor self-help groups.

a. *International Organizations*

International Menopause Society, 8, avenue Don Bosco, 1150 Brussels, Belgium. The primary objective of the IMS is to promote the study of all aspects of the climacteric in both men and women but, in practice, the society (which is composed primarily of gynaecologists) promotes the study of medical intervention in the female menopause. It holds a congress every third year, the next one scheduled for 1990 in Bangkok. Membership is 50 Swiss francs per year entitling one to regular IMS newsletters or, for a membership fee of $129 (U.S.), one may also receive *Maturitas: International journal for the study of the climacteric* (Elsevier Science Publishers, Box 211, 1000 AE Amsterdam, The Netherlands.)

Isis International, Via San Saba 5, 00153 Rome, Italy. A women's information and communication service. Publishes the Isis International Women's Book Series twice yearly, in English and Spanish.

Isis International: the Latin American and Caribbean Women's Health Network, Casilla 2067, Correo Centrale, Santiago, Chile. Publishes the *Women's Health Journal* (English and Spanish) six times yearly, $20 (U.S.) per year, plus $5 (U.S.) for air-mail charges.

WEMOS/HAI, International Women's Network on Pharmaceuticals, P.O. Box 4098, 1009 BA Amsterdam, The Netherlands. Organized to provide information on drugs and to stimulate research on non-drug alternatives.

Women's Global Network on Reproductive Rights, P.O. Box 4098, 1009 AB Amsterdam, The Netherlands.

Women's Health Information Centre, 52 Featherstone St., London, EC1, England. Membership entitles you to WHIC Newsletter (three times yearly) plus fact sheets and broadsheets published during that year. Membership is £7 for individuals, £10 for institutions.

b. *U.S. Organizations*
The Boston Women's Health Book Collective, P.O.Box 192 (240A Elm Street),
West Somerville, MA 02144. Information requests to (617) 625-0271.

The Coalition for the Medical Rights of Women, 2845 24th Street, San
Francisco, CA 94110 U.S.A. Telephone (415) 826-4401. A nonprofit grassroots
organization in operation since 1975.

HERS (Hysterectomy Educational Resources and Services), 422 Bryn Mawr
Avenue, Bala Cynwyd, PA 19004, U.S.A. Publishes a quarterly newsletter ($12
U.S. per year) and sponsors occasional seminars. Will also supply reprints of
articles on specific topics.

HIP (Help for Incontinent People), Box 544, Union, SC 29379, U.S.A. Publishes
a quarterly newsletter and a *Resource Guide of Continence Aids & Services* ($3
U.S.).

Melpomene Institute for Women's Health Research, 2125 E. Hennepin Avenue,
Minneapolis, MN 55413. Sponsors research on women's health with a special
interest in exercise, occasional weekend seminars on a variety of topics, and a
publication appearing three times annually, *Melpomene Report* (see listing under
Newsletters and Periodicals).

National Action Forum for Midlife and Older Women, Box 816, Stony Brook,
NY 11790-0609. Publishes a quarterly newsletter, *Hot Flash* (see Newsletters and
Periodicals), and is in the process of forming an International Action Forum for
Midlife and Older Women.

National Association for Obstetric, Gynecologic, and Neonatal Nurses (NAACOG),
600 Maryland Ave., SW, Suite 200 East, Washington, DC 20024-2589. Publishes
a newsletter and a journal. NAACOG also includes a Canadian group, COGNN.

National Women's Health Network, 1325 G St., N.W., Lower Level,
Washington, D.C. 20005. Membership to the network and receipt of their
bimonthly publication costs $25 (U.S.) per year for individuals, $35 (U.S.) for
consumer groups or women's health organizations (see listing under Newsletters
and Periodicals).

Society for Menstrual Cycle Research, c/o Mary Anna Friederich, M.D., 4304 N.
Cactus, 408B, Phoenix, AZ 85032, U.S.A. Membership is $20 (U.S.) per year,
which entitles you to a quarterly newsletter and news about the annual conference
held early in June.

Women's Association for Research in Menopause (W.A.R.M.), Parkeast Executive
Center, 128 East 56th St., New York, NY 10022, U.S.A. This organization was
founded by Fredi Kronenberg, Ph.D., who does research on hot flashes at
Columbia University College of Physicians and Surgeons. WARM was organized to
form support groups, raise funds for research into hot flashes, and to educate both
the medical and nonmedical communities about menopause.

c. *North American Organizations*
Endometriosis Association, U.S./Canada Headquarters, P.O. Box 92187,
Milwaukee, WI 53202, U.S.A. Telephone 1-800-426-2END (Canada) or
1-800-992-ENDO (U.S.A.) Publishes regular bulletins, leaflets ("How Can I Tell

If I Have Endometriosis?") and a book, *Overcoming Endometriosis* ($8.95). The association acts as a support network, with regional chapters — including four in Canada (B.C., Alberta, Saskatchewan, and Southern Ontario) — and names and numbers of women who are willing to handle "crisis calls." The association will also provide information about doctors skilled in diagnosing and treating endometriosis.

d. *Canadian Organizations*

ADOCE (Association des opérés en chirurgie esthétique), P.O. Box 230, 5135 Jean Talon East, Montreal, PQ H1S 2Z4. A nonprofit agency established to inform, warn, and protect patients who are contemplating cosmetic surgery or who have undergone it. It provides documentation and advice upon request. Membership costs $25.

Allergy Information Association, 65 Tromley Drive, Suite 10, Etobicoke, Ont. M9B 5Y7. Telephone (416) 244-8585. Provides information on all aspects of allergy, organizes seminars, provides resource material. Annual membership fee of $25 includes a quarterly newsletter.

Association of Plastic Surgeons of Quebec, 2 Complexe Desjardins, #3000, Montreal, Que. H5B 1G8. Telephone (514) 845-2474.

Canadian Advisory Council on the Status of Women, 110 O'Connor, 9th floor, Ottawa, Ont. K1P 5M9. Telephone (613) 992-4975. A paragovernmental body, consisting of thirty members appointed by the government, and reporting to the Minister Responsible for the Status of Women. Regional Offices are in Montreal (2021 Union Ave., Suite 875, Montreal H3A 2C1. Telephone 514-283-3123), in Winnipeg (269 Main St., Suite 600, Winnipeg R3C 1B2. Telephone 204-949-3140), and in Calgary (220-465th Ave., Suite 270, Calgary T2P 2L6. Telephone 403-292-6668).

Canadian Cancer Society. Offices in St. John's, Saint John, Halifax, Charlottetown, Montreal, Toronto, Winnipeg, Calgary, and Vancouver. Booklets on breast cancer, breast self-examination, the Pap test, etc.

Canadian College of Natural Healing, 380 Forest St., Ottawa, Ont. K2B 8E6. Telephone (613) 820-0318

Canadian Health Coalition, 2842 Riverside Drive, Ottawa, Ont. K1V 8X7. Telephone (613) 521-3400, Ext. 227. Group formed to educate the general public about threats to the medicare system. Publishes *Medicare Monitor*. Subscriptions are $15.00 annually.

Canadian Heart Foundation. Head Office, 1200-1 Nicholas Street, Ottawa, Ont. K2N 7B7. This organization publishes a booklet, *Your Heart*, a series of pamphlets: "A Statement on Cardiovascular Risk Factors," "Food and Your Heart," "Smoking and Heart Disease," "Children and Smoking: A Message to Parents," etc., as well as a "Fitness Wheel," a way of calculating optimum diet and exercise for a healthy heart. All of these materials are available free of charge either from the head office, or from regional offices in St. John's, Charlottetown, Saint John, Halifax, Montreal, Toronto, Winnipeg, Saskatoon, Calgary, and Vancouver.

Canadian Obstetric, Gynecological and Neonatal Nurses (COGNN), an organization under the umbrella of NAACOG. There are plans to publish a newsletter.

Canadian PID Society, Box 33804, Station D, Vancouver, B.C. V6J 4L6. Telephone (416) 684-5704. Information about pelvic inflammatory disease and its consequences.

Canadian Society of Facial Plastic Surgeons (Dr. Peter Adamson) P.O. Box 47, Toronto-Dominion Centre, Toronto, Ont. M5K 1B7. Telephone (416) 363-1716.

Canadian Society of Plastic Surgeons (Dr. Douglas, Secretary/Treasurer), Room 324, E.K. Jones Bldg., 160 Wellesley St. East, Toronto, Ont. M4Y 1J3. Will provide names of accredited plastic surgeons in your area.

Canadian Coalition on Depo Provera, c/o Women's Health Interaction Manitoba, 1031 Portage Ave., Winnipeg, Man. R3G 0R8. Telephone (204) 786-2106. Women's health activist group lobbying against the approval of Depo Provera (injectable synthetic progesterone) for use as a contraceptive.

Canadian Congress for Learning Opportunities for Women (CCLOW), 47 Main St., Toronto, Ont. M4E 2V6. Telephone (416) 669-1909. Branches in Newfoundland, Nova Scotia, New Brunswick, P.E.I., Ontario, Saskatchewan, and B.C.

Canadian Network for Disease Information, 34 Bayview Dr., St. Catharines, Ont. L2N 4Y6. A new organization to co-ordinate health information so that individuals may enquire about services, organizations, and/or groups available for specific health needs.

Canadian Public Health Association, 1335 Carling Ave., #210, Ottawa, Ont. K1Z 8N8. Telephone (613) 725-3769. Nonprofit organization seeking to improve personal and community health.

Canadian Research Institute for the Advancement of Women (CRIAW), Suite 415, 151 Slater St., Ottawa, Ont. K1P 5H3. Encourages, promotes, and disseminates research into women's experience. Publishes a newsletter, the CRIAW papers, and *Feminist Perspectives*.

Candida Research and Information Foundation (CRIF), 598 St. Clair Ave., West, 3rd floor, Toronto, Ont. M6C 1A6. Telephone (416) 656-0047. Information about diagnosis and treatment of chronic yeast infections.

Council on Aging, 256 King Edward Ave., Ottawa, Ont. K1N 7M1. Telephone (613) 232-3577.

DES Action/Canada, Snowdon P.O. Box 233, Montreal, Que., H3X 3T4. Telephone (514) 482-3204. Dedicated to information about DES, a synthetic estrogen prescribed between 1941 and 1971 to prevent miscarriage; also attempts to locate and counsel the children of women who were given DES. There are DES/Action groups in Port aux Basques, Greenwood, Montreal, Nepean, Ottawa, Toronto, Thunder Bay, Winnipeg, Regina, Calgary and Vancouver. The head office publishes a quarterly newsletter and can put you in touch with your local representatives. DES Action USA also publishes a quarterly newsletter, *DES Action Voice*.

Disabled Women's Network (DAWN), 776 E. Georgia Street, Vancouver, B.C. V6A 2A3. Telephone (604) 254-3585. Organized by and comprised of disabled women.

Endometriosis Toronto, P.O. Box 3135, Markham Industrial Park, Markham, Ont.

L3R 6G5. (For more information, see entry under North American organizations. The Toronto chapter is the first one to have its own mailing address. Other chapters have individual representatives who work from their own homes.)

Health League of Canada, 1560 Bayview Ave., Suite 304, Toronto, Ont. M4G 3B8. Telephone (416) 486-6023. A citizens' committee of the World Health Organization, the Health League promotes health education and information; membership is $10 and includes a newsletter, *Health News Digest*, published six times yearly.

Interstitial Cystitis Association, Box 5814, Station A, Toronto, Ont. M5W 1P2. Provides information and/or help in forming support groups.

The Migraine Foundation, 390 Brunswick Avenue, Toronto, Ont. M5R 2Z4. Telephone (416) 920-4916. This organization will provide information about migraine, in all its forms, and names of neurologists who specialize in its diagnosis and treatment.

National Action Committee on the Status of Women, Health Committee, 344 Bloor St. W., Suite 505, Toronto, Ont. M5S 1W9. Telephone (416) 922-3246. NAC is a voluntary, feminist, nongovernmental organization and represents more than five hundred nongovernmental groups.

National Cancer Institute of Canada, 77 Bloor St. West, Suite 1702, Toronto, Ont. M5S 3A1 (see also the Canadian Cancer Society).

Older Women's Network, P.O. Box 317, Station Z, Toronto, Ont. M5N 2Z5. Telephone (416) 483-3234. Organized to encourage and correspond with small groups of women aged 55+, meeting in each other's homes, with a view to public discussion of and action on issues affecting older women.

One Voice, 350 Sparks St., Ottawa, Ont. K1R 7S8. A lobbying organization for seniors.

Osteoporosis Society of Canada, Suite 502, 76 St. Clair Ave. W., Toronto, Ont. M4V 1N2. Telephone (416) 922-1358. There are chapters of the Society in Alberta (Box 226, Calgary, Alta. T2G 0W2. Telephone 403-284-3113), Manitoba (P.O. Box 2099, Winnipeg, Man. R3C 3R4. Telephone 204-888-3928) and Quebec (2170 Lincoln Ave., PH2, Montreal, Que. H3H 2N5. Telephone 514-935-3726).

Sex Information and Education Council of Canada (SIECCAN), 150 Laird Dr. Toronto, Ont. M4G 3V7. Publishes the SIECCAN *Journal*.

WHOLE (Holistic Health Organization and Learning Exchange), 75 Rosemount Dr., Scarborough, Ont. M1K 2X4. Telephone (416) 759-4595. Organizes meetings and workshops on organic, holistic, and alternative health practices.

Women's Health Interaction, 58 Arthur St., Ottawa, Ont. K1R 7B9. Telephone (613) 563-4801. Publishes an occasional newsletter.

e. *Regional and Local Organizations.* Some of these have been formed to deal with general issues of interest to women; some focus on health issues. The listings run from east to west.

East Prince Women's Information Centre, 240 Water St., Summerside, P.E.I. C1N 1B3. Telephone (902) 436-9856

Second Story Women's Centre, 9 Dominion St., Bridgewater, N.S. B4V 2J6. Telephone (902) 543-1315

Women Unlimited, P.O. Box 368, Sydney, N.S. B1P 6H2

Women's Health Education Network, Box 2280, Stellarton, N.S. B0K 1S0 Publishes a quarterly bulletin, *Vitality* (Box 99, Debert, N.S. B0M 1G0). $10 per year.

Healthfest, c/o Jane Haliburton, Box 772, Middleton, N.S. B0S 1P0. Telephone (902) 825-6875

Reproductive Health Centre, 74 Water St., P.O. Box 278, Campbellton, N.B. E3N 1B1

PMS Self-Help, R.R. #1, Alcove, Que. J0X 1A0. Telephone (819) 459-3388

Women's Information and Referral Centre, 3585 St-Urbain, Montreal, Que. H2X 2N6. Telephone (514) 844-1761. Home of *Communiqu'ELLES*, published monthly by Les Editions Communiqu'ELLES, $12 per year.

Association of Concerned Citizens for Preventive Medicine, 415B McArthur Avenue, Ottawa, Ont. K1K 1G5. Telephone (613) 749-1002

Ottawa Holistic Living Association, Box 147, Station B, Ottawa, Ont. K1P 6C3. Telephone (613) 837-2690

Women's Place, 242 Besserer, Ottawa, Ont. K1N 6B1. Telephone (613) 238-2882

OSTOP Ottawa, a self-help group for women interested in knowing more about osteoporosis, how to prevent it or how to deal with it. c/o Good Campanion Centre, 670 Albert St., Ottawa K1R 6L2. Telephone (613) 236-0428

Kingston Women's Health Collective, 99 York St., Kingston, Ont. K7K 1P9. Telephone (613) 542-1136

Sudbury Women's Centre, 160 Minto St., Sudbury, Ont. P3E 3G7. Telephone (705) 673-1916

Women's Health Care Centre, Peterborough Civic Hospital, Weller Street, Peterborough, Ont. K9J 7C6. Director: Susan Law.

Ontario Herbalist Association, General Delivery, Jackson's Point, Ont. L0E 1L0. Telephone (416) 722-8604. Information and educational organization for use of herbs and herbal medicines.

Hersize: A weight prejudice action group, 223 Concord Avenue, Toronto, Ont. M6H 2P4. Telephone (416) 535-4653 or 535-2722. Dedicated to increasing public awareness of fat oppression, freeing women from over-concern with body size and shape, and preventing eating disorders.

Toronto Women's Health Network, c/o L. Spring, 1884 Davenport Road, Toronto, Ont. M6N 4Y2. Telephone (416) 392-0898. Umbrella network of individuals and women's health organizations. Publishes a monthly newsletter. $15 annually.

Medical Reform Group, P.O. Box 366, Station J, Toronto, Ont. M4J 4Y8. A group of physicians committed to more equal access to health care and more emphasis on preventive aspects.

Ontario College of Naturopathic Medicine, 60 Berl Ave., Toronto, Ont. M8Y 3C7. Telephone (416) 251-5261. A training facility for practitioners of naturopathy.

Patients' Rights Association, 40 Homewood Avenue, No. 315, Toronto, Ont. M4Y 2K2. Telephone (416) 923-9629. Formed to protect the rights of Ontario patients; membership is $15, entitling you to their newsletter *The Patient's Advocate*.

Women's Health Centre, St. Joseph's Hospital, 30 The Queensway, Toronto, Ont. M6R 1B5. Director: Suzanne Boggild.

Women's Health Centre, Women's College Hospital, 790 Bay Street, 8th Floor, Toronto, Ont. M5G 1N9. Program Director: Zubeida Ramji.

Women's Health Bureau, Ontario Ministry of Health. Telephone (416) 965-0460. A policy advising group within the ministry that works with government officials and community groups.

Women Today, Box 1405, Clinton, Ont. N0M 1L0. Telephone (519) 482-9706

Northwestern Ontario Women's Health Information Network, 8A N. Cumberland St., Suite 17, Thunder Bay, Ont. P7A 4L1. Telephone (807) 345-1410. Publishes a quarterly newsletter, *Health Network News*, $5 per year.

Women's Health Interaction Manitoba, 1031 Portage Ave., Winnipeg, Man. R3G 0R8. Telephone (204) 786-2106.

Women's Health Clinic 304-414 Graham Ave., Winnipeg, Man. R3C 0L8. Telephone (204) 947-1517. A comprehensive health centre for women offering a wide range of medical, educational, counselling, and support services.

Gatekeepers, 301-83 Churchill Dr., Thompson, Man. R8N 0L6. Telephone (204) 778-8713

Regina Healthsharing, P.O. Box 734, Regina, Sask. S4P 3A8. Telephone (306) 352-8397

Regina OSTOP, #8-2700 Montague St., Regina, Sask. S4S 0J9. Telephone (306) 584-5866. Meetings are announced in the local press.

Saskatoon Women's Reproductive Rights Movement, P.O. Box 8718, Saskatoon, Sask. Telephone (306) 244-9724

Calgary Women's Health Collective, 2340 1st Avenue, N.W. Calgary, Alta. T2N 0B8. Telephone (403) 264-7977

Women's Resource Centre, YWCA, 320-5th Ave. S.E., Calgary, Alta. T2G 0E5. Telephone (403) 263-1550, local 397

Fernie Women's Resource and Drop-In Centre, Box 2054, Fernie, B.C. V0B 1M0. Telephone (604) 423-4819

Okanagan Women's Coalition, P.O. Box 1242, Vernon, B.C. V1T 6N6

Health Action Network Society (HANS), 5338 Ewart St., Burnaby, B.C. V5J 2W4. Telephone (604) 437-4008 or 435-0512

Women's Resource Centre, #1-1144 Robson St., Vancouver, B.C. V6E 1B2

Vancouver Women's Health Collective, 1720 Grant St., 3rd floor, Vancouver, B.C. V5L 3Y2. Telephone (604) 682-4805

First Mature Women's Network Society, 411 Dunsmuir Street, 2nd Floor, Vancouver, B.C. V6B 1X4.

Status of Women Action Group, Suite 213, 620 View St., Victoria, B.C. V8W 2N2. Telephone (604) 381-1012

Victoria Faulkner Women's Centre, 302 Steele St., Suite 103, Whitehorse, Yukon Y1A 2C5

6. Publications that specialize or touch on issues of interest to the woman seeking to understand her body.

a) Magazines about health. Some of these are better than others. *Medical Self Care* is the most consistently interesting of the American magazines. *Healthsharing*, which is Canadian and devoted to women's health, is a unique publication appreciated in the United States as well as in Canada.

Alive: Canadian Journal of Health and Nutrition. Published eight times a year by Canadian Health Reform Products Ltd., Box 67333, Vancouver, B.C. V5W 3T1. $12 a year.

American Health: Fitness of Body and Mind. Sometimes referred to as the "People Magazine" of health publications. Published monthly, except February and August, by American Health Partners, 80 Fifth Ave., New York, NY 10011 U.S.A. $17.95 (U.S.) per year.

FDA Consumer. Published ten times a year (combined issues in July/August and December/January) by the U.S. Food and Drug Administration, Superintendent of Documents, Government Printing Office, Washington, DC 20402 U.S.A. $11.90 (U.S.) per year.

Healthsharing: A Canadian Women's Health Quarterly, 14 Skey Lane, Toronto, Ont. M6J 3S4. $9.00 per year (individual subscription).

Let's Live: Health and Preventive Medical Magazine. Published monthly by Oxford Industries, P.O. Box 2032, Marion, OH 43305, U.S.A. $22.95 (U.S.) per year.

Medical Self Care. Published quarterly by Medical Self Care, P.O. Box 1000, Pt. Reyes, CA 94956, U.S.A. $17 (U.S.) per year.

Prevention: America's leading health magazine. Published monthly by Rodale Press, 33 East Minor St., Emmaus, PA 18049, U.S.A. $18.97 (U.S.) per year.

Today's Health. Published six times a year by Daycal Publishing, 273 Richmond St. W., Toronto, Ont. M5V 1X1. $11 per year.

b) Newsletters and Periodicals. Some of these deal with women's interests generally; some are medical bulletins. Many American hospitals are making extra money by publishing and selling newsletters; it is hard to pick one over another. *Healthfacts* is the best independent newsletter; *The National Women's Health Report* and the *National Women's Health Network News* specialize in women's health generally; *A Friend Indeed* is the only one focusing on menopause and mid-life.

Broomstick: By, For and About Women over Forty. A literary slant, featuring poems, short stories, and commentary by readers. Published bimonthly by Broomstick, 3543 18th St. #3, San Francisco, CA 94110 U.S.A. $20 (U.S.) per year.

Cassandra: Radical feminist nurses' newsjournal. Published three times a year (January, May, and September) by the organization of the same name, P.O. Box 341, Williamsville, NY 14221. $25 (U.S.) per year.

A Fit Third Age, Secretariat for Fitness in the Third Age, c/o Canadian Parks and Recreation Association, 333 River Road, Vanier, Ont. K1L 8H9. Newsletter published three times per year to encourage fitness of older citizens.

A Friend Indeed . . . for women in the prime of life. A newsletter about menopause and mid-life. Published ten times a year (monthly except July and August) by A Friend Indeed Publications Inc., Box 515, Place du Parc Station, Montreal, Que. H2W 2P1. $30 per year. The newsletter is also available in French as *Une Véritable Amie.*

Harvard Medical School Health Letter. Published monthly by the Department of Continuing Education, Harvard Medical School Letter, 79 Garden St., Cambridge, MA 02138, U.S.A. $24 (U.S.) per year.

Healthfacts. Published by the Center for Medical Consumers, 237 Thompson St., New York, NY 10012, U.S.A. $18 (U.S.) per year.

Health News: Your authoritative guide to current health issues. Published bimonthly by Faculty of Medicine, Medical Science Building, University of Toronto, Toronto, Ont. M5S 1A8. $12 per year.

Hot Flash: Newsletter for Midlife and Older Women. Despite its name, this newsletter does not focus on menopause. The official publication of the National Action Forum for Mid-Life and Older Women (see listing under U.S. Organizations).

In Control: A PMS Newsletter. R.R. #2, Box 3255, Yarmouth, N.S. B5A 4A6. Telephone (902) 742-8663. Published six times a year by the Canadian Association for Understanding Premenstrual Changes. A one-year subscription is $20.

Initiative: The self-help newsletter. Published quarterly by the Canadian Council on Social Development, 55 Parkdale Ave., Box 3505, Station C, Ottawa, Ont. K1Y 4G1. Free.

IPPF Open File. Published biweekly by International Planned Parenthood Federation International Office, Regent's College, Inner Circle, Regent's Park, London NW1 4NS England. Summarizes medical and news reports related to Planned Parenthood's mandate. Free.

Mayo Clinic Health Letter: Reliable information for a healthier life. Published monthly by Mayo Medical Resources, Rochester, MN 55905, U.S.A. $24 (U.S.) per year.

Melpomene Report: A journal for women's health research. Focuses on the relationship between exercise and women's health; published three times yearly by Melpomene Institute. Canadian subscriptions are $30.00 (U.S.) per year (see listing under U.S. Organizations).

National Women's Health Network News. 1325 G St., N.W., Lower Level, Washington, DC 20005. Membership to the network and receipt of the bimonthly publication costs $25 (U.S.) per year for individuals, $35 (U.S.) for consumer groups or women's health organizations (see listing under U.S. Organizations).

National Women's Health Report. Published bimonthly by the NWHR Publications, P.O. Box 25307, Georgetown Station, Washington, DC 20007. $15 (U.S.) per year.

Network News. A newsletter of the Global Link for Midlife and Older Women, published quarterly by the Women's Initiative of the American Association of Retired Persons, 1909 K Street, N.W., Washington, D.C. 20049.

Option: Journal of Complementary Medicine. Published four times yearly by HANS (Health Action Network Society), 311-3856 Sunset Street, Burnaby, B.C. V5G 1T3. Subscriptions are $15 per year and subscribers automatically become members of HANS

SIECCAN Journal, the publication of the Sex Information and Education Council of Canada (see listing under Canadian Organizations).

Resources Guide Resources, 810 Duluth St. East, Montreal, P.Q. H2L 1B3. Telephone (514) 521-7728. A quarterly bilingual publication devoted to natural health. $6 per year.

Tufts University Diet and Nutrition Letter. Published monthly by Tufts University Diet and Nutrition, P.O. Box 10948, Des Moines, IA 50940, U.S.A. $19 (U.S.) per year.

University of California, Berkeley Wellness Letter: The newsletter of nutrition, fitness, and stress management. Published monthly by Health Letter Associates, P.O. Box 10922, Des Moines, IA 50340, U.S.A. $20 (U.S.) per year.

Women & Health. The Haworth Press, 112 West 32nd St., New York City, NY 10001, U.S.A. Subscriptions are $39 (U.S.) in Canada.

Women's Global Network on Reproductive Rights. Periodical published quarterly (in English and Spanish) by the organization of the same name, P.O. Box 4098, 1009 AB Amsterdam, The Netherlands. 40 Dutch guilders or $20.00 (U.S.) per year.

The Women's Letter. Sköl Publishing Corp., P.O. Box 6036, Newburyport, MA. Telephone (617) 465-6026. A new publication covering synopses of studies relating to women's health. Twelve monthly issues for $69 U.S.

7. Bookstores (listed east to west) that stock or order books on women's issues. Many will take mail or telephone orders. Have a Visa credit card number on hand when you call.

Idle Hands Book Store, 1423 Prince St., Charlottetown, P.E.I. C1A 4R6. Telephone (902) 892-6446

Bibliophile, 5474 Queen Mary Rd., Montreal, Que. H3X 1V6. Telephone (514) 486-7369

Ottawa Women's Bookstore, 380 Elgin St., Ottawa, Ont. K2P 1N1. Telephone (613) 230-1156

Mrs. Dalloway's Books, 38A Princess St., Kingston, Ont. K7L 1A4. Telephone (613) 544-4243

S.C.M. Bookroom, 333 Bloor St. West, Toronto, Ont. M5S 1W7. Telephone (416) 979-9624

Toronto Women's Bookstore, 73 Harbord St., Toronto, Ont. M5S 1G4. Telephone (416) 922-8744

Women's Bookstop, 333 Main St. West, Hamilton, Ont. L8P 1K1. Telephone (416) 525-2970

The Bookshelf Café, 41 Quebec Street, Guelph, Ont. N1H 2T1. Telephone (519) 821-3311

Northern Women's Bookstore, 69 North Court St., Thunder Bay, Ont. P7A 4A9. Telephone (807) 344-7979

Prairie Sky Books, 871 Westminster Ave., Winnipeg, Man. R3G 1B3. Telephone (204) 774-6152

Bold Print, Inc. The Women's Bookshop, 478A River Ave., Winnipeg, Man. R3L 0C8. Telephone (204) 452-9682

Tumbleweed Books, 2210 Albert St., Regina, Sask. S4P 2V2

A Woman's Place Bookstore, 1412 Centre St., S., Calgary, Alta. T2G 2E4. Telephone (403) 263-5256

Self Connection Books, Triwood Plaza, 4004–19th Street N.W., Calgary, Alta. T2L 2B6. Telephone (403) 284-1486.

Common Woman Books, 8724-109 Street, Edmonton, Alta. T6G 1E9. Telephone (403) 432-9344

The Compleat Reader Bookstore, 65B Prairie Mall, 11801-100 St., Grande Prairie, Alta. Telephone (403) 532-3649

Vancouver Women's Bookstore, 315 Cambie St., Vancouver, B.C. V6B 2N4. Telephone (604) 684-0523

Ariel Books Ltd., 2766 West 4th Ave., Vancouver, B.C. V6K 1R1. Telephone (604) 733-3511

Every Woman's Books, 641 Johnston St., Victoria, B.C. V8W 1M7. Telephone (604) 388-9411

GENERAL REFERENCES

(Please see selected references and resources for citations relevant to each chapter.)

Al-Issa, Ihsan. *The Psychopathology of Women.* Englewood Cliffs, N.J.: Prentice-Hall, 1980.

Anderson, Evelyn, et al. "Characteristics of menopausal women seeking assistance." *American Journal of Obstet. & Gynecol.*, 156(2): 428–433, February 1987.

Anderson, Mary. *The Menopause.* London: Faber and Faber, 1983.

Bart, P.B., and M. Grossman. "Menopause." *Women & Health*, 1(2): 3–10, 1976.

Baruch, Grace, and Jeanne Brooks-Gunn, eds. *Women in Midlife.* N.Y.: Plenum Press, 1984.

Berland, Theodore. *Fitness for Life: Exercise for People over 50.* Illinois: AARP Books, Scott Foresman & Co., 1986.

Bolton, Valerie. *Women Being Well Training Guide: Facilitator training and organizational skills for women establishing mutual aid support groups.* P.O. Box 1405, Clinton, Ontario N0M 1L0.

Boston Women's Health Book Collective. *The New Our Bodies Ourselves.* N.Y.: Simon and Schuster, 1984.

Bricklin, Mark, exec. ed. *Rodale's Encyclopedia of Natural Home Remedies.* Emmaus, PA.: Rodale Press, 1982.

Brown, Judith K., and Virginia Kerns. *In Her Prime.* Massachusetts: Bergin & Garvey, 1985.

Brown, Mackey. "Keeping marriage alive through middle age," in *Growing Older,* M.H. Huyck, ed., *Growing Older.* Englewood Cliffs, N.J.: Prentice-Hall, 1974.

Budoff, Penny Wise. *No More Menstrual Cramps and Other Good News.* Markham, Ont.: Penguin, 1981.

_____. *No More Hot Flashes and Other Good News.* N.Y.: G.P. Putnam's Sons, 1983.

Cadmus, R.R. *Caring for Your Aging Parents.* N.J.: Prentice-Hall, 1984.

Canadian Woman Studies, Special Issue on Aging, 5(3), Spring 1984. 212 Founders College, York University, 4700 Keele St., Downsview, Ont. M3J 1P3.

Carson, Ruth. *Your Menopause.* N.Y.: Public Affairs Pamphlets, 1978.

Carver, Cynthia. *Patient Beware.* Ontario: Prentice-Hall, 1984.

Chernin, Kim. *The Obsession: Reflections on the Tyranny of Slenderness.* N.Y.: Harper Colophon, 1981.

Cherry, Sheldon. *The Menopause Myth.* N.Y.: Ballantine Books, 1976.

Chesler, Phyllis. *Women and Madness.* N.Y.: Doubleday, 1972.

Clarkes, Rebecca. *Directory of Health Care Practitioners: A Listing of Nutritionally Oriented Doctors across Canada.* Vancouver: Alive Books, Box 67333, 1984.

Clay, Vidal S. *Women: Menopause and Middle Age.* Pennsylvania: Know Inc, 1977.

Cobb, Janine O'L. *A Friend Indeed.* Newsletter founded 1984. Issued ten times annually, April 1984 onwards (Box 515, Place du Parc Station, Montreal H2W 2P1).

_____. "The great hormone debate." *Healthsharing,* 8(1): 17–20, Winter 1986.

_____. "Demystifying menopause." *Canadian Nurse,* 83(7): 16–20, August 1987.

Cohen, Joan Z., Karen L. Coburn; and Joan Pearlman. *Hitting Our Stride: Good News About Women in Their Middle Years.* N.Y.: Delacorte Press, 1980.

Cohen, Leah. *Small Expectations.* Toronto: McClelland and Stewart, 1984.

Coope, Jean. *The Menopause: Coping with the Change.* Ontario: Prentice-Hall,

Cooperstock, R., and J. Hill. *The Effects of Tranquillization: Benzodiazepine use in Canada.* Ottawa: Health and Welfare, 1982.

Corea, Gina. *Women's Health Care: The Hidden Malpractice.* N.Y.: Wm. Morrow, 1977.

Costlow, Judy, Maria Christina Lopez; and Mara Taub. *Menopause: A Self-Care Manual* (2nd rev. ed.). Available for $5 (U.S.) plus $1.50 postage and handling from the Santa Fe Health Education Project, P.O. Box 577, Santa Fe, NM 87504-0577 U.S.A.

Curtis, L.R., G.B. Curtis; and M.K. Beard. *My Body — My Decision: What You Should Know about the Most Common Female Surgeries.* Tucson, AZ: The Body Press (HPBooks), 1986.

Cutler, W.B., C.R. Garcia; and D.A. Edwards. *Menopause: A Guide for Women and the Men Who Love Them.* N.Y.: W.W. Norton, 1983.

Cutler, W.B., and C.R. Garcia. *The Medical Management of Menopause and Premenopause.* Philadelphia: J.P. Lippincott, 1984.

Dalton, Katharina. *The Premenstrual Syndrome and Progesterone Therapy* (2nd ed.). Chicago: Year Book Medical Publishers, 1984.

Davis, Donna Lee. *Blood and Nerves.* Newfoundland: Memorial University of Newfoundland, 1983.

DeMarco, Carolyn. *Take Charge of Your Body: A Woman's Guide to Health.* Available from the author for $6.95 at 598 St. Clair Ave. West, Toronto, Ont. M6C 1A7.

Dennerstein, Lorraine, Carl Wood; and Graham Burrows. *Hysterectomy: How to Deal with the Physical and Emotional Aspects.* Melbourne, Australia: Oxford Univ. Press, 1982.

Doan, Helen. *Every Woman: Adapting to Mid-Life Change.* Toronto: Stoddart Publishing, 1987.

Donohugh, Donald L. *The Middle Years.* N.Y.: Berkley Books, 1983.

Doress, Paula Brown, and Diana Laskin Siegal (and the Midlife and Older Women Book Project). *Ourselves, Growing Older.* N.Y.: Simon and Schuster, 1987.

Dreifus, Claudia, ed. *Seizing Our Bodies: The Politics of Women's Health.* N.Y.: Random House, Vintage Books, 1977.

Dudley, R., and W. Rowland. *How to Find Relief from Migraine.* Toronto: Collins, 1982.

Edelstein, Barbara. *The Woman Doctor's Medical Guide for Women.* Toronto: Bantam Books, 1982.

Ehrenreich, Barbara, and Deirdre English. *Complaints and Disorders: The Sexual Politics of Sickness.* (Glass Mountain Pamphlet No. 2). Brooklyn, N.Y.: Faculty Press, 1973.

————. *For Her Own Good: 150 Years of the Experts' Advice to Women.* N.Y.: Anchor Books, 1979.

Eichenbaum, Luise, and Susie Orbach. *What Do Women Want.* N.Y.: Coward-McCann Inc., 1983.

Evans, Dr. Barbara. *Life Change: A Guide to the Menopause, Its Effects and Treatment.* London: Pan Books, 1979.

Farrell, M.P., and S.D. Rosenberg. *Men at Midlife.* Boston: Auburn House, 1981.

Federation of Feminist Women's Health Centers. *How to Stay Out of the Gynecologist's Office.* California: Peace Press, 1981.

Feltin, Marie. *A Woman's Guide to Good Health After 50.* Glenview, Ill.: Scott Foresman, 1987.

Fisher, A. *The Healthy Heart.* Alexandria, VA.: Time-Life Books, 1981.

Ford, Anne Rochon. "When women outlive their ovaries." *The New Internationalist,* No. 165, November 1986.

Fremes, R., and Z. Sabry. *NutriSCORE: The Rate Yourself Plan for Better Nutrition* (2nd ed.). Toronto: Methuen, 1981.

Frey, Karen A. "Middle-aged women's experience and perceptions of menopause." *Women and Health,* 6(1-2): 25–36, 1981.

Fromer, Margot Jean. *Menopause: The Latest Discoveries about the Time of Life Every Woman Will Face.* N.Y.: Pinnacle Books, 1985.

Gannon, Linda R. *Menstrual Disorders and Menopause: Biological, Psychological and Cultural Research.* N.Y.: Praeger Publishers, 1985.

Gilligan, Carol. *In A Different Voice: Psychological Theory and Woman's Development.* Cambridge, MA.: Harvard Univ. Press, 1982.

Graedon, Joe. *The People's Pharmacy.* N.Y.: St. Martin's Press, 1986.

Gray, Madeline. *The Changing Years: The Menopause Without Fear.* N.Y.: Signet/Doubleday, 1981.

Greenblatt, R.B. *The Menopausal Syndrome.* N.Y.: Medcom Press, 1974.

Greenwood, Sadja. *Menopause Naturally: Preparing for the Second Half of Your Life* (2nd edition). San Francisco: Volcano Press, 1988.

Hailes, Jean, Richard J. Doran; and P. Andream Lum-Doran. *Middle Years: The Female Menopause.* Toronto: Copp Clark Pitman, 1982.

Hanington, E. *The Headache Book.* N.Y.: Technomic, 1980.

Hartmann, Ernest. *The Sleep Book: Understanding and Preventing Sleep Problems in People over 50.* Illinois: AARP Books, Scott Foresman & Co., 1987.

Hausman, Patricia. *The Calcium Bible: How to Have Better Bones All Your Life.* N.Y.: Rawson Associates, 1985.

Henig, Robin Marantz. *How a Woman Ages: What to Expect and What You Can Do About It.* N.Y.: Ballantine Books, 1985.

————. *The Myth of Senility: The Truth about the Brain and Aging.* Illinois: AARP Books, Scott Foresman & Co., 1985.

Hepworth, Mike, and Mike Featherstone. *Surviving Middle Age.* Oxford, England: Basil Blackwell, 1982.

Hill, Karen. *Helping You Helps Me: A Guide Book for Self-help Groups.* Canadian Council on Social Development, P.O. Box 3505, Station C, Ottawa, Ontario K1Y 4G1.

Holte, Arne, and A. Mikkelsen. "The Menopause: The predictors of good and bad outcome. Lessons from a prospective longitudinal study." Paper presented at The Future of Adult Life: 1st International Conference, Amsterdam, 1987.

Hunter, D.J.S. "Oophorectomy and the surgical menopause," in R.J. Beard, ed., *The Menopause: A Guide to Current Research and Practice.* Baltimore: Univ. Park Press, 1976.

Huyck, Margaret Hellie. *Growing Older: What You Need to Know about Aging.* N.J.: Prentice-Hall, 1974.

Jamison, DeeDee, and Roberta Schwalb. *Every Woman's Guide to Hysterectomy: Taking Charge of Your Own Body.* N.J.: Prentice-Hall, 1978.

Kahn, Ada P., and Linda Hughey Holt. *Midlife Health.* N.Y.: Facts on File Publications, 1987.

Kaufert, Patricia. "The perimenopausal woman and her use of health services." *Maturitas,* 2: 191–205, 1980.

_____. "Myth and the menopause." *Sociology of Health and Illness,* 4(2), July 1982.

_____, and John Syrotiuk. "Symptom reporting at the menopause." *Soc. Sci. Med.,* 151: 173–184, 1981.

_____. "The Menopausal Transition: The Use of Estrogen." *Cdn. Jrnl. of Public Health,* Vol. 77, Suppl. 1, May/June 1986.

_____. "Menstruation and menstrual change: Women in midlife." *Health Care for Women International,* 7(1–2), 1986.

Kinsey, A., et al. *Sexual Behaviour in the Human Female.* Philadelphia: W.G. Saunders, 1953.

Kirkpatrick, M., ed. *Women's Sexual Experience: Exploration of a Dark Continent.* N.Y.: Plenum Press, 1982.

Kitzinger, Sheila. *Woman's Experience of Sex.* N.Y.: G.P. Putnam's Sons, 1983.

Lalinec-Michaud, M., and F. Engelsmann. "Anxiety, fears and depression related to hysterectomy" in *Can. Jrnl. of Psychiatry,* 30: 44–47, Feb. 1985.

Lauerson, Niels, and Steven Whitney. *It's Your Body: A Woman's Guide to Gynecology.* N.Y.: Berkley Books, 1977.

Levinson, D.J., et al. *The Seasons of a Man's Life.* N.Y.: Alfred A. Knopf, 1978.

Lewinsohn, P.M., E.M. Duncan, A.K. Stanton; and M. Hautzinger. "Age at first onset for nonpolar depression." *Jrnl. of Abnormal Psych.,* 95(4), 378–383, 1986.

Lexchin, Joel. *The Real Drug Pushers: A Critical Analysis of the Canadian Drug Industry.* Vancouver: New Star Books, 1985.

Lock, Margaret. "Ambiguities of aging: Japanese experience and perceptions of menopause." *Culture, Medicine & Psychiatry,* 10: 23–46, 1986.

Lowenthal, M.F., M. Thurnher; and D. Chiriboga. *Four Stages of Life: A Comparative Study of Women and Men Facing Transitions.* San Francisco: Jossey-Bass, 1977.

Luce, Gay Gaer. *Your Second Life: Vitality and Growth in Middle and Later Years.* N.Y.: Delta Books, 1979.

MacPherson, Kathleen I. "Menopause as disease: The social construction of a metaphor." *Annals of Nursing Science,* 3: 95–113, 1981.

MacPherson, Kay. "Thoughts on growing old," in *Canadian Woman Studies,* Spring 1984.

Martin, Emily. *The Woman in the Body: A Cultural Analysis of Reproduction.* Boston: Beacon Press, 1987.

Martin, Michael. "Malady and menopause." *The Jrnl. of Medicine and Philosophy,* 10: 329–337, 1985.

Masters W., V. Johnson, and R. Kolodny. *Human Sexuality (2nd ed.).* Boston: Little, Brown, 1985.

Mastroianni, Luigi Jr., and C. Alvin Paulsen, eds. *Aging, Reproduction and the Climacteric.* N.Y.: Plenum Press, 1986.

McCauley, Carole Spearin. *Surviving Breast Cancer.* Toronto: Bantam Books, 1986.

McCrea, Frances B. "The politics of menopause: The 'discovery' of a deficiency disease." *Social Problems, 31*(1), October 1983.

McDonnell, Kathleen, ed. *Adverse Effects: Women and the Pharmaceutical Industry.* Toronto: Women's Educational Press, 1986.

McDonnell, Kathleen, and Mariana Valverde. *The Healthsharing Book: Resources for Canadian Women.* Toronto: The Women's Press, 1985.

McGowan, Larry. "Ovarian cancer after hysterectomy." *Obs. & Gyne.,* 69(3), March 1987.

McKinlay, J.B., S.M. McKinlay, and D.J. Brambilla. "Health status and utilization behavior associated with menopause." *Am. Jrnl. of Epidemiology, 125*(1), 1987.

McKinlay, S.M., and M. Jeffreys. "The menopausal syndrome." *British Jrnl. of Prev. Soc. Med.,* 28, 1976.

————, and J.B. McKinlay. "Selected studies of the menopause." *Jrnl. of Biosocial Sciences,* 5: 533–555, October 1973.

Melamed, Elissa. *Mirror, Mirror: The Terror of Not Being Young.* N.Y.: Linden Press 1983.

Mindell, Earl. *Vitamin Bible.* New York: Warner Books, 1979.

Millette, Brenda, and Joellen Hawkins. *The Passage through Menopause: Women's Lives in Transition.* Virginia: Reston Publishing Co., 1983.

Montreal Health Press. *The Book about Menopause,* Rosemary Byrne-Hunter and Miryam Gerson, C.P. 1000, Station Place du Parc, Montreal H2W 2N1, 1987.

Morgan, Susanne. *Coping With A Hysterectomy: Your Own Choice, Your Own Solutions.* N.Y.: Dial Press, 1982 and New American Library, 1986.

Musgrave, Beatrice, and Zoe Menell, eds. *Change and Choice: Women and Middle Age.* London: Peter Owen, 1980.

Napholz, L. "A descriptive study on working women's knowledge about midlife menopause and health care practices." *Occupational Health Nursing*, October 1985.

Napoli, Maryann. *Health Facts.* New York: Overlook Press, 1981.

Nellis, Muriel. *The Female Fix.* Pennsylvania: Penguin Books, 1980.

Nett, Emily M., ed. "Women as Elders." *Resources for Feminist Research*, *11*(2), July 1982.

Neugarten, B.L., and R.J. Kraines. "Menopausal symptoms in women of various ages." *Psychosomatic Medicine*, *27*: 266, 1965.

————, ed. *Middle Age and Aging.* Chicago: University of Chicago Press, 1968.

Northrup, C., and S.S. Lowy. "The challenge of menopause." *East West Journal*, December 1985.

Notelovitz, Morris, and Marsha Ware. *Stand Tall: The Informed Woman's Guide to Preventing Osteoporosis.* Florida: Triad Publishing, 1982.

Novak, Mark. *Successful Aging: The Myths, Realities and Future of Aging in Canada.* Markham, Ontario: Penguin, 1985.

Older, Julia. *Endometriosis: A Woman's Guide to a Common But Often Undetected Disease That Can Cause Infertility and Other Major Medical Problems.* N.Y.: Scribner's, 1984.

Padus, Emrika, Sr., ed. *The Woman's Encyclopedia of Health and Natural Living.* Emmaus, PA.: Rodale Press, 1981.

Paxton, Mary J.W. *The Female Body in Control.* New Jersey: Prentice-Hall, 1981.

Payer, Lynn. *How to Avoid a Hysterectomy: An Indispensable Guide to Exploring All Your Options Before You Consent to a Hysterectomy.* Toronto: Random House, 1987.

Pengelly, Eric T. *Sex and Human Life.* Don Mills, Ont.: Addison-Wesley, 1974.

Pesmen, C., et al. *How a Man Ages.* N.Y.: Ballantine, 1984.

Poon, Leonard W., ed. *Aging in the 1980's: The Psychological Issues.* Washington, D.C.: American Psychology Association, 1980.

Porcino, Jane. *Growing Older, Getting Better.* Reading, MA.: Addison-Wesley, 1983.

Pritikin, N., and P.M. McGrady, Jr. *The Pritikin Program for Diet and Exercise.* Bantam Books, 1979.

Prudden, Bonnie. *Bonnie Prudden's After Fifty Fitness Guide.* N.Y.: Ballantine Books, 1986.

Ragan, P.K., ed. *Aging Parents.* California: Ethel Percy Andrus Gerontology Center, U. Of Cal. Press, 1979.

Reimer, Beth L. *The Menopausal Years.* Daly City, CA: Krames Communications, 1980.

Reitz, Rosetta. *Menopause: A Positive Approach.* Markham, Ont.: Penguin, 1979.

Resnick, J.L.; M.C. Dougherty; and M. Notelovitz. "Significant life events and sources of stress in healthy climacteric women." Paper presented at the Fourth International Congress on the Menopause, Buena Vista, Florida, October 1984.

Richardson, Laurel Walum. *The Dynamics of Sex and Gender*. Boston: Houghton Mifflin, 1981.

Ritz, Sandra. "Growing through menopause." *Medical Self-Care*, Winter 1981.

Roadburg, Alan. *Aging, Retirement, Leisure and Work in Canada*. Toronto: Methuen, 1985.

Rodgers, Joann. "Rush to Surgery." *N.Y. Times Magazine*, September 21, 1975.

Rose, Louise, ed. *The Menopause Book*. N.Y.: Hawthorn Books, 1977.

Rosenberger, Nancy. "Menopause as a symbol of anomaly: The case of Japanese women." *Health Care for Women International*, 7, nos. 1–2, 1986.

Rubin, L.B. *Women Of a Certain Age: The Midlife Search for Self*. N.Y.: Harper Colophon, 1979.

————. "Sex and sexuality: Women at mid-life," in M. Kirkpatrick, ed., *Women's Sexual Experience*.

Ruebsaat, H.J., and R. Hull. *The Male Climacteric*. N.Y.: Hawthorn, 1975.

Ryan, M.M., and Dennerstein, L. "Hysterectomy and tubal ligation," *Advances in Psychosomatic Med.*, 15: 186–198, 1986.

Sacks, Oliver. *Migraine: Evolution of a Common Disorder*. London, Faber and Faber, 1970.

Sanford, Linda Tschirhart, and Mary Ellen Donovan. *Women and Self-Esteem*. N.Y.: Anchor Press, 1984.

San Francisco Women's Health Center. *Menopause: A Natural Process*. 364 Collingwood St., San Francisco, CA 94114, U.S.A. $2.00 U.S.

Saper, J.R., and K.R. Magee. *Freedom from Headaches*. New York: Simon & Schuster, 1978.

Satir, Virginia. *Peoplemaking*. Palo Alto, CA: Science and Behavior books, 1972.

Scarf, Maggie. *Unfinished Business: Pressure Points in the Lives of Women*. Doubleday, 1980.

Scully, Diana H. *Men Who Control Women's Health*. Boston: Houghton, Mifflin 1980.

Seaman, Barbara, and Gideon Seaman. *Women and the Crisis in Sex Hormones*. N.Y.: Rawson Associates, 1977.

Shainess, Natalie. *Sweet Suffering: Woman as Victim*. New York: Wallaby Books (Simon & Schuster), 1982.

Seigel, Diane, and Patricia Boyle. *Facing the Change of Life: A Resource Kit on Menopause*. Newfoundland: Planned Parenthood Newfoundland/Labrador, 1984.

Sheehy, G. *Passages: Predictable Crises of Adult Life*. N.Y.: Bantam, 1976.

Sherwin, B.B., and M.M. Gelfand. "Differential symptom response to pareneral estrogen and/or androgen administration in the surgical menopause." *American Journal of Obstetrics and Gynecology*, 151, no. 2 (January 15, 1985).

Shreeve, Caroline M. *Overcoming the Menopause Naturally*. England: Arrow Books, 1986.

Silverstone, B., and H.K. Hyman. *You and Your Aging Parent*. N.Y.: Pantheon, 1976.

Sontag, Susan. "The Double Standard of Aging." *Saturday Review*: 182–190, Sept. 23, 1972.

Stokes, Naomi Miller. *The Castrated Woman: What Your Doctor Won't Tell You about Hysterectomy*. N.Y. & Toronto: Franklin Watts, 1986.

Stopes, Marie Carmichael. *Change of Life in Men and Women*. N.Y.: G.B. Putnam's Sons, 1936.

Stoppard, M. *The Best Years of Your Life*. New York: Villard, 1984.

Sullivan, Kay. *Alive and Well and Over Forty*. New York: Bantam, 1984.

Tamir, L.M. *Men in Their Forties*. New York: Springer, 1982.

The Time of Our Lives: A Booklet on Menopause. Published by the Ad Hoc Committee on Women's Health Issues, c/o Ann Thurlow, P.O. Box 4, Souris, P.E.I. C0A 2B0.

Todres, Rubin. *Self-Help Groups: An Annotated Bibliography 1970–1982*. National Self-Help Clearinghouse, The Graduate School and University Center of the City of New York, 33 West 42nd Street, Room 1222, New York, N.Y. 10036.

Trien, Susan Flamholtz. *Change of Life: The Menopause Handbook*. N.Y.: Fawcett, Columbine, 1986.

Vancouver Women's Health Collective. *The Menopause Kit*. 1720 Grant St., 3rd floor, Vancouver, B.C. V5L 3Y2.

Vancouver Women's Health Collective. *Breast Health Kit*. 1720 Grant St., 3rd floor, Vancouver, B.C. V5L 3Y2.

Voda, Ann M., D. Dinnerstein, and S. O'Donnell, eds. *Changing Perspectives on Menopause*. Austin, Texas: University of Texas Press, 1982.

————, and M. Eliasson. "Menopause: The closure of menstrual life." *Women and Health*, 8(2–3), Summer-Fall, 1983.

————. *Menopause Me & You: A Personal Handbook for Women*. Salt Lake City: School of Nursing, U. of Utah.

————, and T. George. "Menopause." *Annual Review of Nursing Research*, 4: 55–75, 1986.

Weideger, Paula. *Menstruation and Menopause: The Physiology and Psychology, the Myth and the Reality*. N.Y.: Alfred Knopf, 1976.

Weiss, Kay, ed. *Women's Health Care: A Guide to Alternatives*. Reston, VA.: Reston Publishing Co., 1984.

Whitehead, M.I. "The menopause." *The Practitioner*, 231 (January 8, 1987).

Wigfall-Williams, Wanda. *Hysterectomy: Learning the Facts, Coping with the Feelings, Facing the Future*. N.Y.: Michael Kesend, 1986.

Witkin-Lanoil, Georgia. *The Female Stress Syndrome: How to Recognize and Live with It*. N.Y.: Berkley Books, 1985.

Women's Counselling Referral and Education Centre (WCREC). *Helping Ourselves: A Handbook for Women Starting Groups.* 525 Bloor St. West, Toronto, Ontario M5S 1Y4.

Woods, Nancy Fugate. "Menopausal distress: A model for epidemiological investigation," in Voda, et al., eds., *Changing Perspectives on Menopause,* 1982.

GLOSSARY

.

abdominoplasty	Medical term for a "tummy tuck," a cosmetic surgical procedure during which skin and fat are removed from the lower abdomen.
adenomyosis	Condition where tissue from the endometrium becomes embedded in the muscle of the uterus itself.
adenosis	Abnormal development of a gland.
adhesions	Fibrous tissue that may form in any part of the body as a result of surgery, infection, or bleeding. Adhesions may scar organs together and, when removed surgically, may cause new adhesions to grow.
adrenal glands	Flattened body above both kidneys that produce steroid hormones. The adrenals consist of a cortex and medulla. The cortex is responsible for many hormones; the medulla primarily for epinephrine (adrenaline).
agoraphobia	An irrational fear of being away from a known place. A common phobia among women, agoraphobia is diagnosed when panic attacks dictate a restricted area of activity for the phobic person. It can be effectively treated by behaviour therapy.
air hunger	The temporary sensation of being starved of oxygen. Lasting only a few moments, this sensation is characteristic of pregnancy and menopause.
alopecia areata	Patchy hair loss, often reversible, in sharply defined areas, usually involving the scalp.
amenorrhea	Absence of menstruation for more than three cycles, usually caused by fluctuating estrogen levels during breast feeding, heavy exercise, illness, stress, weight change, etc. Episodes of amenorrhea are characteristic of the peri-menopause.
amines	Organic compounds containing nitrogen.
androgen	The hormone that stimulates male characteristics. The major androgens are testosterone and androsterone. Females produce small but essential amounts of androgen.
angioma	Round, bright red spot made up of blood vessels. Angiomas are usually noticed on the skin as small red dots (cherry or senile angioma) or as a tracery of dilated blood vessels (spider or telangiactic angioma). A common feature of ageing.

216

angina	Spasmodic choking, or suffocating pain. Term used almost exclusively for chest pain ("angina pectoris") usually due to interference with the supply of oxygen to the heart muscle and precipitated by excitement or effort.
aneurysm	A balloon-like swelling in the walls of a damaged artery.
anorexia nervosa	Condition based on fear of gaining weight, leading to extreme weight loss and amenorrhea. Anorectic patients are typically women in their late teens or early twenties. If not overcome, anorexia can lead to osteoporosis, heart disease and, in some cases, to death as a result of self-starvation.
apnea	The cessation of breathing for a few seconds. Cause is unknown. Sleep apnea is believed responsible for some kinds of very loud snoring and may also be responsible for temporary episodes of "air hunger" during menopause.
areola	Area around the nipple of the breast. May be pink to dark brown.
arrhythmia	Any variation from a regular heartbeat, including tachycardia (rapid) and bradycardia (too slow).
arteriosclerosis	Hardening of the arteries, a condition in which deposits form inside the arteries and affect blood flow from the heart.
artery/arteriole	Blood vessels that carry freshly oxygenated blood from the heart to all cells of the body.
aspirated	Drained of fluids by suction.
atheroma	Deposit of fats (or lipids) in the artery.
atherosclerosis	The formation of atheromas inside the walls of the arteries; part of the condition known as arteriosclerosis.
atrophic vaginitis	*See* dry vagina
aura	A strange sensation that precedes the onset of a hot flash, a migraine headache, an epileptic seizure. Auras may consist of visual disturbances, feelings of nausea, sudden changes in mood. The person experiencing the aura learns that it is a signal of the onset of a flash, headache, etc.
basal skin cancer	Small, pink growth in the head or neck area. Over time, these change to a cluster of pimples and then to a deep, crusty sore.
biofeedback	Method of training people to control bodily processes once thought to be involuntary. For instance, if a

tone sounds each time an individual succeeds in raising or lowering blood pressure, that individual may learn to manipulate blood pressure at will.

blepharoplasty	Medical term for eyelift.
bloat	The sudden distension of the waist or abdomen. Bloat may occur simultaneously with wind, or for no discernible reason. After a period of some discomfort (often two to three hours) it goes away. Common during premenstrual phase and menopause.
breakthrough bleeding	Bleeding or spotting between periods or after a long absence of periods (twelve months or more). Should be reported to a doctor.
breast self-examination	Practice advocated by the Cancer Society to reduce the incidence of breast cancer. BSE should be practised once a month and often locates lumps too small to be felt by an experienced physician.
bursitis	Inflammation of a fluid-filled sac or sac-like cavity (bursa). Bursae are situated in places like joints where friction would otherwise occur.
calcitonin	A hormone produced by the thyroid that influences levels of calcium in the blood.
Candida albicans	Type of yeast-like fungus that is normally part of the mouth, skin, intestinal tract and vagina, but that can cause problems if over-abundant.
carcinoma in situ	A tumour where the cells have not invaded the deepest membrane and are confined to the surface of the organ involved.
cerebral infarction	Death of brain tissue, often as a result of a stroke.
cerebral thrombosis	Blood clot in the brain.
cerebrovascular accident	*See* stroke
cervicitis	Inflammation of the neck of the uterus.
cervix	The bottom third of the uterus that projects into the vagina. Viewed through the vagina, the cervix resembles a doughnut.
cholesterol	Type of animal fat that is manufactured by the liver and circulated in the blood. Cholesterol is also eaten, primarily in the form of animal or dairy fats.
climacteric	Generally used to refer to the middle years in both males and females, loosely the years from about forty to sixty. The word comes from a Greek term for ladder and signifies a new step every seven years. The climacteric should be the years from forty-two to sixty-three, and the grand climacteric at the latter age.

218

Climacteron	Trademark name (Frosst) of an injectable form of estrogen replacement therapy, made up of testosterone and estradiol in oil. Used as one form of ERT, particularly for the surgically menopaused woman.
clitoris	Female organ of sexual arousal equivalent to male penis.
clomiphene citrate	Generic drug widely known as the "fertility drug" and prescribed as Clomid, an ovulatory agent that stimulates the release of gonadotropins (FSH and LH).
clonidine	Generic drug prescribed as Catapres or Dixarit. A drug used to control hypertension, which also acts to control hot flashes for some women.
collagen	A main supportive protein of skin, tendon, bone, cartilage, and connective tissue.
colporrhaphy	An operation that tightens the supports under the neck of the bladder and removes the slack tissue of the vagina.
comedomastitis	*See* duct ectasia
conization	The removal of a cone of tissue from the cervix for inspection and analysis.
corticosteroid	Any of the steroids produced by the adrenal cortex, or other natural or synthetic compounds with similar activity.
cystitis	Inflammation of the bladder, often producing a burning sensation when urinating.
danazol	Generic term for drug (Danocrine in U.S.A., Cyclomen in Canada) often prescribed for endometriosis, sometimes for premenstrual syndrome (PMS). It impedes ovulation and causes pseudo-menopause.
deremabrasion	Planing of the skin done by mechanical means, e.g., with sandpaper, wire brushes, etc..
dermis	The skin.
diaphanography	Illuminating the breasts with a very bright light to reveal the darker masses (potential tumours).
diastole	Force of the heart at rest.
diazepam	Generic tranquillizer (*Valium*) prescribed for relief of anxiety. Often prescribed to menopausal women, diazepam is addictive and acts as a depressant.
digitalis	A genus of herbs (from the foxglove plant) used in the treatment of congestive heart failure.
D&C (dilatation & curettage)	Minor surgical procedure involving opening of the cervix (the mouth of the uterus) for insertion of a

	curette (a long-handled, spoon-like device) in order to scoop out the lining of the uterus.
Dixarit	Trademark name (Boeringer) of clonidine.
dry vagina	A condition resulting from the thinning out of the vaginal walls and occurring either post-menopausally or as a result of surgical menopause (oophorectomies). Also known as "mature vagina." Unacceptable terms are "atrophic" or "senile vagina."
duct ectasia	Dilation of the collecting (milk) ducts of the breasts. Serious forms of this are comedomastitis and plasma cell mastitis.
duct hyperplasia	Abnormal growth of normal cells of the lining of the milk ducts of the breasts.
ductal papillomas	Benign growths (warts) in the milk ducts of the breasts.
emphysema	A pathological accumulation of air in tissues or organs.
endocrine	Bodily system comprising glands that release hormones into the bloodstream — i.e., pituitary, thyroid, parathyroid, adrenals, pineal body, gonads (ovaries or testes), pancreas, and paraganglia.
endocrinologist	A doctor of internal medicine who specializes in diagnosis and treatment of disorders of the endocrine glands.
endometriosis	Abnormal occurrence of tissues which more or less perfectly resemble the endometrium, in various locations in the pelvic cavity.
endometrium	Tissue lining the uterus or womb.
epidemiologist	One who studies the relationships of various factors determining the frequency and distribution of diseases in the human community.
epidermis	The outermost layer of skin.
ergotamine	Tartrate salt used for the relief of migraine.
estradiol	A strong estrogen produced by the ovaries. The major estrogen in pre-menopausal women.
estriol	The least powerful form of estrogen, a byproduct of estrone.
estrogen	Hormone classified as "female sex hormone" although it is produced by both men and women. There are three different kinds of hormones, the major one produced in the ovaries.
estrogen replacement therapy (ERT)	The most common form of supplementary estrogen prescribed to menopausal women, usually consisting of one tablet (to be taken orally) once a day for

(a) three weeks with one week off or (b) twenty-five days, with the balance of the month off. (*See also* hormone replacement therapy.)

estrone	A weak hormone produced partly by the ovaries and partly through the conversion, in body fat, of a precursor from the adrenal glands. Estrone is the main post-menopausal estrogen and the conversion process becomes more efficient with age.
ethynyl estradiol	A common form of synthetic estrogen used in the contraceptive pill and, in much smaller quantities, in some forms of estrogen replacement therapy.
fallopian tubes	Tubes with hair-like ends which pick up eggs erupting from the ovary and carry them down into the uterus.
fibrocystic	Characterized by an overgrowth of fibrous tissue and development of cystic spaces, especially in a gland.
fibroids	Colloquial clinical term for leiomyomas (benign tumours most often derived from smooth muscle) in or around the uterus.
fibromyalgia	A "sore-all-over" condition, also referred to as fibrositis. Symptoms include aching, pain, stiffness, sore spots that may continue for months or years. Treated with anti-inflammatory drugs, exercise, relaxation, etc.
fibrosis	Firm mass in the breasts, difficult to distinguish from normal tissue. Usually benign.
fibrous dysplasia	*See* fibrosis
follicle	Seed pod, or pouch-like covering surrounding the egg, or ovum, produced by the ovaries. When the follicle bursts, an egg is released to be picked up by the fallopian tube.
formication	A word used to describe the sensation of ants crawling on the skin, a common experience during menopause.
geriatrics	Department of medicine dealing with the problems of ageing and diseases of the elderly.
gerontology	The scientific study of the problems of ageing in all its aspects.
giant fibroadenoma	Rapidly growing rubbery tumour in the breasts.
gonadotropin	A substance that has a stimulating effect upon the ovaries, especially the hormone secreted by the anterior pituitary.
gynaecologist	Medical doctor specializing in the treatment of conditions or diseases affecting women.

histamine	Amine that causes dilation of capillaries, constriction of the muscles in the lungs, increased gastric secretion.
hormone	Substance produced by a gland and circulating through the bloodstream.
hormone replacement therapy (HRT)	Usually understood to comprise estrogen replacement therapy (ERT) with the addition of a pregestational agent (progestin or progestogen) taken for at least ten days *with* the estrogen for an optimum of thirteen days before both drugs are withdrawn and a "withdrawal bleed" follows.
hot flash	The subjective sensation of heat, often through the chest and over the head but felt, by some women, to the ends of their fingertips and to the soles of the feet. There may be an accompanying rise in temperature. The most common menopausal complaint, its cause is unknown.
hot flush	The evidence (red neck, face, enlarged veins, etc.) that often accompanies a hot flash. Not all hot flashes produce a flush. Not all flushes are felt as a flash.
hyperplasia	Abnormal increase in the number of normal cells in normal arrangement in an organ or tissue, which increases in volume.
hysterectomy	Surgical removal of the uterus. A complete hysterectomy involves removal of uterus and cervix. A partial hysterectomy involves removal of the uterus only. A radical hysterectomy involves removal of uterus, cervix, lymph nodes, and sometimes part of the vagina.
intraductal papillomas	Wart-like growths in the breasts that may produce a discharge from the nipple.
kwashiorkor	A syndrome due to severe protein deficiency; symptoms include retarded growth, changes in skin and hair pigment, and pathologic changes in the liver.
labia	Lips (outer and inner) that cover female genitals.
laparoscopy	Procedure, which may be diagnostic or operative. When used for diagnosis, it involves examination of the abdominal or pelvic cavity. A small incision is made in the navel and carbon dioxide or nitrous oxide is pumped into the abdomen to give the doctor a better view of the pelvic organs. A laparoscope is then inserted, through which the doctor examines the pelvic organs. A second incision on the pubic line may be required for operative laparoscopy.

laparotomy	Incision through the abdominal wall.
lipectomy	Medical term for fat suction.
lipoma	A benign fatty tumour, usually composed of mature fat cells.
lipoprotein	A combination of a lipid and a protein, having the general properties of proteins, but categorized as high-density, low-density, or very-low-density, etc. (HDLs, LDLs, VLDLs).
lithotomy position	Term used to describe position of woman during standard gynaecological examination (i.e., knees spread, feet up on stirrups). This position is also used for certain types of hysterectomies, particularly for prolapsed uterus, but may also involve tipping of the operating table so that the surgeon has a better view of the operating field. The result is often severe post-operative backache for the patient.
lorazepam	Generic tranquillizer (Ativan) prescribed for relief of excessive anxiety. Often prescribed to menopausal women, lorazepam is addictive and acts as a depressant.
lypolysis	Medical term for fat suction.
malignant melanoma	Form of cancer resulting from overexposure to the sun, it begins as a raised, bumpy darkened area of skin. Its shape and colour may change, and it may be itchy or sore.
mastitis	Inflammation of the breast.
menopause	Medical definition: the cessation of menstruation. Non-medical definition: the years surrounding the cessation of menstruation.
Menrium	Trademark name (Roche) of esterified estrogen and diazepam (a tranquillizer), sometimes prescribed for menopausal women. Addictive.
mitral valve	The valve between the left atrium and the left ventricle of the heart.
myomectomy	Surgical procedure involving the removal of myomas (also known as leiomyomas or fibroids) from in or around the uterus. This procedure is more common in Europe and often avoids the necessity of a hysterectomy.
naturopathy	A drugless system of healing by the use of physical methods.
necrosis	Hard lump consisting of dead cells, often resulting from a blow.

oophorectomy	Excision of one or both ovaries.
osteoarthritis	Degenerative joint disease accompanied by pain and stiffness.
osteomalacia	Softening of the bones due to a Vitamin D deficiency.
osteopenia	Any condition involving reduced bone mass.
osteoporosis	Abnormal thinning out of bone; porous bones.
ovary	One of a pair of female glands in which the ova (eggs) are produced. Major source of estrogen during the reproductive years.
palpitations	Disagreeable subjective awareness of the heartbeat.
pelvic inflammatory disease (P.I.D.)	Any inflammation of the reproductive organs. Symptoms may be pain, swelling, fever, nausea, unusual vaginal discharge, unusual bleeding, etc. Sometimes caused by sexually transmitted diseases.
peri-menopause	Period of time surrounding menopause when menstruation is irregular.
petrolatum	A purified mixture of hydrocarbons obtained from petroleum used as an ointment base or soothing application to the skin. Effective ingredient in products used to relieve dry skin.
phlebitis	Inflammation of a vein.
placebo	Inactive substance given to satisfy the patient's symbolic need for drug therapy or to test effectiveness of an experimental drug.
post-menopause	Period of time when menstruation has definitely ceased. Post-menopause is usually understood to begin when a woman has not had a menstrual period for twelve months.
plasma cell mastitis	*See* duct ectasia
Premarin	Trademark name (Ayerst) of conjugated estrogen used in estrogen replacement therapy to treat menopause ailments such as hot flashes and dry vagina. Often prescribed in conjunction with synthetic progesterone (Provera).
pre-menopause	Period of time when some menopausal symptoms occur but before menstrual periods become irregular.
premenstrual syndrome (PMS)	A wide range of physical and emotional symptoms which occur usually seven to ten days before the menstrual period.
prodrome	*See* aura
progesterone	Hormone produced by the corpus luteum (yellow body) that is left after a follicle bursts from

the ovary. This hormone paves the way for menstruation.

progestin

Synthetic form of progesterone. Generic names are "medroxyprogesterone acetate," or "megestrol acetate."

progestogen

Synthetic hormone derived from the male hormone, testosterone. Generic names are "norethindrone" or "norethisterone."

prostate

A gland surrounding the neck of the bladder and urethra in the male; it contributes a secretion to the semen.

Provera

Trademark name (Upjohn) of a progestogen that causes the endometrium to shed. May be prescribed to accompany estrogen (to control severe menopausal symptoms) or to help regulate unusual bleeding.

reserpine

An alkaloid used as an antihypertensive and tranquillizer. Increases risk of breast cancer.

rhytidectomy

Medical term for a facelift.

rickets

A condition caused by Vitamin D deficiency. Bones do not harden normally but are bent and distorted and the bones have enlarged nodes at the end and sides.

scurvy

Severe nutritional deficiency due to lack of Vitamin C. Symptoms are anaemia, spongy gums, hard spots on calf or leg muscles, etc.

senile lentigos

Liver spots caused by melanin (the dark pigment of the skin) deposits, a common sign of ageing.

spironolactone

An aldosterone (steroid hormone) inhibitor used as a diuretic (water pill).

squamous cell cancer

Form of cancer that starts as a small, red, hard pimple and then becomes a hard, crusted sore that refuses to heal.

stilbestrol

Synthetic non-steroidal estrogen. Effects are similar to those of natural estrogens. Once used to prevent miscarriage, to dry up breast milk, and as a morning-after pill. Its legal use is now limited to the treatment of breast and prostate cancer.

stroke

A condition with sudden onset due to acute vascular lesions of the brain (hemorrhage, embolism, thrombosis, rupturing aneurysm), which may be marked by partial or total paralysis of one side of the body, vertigo, numbness, partial or total loss of speech, often followed by permanent neurologic damage. Medical terms are CVA (cerebro-vascular

	accident) or, in its milder form, TIA (transient ischemic accident).
suction curettage	Another term for fat suction.
systole	Force of the heart while pumping.
temporomandibular joint syndrome (TMJ)	Faulty articulation of the hinged joint of the jaw; a condition that may cause headache, dizziness or ringing in the ears.
testosterone	A hormone secreted by the testes, which functions in the induction and maintenance of male secondary sex characters. A synthetic version is produced from cholesterol or isolated from bull testes.
thermography	Diagnostic technique that measures temperature differences between normal and abnormal (warmer) tissues. Useful but, by itself, not accurate enough for diagnosing breast cancer.
thromboembolism	Obstruction of a blood vessel with thrombotic material carried by the blood from the site of origin to plug another vessel.
touch impairment	Sensitivity to being touched that makes one shrink from human contact or impedes responses to touch. Nearly always temporary. Treatable with estrogen replacement therapy.
transillumination	*See* diaphanography
tubal ligation	Surgical technique of sterilization. The fallopian tubes are cut and bound, or plugged. Rarely reversible.
ultrasound	Technique that sends sound waves into the body that are reflected back onto a screen for display.
uterus	A muscular organ, pear-sized and -shaped, part of the same structure as the cervix. Also known as the womb. The lining of the uterus is the endometrium. As well as holding the developing foetus, the uterus influences the capacity for sexual response.
vagina	Canal leading from the opening of the uterus (the cervix) to the outside of the female body. Highly elastic, the vagina lubricates during sexual arousal.
vasodilator	Causing dilation of blood vessels.
vitamin A	(Retinol) Fat-soluble vitamin which helps to form and maintain the tissues of the skin and mucous linings of mouth, digestive, and genito-urinary tracts. Sources are yellow and green vegetables, liver, fish liver oils, eggs. Toxic in overdose.
vitamin B_6	(Pyridoxine) Water-soluble vitamin aiding metabolism of protein. The more protein in the diet, the more B_6 needed. Not stored in the body. Use of supplementary

	hormones (for contraception or menopause) interferes with absorption of this vitamin. Sources are whole grain cereals or breads, liver, kidney, other meats.
vitamin D	(Calciferol) Fat-soluble vitamin essential in the formation and maintenance of healthy bone. Formed by the action of sunlight on a lubricating substance in the skin. Major source is sunlight or milk with Vitamin D added. Fish oil supplements may be required to maintain adequate levels of Vitamin D in our climate, particularly since this vitamin is processed less efficiently with age.
vitamin E	(Tocopherol) Fat-soluble vitamin stored in the liver, fatty tissue, heart, muscles, uterus, blood, adrenal and pituitary glands. An anti-oxidant, Vitamin E enhances the activity of Vitamin A and acts as a vasodilator and anticoagulant. Often helpful in alleviating hot flashes. Sources are wheat germ, soybeans, broccoli, and leafy green vegetables.
withdrawal bleed	An artificial menstrual period, induced by ERT or HRT, assumed to eliminate the build-up of pre-cancerous cells in the uterus.

INDEX

.